COMMUNITY COLLEGES AS CULTURAL TEXTS

SUNY series

FRONTIERS IN EDUCATION

Philip G. Altbach, Editor

The Frontiers in Education Series draws upon a range of disciplines and approaches in the analysis of contemporary educational issues and concerns. Books in the series help to reinterpret established fields of scholarship in education by encouraging the latest synthesis and research. A special focus highlights educational policy issues from a multidisciplinary perspective. The series is published in cooperation with the School of Education, Boston College. A complete listing of books in the series can be found at the end of this volume.

COMMUNITY COLLEGES AS CULTURAL TEXTS

QUALITATIVE EXPLORATIONS OF ORGANIZATIONAL
AND STUDENT CULTURE

Edited by
KATHLEEN M. SHAW
JAMES R. VALADEZ
ROBERT A. RHOADS

State University of New York Press

Published by
State University of New York Press, Albany

For information, address State University of New York Press,
State University Plaza, Albany, NY 12246

Production by Laurie Searl
Marketing by Anne M. Valentine

Library of Congress Cataloging-in-Publication Data

Community colleges as cultural texts : qualitative explorations of
   organizational and student culture / Kathleen M. Shaw, James R.
   Valadez, and Robert A. Rhoads, eds.
      p.   cm. — (SUNY series, frontiers in education)
   Includes bibliographical references and index.
   ISBN 0-7914-4289-6 (alk. paper). — ISBN 0-7914-4290-X (alk.
paper)
      1. Community colleges—United States—Administration.
   2. Community colleges—United States—Sociological aspects.
   3. Multicultural education—United States.   4. Minority college
   students—United States.   5. Critical pedagogy—United States.
   6. Educational change—United States.   I. Shaw, Kathleen M.
   II. Valadez, James R.   III. Rhoads, Robert A.   IV. Series.
   LB2328.15.U6C656   1999
   378.1'543'0973—dc21   98-54287
                                                                CIP
                                                                AC

10 9 8 7 6 5 4 3 2 1

Contents

v

Figures and Tables

Acknowledgments

A variety of generous individuals have helped us in developing and refining this manuscript. We are especially grateful to Philip Altbach, series editor, whose reassurance and gentle guidance was invaluable. Howard London and John Noakes were extremely supportive throughout the conceptualization and writing of the manuscript. Anonymous reviewers provided us with constructive and detailed feedback on earlier drafts of the book. And finally we wish to thank the editorial staff at SUNY Press for their professionalism and guidance.

CHAPTER 1

Community Colleges as Cultural Texts:
A Conceptual Overview

KATHLEEN M. SHAW, ROBERT A. RHOADS,
AND JAMES R. VALADEZ

Overview

Community colleges are positioned to play a critical role in the process of upward mobility in American society. While higher education traditionally has been the realm of the white and middle class, over the past 30 years the poor, the working-class, and ethnic and racial minorities have enjoyed increased access to postsecondary education, largely through the doors of community colleges. Despite the "open-door" accessibility of these institutions, the question of whether community colleges enhance the social mobility of working-class and minority students remains an open one. In recent years, a spate of critical educational researchers has asserted that these colleges sort students into educational and career tracks that "cool out" the ambitions of working-class students (e.g., Brint & Karabel, 1989; Nora, 1993; Zwerling, 1989; Rhoads and Valadez, 1996). Yet current research by critical scholars has also uncovered community colleges whose cultures and educational practices are aimed at transforming students into active, empowered participants in the educational process (Shaw, 1997; Rhoads & Solorzano, 1995; Shaw and London, 1995).

The contradictory and often paradoxical nature of this research suggests that making generalizations about the community-college sector as a whole is perhaps misguided (Dougherty, 1994). In fact, organizational, programmatic and cultural differences exist not only within the sector as a whole, but also within individual community colleges, and even among specific compo-

1

nents of individual colleges. However, our knowledge of the inner workings of community colleges remains rudimentary, in large part due to the macro-level, often quantitative analyses that have dominated research on these institutions. This work, while important, is not enough. Clearly, our understanding of community colleges needs to progress past the sweeping portraits that have been drawn of them thus far.

This book is designed to take an important step toward developing a more nuanced understanding of the complexity of community colleges. We approach this task by using critical qualitative frameworks to examine, through a variety of lenses, the elements of community college culture that contribute to the stratification of students' opportunities. The broad question of how these institutions address the challenges inherent in their diverse missions and student populations is explored using site-specific qualitative analyses of the cultures of these institutions. This type of analysis does not disregard the influence of either internal or external structural factors. However, it is based on the premise that if we are to more fully understand how inequality is both reproduced and overcome, we must examine the interaction of individuals within the social and organizational context of the institution (Giddens, 1978; Tierney, 1993).

Rhetoric and Research on the Community College

Defenders of community colleges have described these institutions as the "people's colleges" or "democracy's colleges." Community colleges have indeed opened their doors to a broad range of the populace, resulting in a student population that is more heavily working-class, minority and female than that of four-year institutions. For example, 22 percent of community college students are minority, compared with 18 percent in four-year schools; 10 percent have family incomes below $15,000, compared with 6 percent in four-year schools; and 37 percent of the students are more than 30 years of age, compared with 25 percent in four-year schools (Dougherty, 1994).

The diverse students attending community colleges bring with them an array of experiences and attitudes which distinguish them from more traditional students and may place them at odds with the values and mores embodied by these institutions (Weis, 1985; London, 1978; Rhoads & Valadez, 1996). Differences in cultural capital—cultural knowledge, skills, norms, and linguistic facilities (Bourdieu, 1973)—are seen among members of various minority and ethnic groups as well as among people of different social classes and subcultures. When such students do not possess the cultural capital valued by the dominant culture, they may attempt to adopt dominant values, which are often reflected in the culture of institutions such as community colleges. However, they may also develop an oppositional culture which directly challenges the legitimacy of the dominant culture.

The idea of resistance to institutional culture is reflected in Paul Willis' (1977) ethnographic study of English working class boys, and also in the theoretical advances posed by Henry Giroux (1983). Giroux considers resistance to be a sociopolitical response to an educational system that has failed minority and other oppressed students. This resistant and oppositional behavior is not easily characterized, but is rooted in the students' explanations of their behavior. In the end, the rejection of the ideology of the dominant culture leads to students' acceptance of their own social class position, ensures their economic fate, and contributes to the reproduction of the class structure. More recently, research on students in public schools (e.g., Mehan, Villanueva, Hubbard and Lintz, 1996) suggests a theoretical middle ground of sorts, in which students do not entirely resist the dominant cultural norms. Instead, these students choose to adapt to them in selected situations for their own benefit, while maintaining a critical stance toward such norms in general.

Community colleges have been criticized for failing to acknowledge or adapt to the diversity in their student populations, resulting in stubbornly low transfer rates and consistently high dropout rates. While numerous sociological and structural analyses effectively highlight the general failure of community colleges to contribute to social mobility (e.g., Dougherty, 1994; Brint & Karabel, 1988; Richardson & Bender, 1987), few do so at a cultural and phenomenological level. As their focus is largely structural, these studies capture the meta-level processes contributing to social inequality; however, they fail to examine the lived experiences and interactions that make up the culture of these institutions.

Yet in recent years a number of scholars have begun to use interpretive frameworks to examine community college education (Hull, 1993; London & Shaw, 1995; Weis, 1985). Rhoads and Valadez (1996), for example, employ a critical framework to identify the ways in which community colleges invalidate or ignore the diversity of student experiences and lifestyles. Yet they also uncover institutional practices that embrace student diversity. It is our intention to build upon these studies, along with several others currently underway. In presenting examples of how an array of community colleges can either reproduce or help dismantle inequality, we hope with this volume to suggest ways in which community colleges can adopt a culture and set of educational practices that empower and transform students.

Understanding the Cultural Texts of Community Colleges

As is true of all complex organizations, the culture of a community college is made up of formal attributes, such as administrative structure and curriculum, as well as informal aspects, such as the interactions between faculty, students, and staff, and the attitudes, beliefs and norms of these

groups. The dialectic interaction between individuals and organizations results in a complex, multi-layered culture which is continuously revised through
these interactions (Geertz, 1973). In this volume, we refer to the complex
interaction between individuals and organizational structures as a "cultural
text," and use this construct to explore the ways in which educational practices, and students' experiences of them, are shaped by these factors. We
choose the metaphor of "text" to suggest that, in the same way that a novel
or poem is subject to multiple readings, so too are community colleges. There
is no one "correct" reading of an institution or any component of it; rather,
a multiplicity of interpretations can, and do, exist. Yet in choosing to utilize
a critical theoretical framework within which to conduct our "readings," we
hope to provide detailed portraits of the ways in which community colleges
grapple with issues of diversity, power, and educational equity.

The diversity of the textual readings included in this volume are in large
part the result of a rich array of analytical approaches. While all of the
chapters of this manuscript view qualitative data through a critical lens to
explore various aspects of community college culture, the authors differ with
regard to the importance placed on data relative to theory. Several authors
employ a straightforward, traditional approach to qualitative analysis, in which
primary importance is placed on the data. This approach results in chapters
which are "grounded" in the tradition of Glaser and Strauss (1967), and
provide thick descriptions of institutional and student culture. As such, they
are valuable tools in exploring and understanding the inner workings of these
institutions and their cultures.

In contrast, other chapters place primary emphasis on theory, utilizing
data to expand, support, or refute various theoretical constructs. In doing so,
these authors are engaging in what we call "critical qualitative research."
While data is still a vital aspect of this analytical approach, these chapters are
somewhat unorthodox in their emphasis on theory. A critical qualitative analysis
challenges the researcher to examine the positions from which faculty, staff,
and students speak. Where does their authority derive? How do they envision
knowledge within the educational context? What opportunities do various
groups have to construct knowledge for themselves? And relatedly, how do
we construct community colleges in a manner that students become equal
participants in knowledge construction?

This emphasis on issues tied to culture, identity, and power follows a
tradition of social science research described by many as "critical social
science" or "critical theory" (Bernstein, 1976; Fay, 1988; Tierney & Rhoads,
1993). While there are many assumptions undergirding critical social science,
a key point stressed in several of the chapters in this book is that research
itself is not simply a matter of objective, empirical inquiry. Knowledge does
not fall from the tree of life as researchers explore the universe from positions
of neutrality. Instead, critical scholars believe that inquiry begins from a

specific location. Hence, the findings one constructs throughout a study relate in large part to the theoretical stance brought to the work. However, theory should not be seen as static: Critical researchers are charged with continually rethinking their theories as they proceed and as knowledge gets constructed between the researchers and the research participants. Thus, the conclusions and implications in critical qualitative research are not drawn from "pure" empiricism, but rather are the result of the interplay between data and theory.

The complexity of community college culture demands such a diversity of analytical approaches. Indeed, when taken as a whole, the blend of theoretical and empirical examples represented in this volume provides a portrait of the community college which recognizes the complexity, nuance, and paradox inherent in this diverse sector of education.

An Overview of Chapters

As we mention above, the chapters which comprise this book explore the cultural texts of community colleges from a variety of theoretical perspectives and levels of analysis. Although we provide a more detailed summary of each chapter at the end of this section, a look at the ways in which the various studies included in this volume overlap and intersect is instructive. While each chapter presents a unique reading of the cultural text of the community college, thematic strands surface repeatedly across several chapters. For example, many of the chapters address issues of diversity, multiculturalism and identity, and focus on students for whom these issues are most salient. Another identifiable theme explores the role that different types of "capital" play in the educational experience of community college students. Because of these thematic strands, the book is best approached as a coherent whole, rather than a set of unrelated chapters. It is our belief that, when read in this way, this manuscript presents an uncommonly detailed and nuanced portrait of community college texts in all of their complexity and contradiction.

The book achieves this goal by examining these institutions with a wide array of lenses, ranging from the most micro explorations of individual experience to broader, institutional-level analysis. For example, the experiences of a few individuals within a single community college are portrayed in chapters by Amey and Valadez; portraits of individual classrooms and programs are seen in the work of Goto and McGrath and Buskirk; Rhoads and Trujillo and Diaz explore the cultures of individual community colleges; Laden conducts comparative institution-level analyses of the cultures of several community colleges; and Shaw combines portraits of a few students with comparisons of institutional culture.

The chapters represent a broad range of topics and critical theoretical frames as well, which afford the reader multiple tools with which to interpret the community college setting. For example, curricular and pedagogical is-sues are examined from the vantage points of two vastly different approaches to education: the implementation of a democratic pedagogy examined in Stan Goto's description of a basic writing classroom, and the more oppressive effects of a traditional vocational program described by James Valadez. Whereas Goto utilizes a semiotic analysis of how writers and faculty make sense of their tasks, Valadez relies on Bourdieuian theories of cultural capital and habitus to examine the ways in which African-American females make sense of an employment training program within the context of our postmodern economy. Although both portraits emphasize a dialectical interplay between structure and the individual, Goto's basic writing teacher creates a far more flexible and responsive environment for his students than does the vocational program portrayed by Valadez. The contrast between the two chapters points to the capacity of curriculum and pedagogy to either limit or expand the hopes and aspirations of community college students.

The differences seen between these two approaches to education may well reflect what Robert Rhoads labels monocultural and multicultural educational environments. In the former, authoritarian pedagogical styles dominate the educational landscape, whereas multicultural education embraces the diversity of the student body and results in a more flexible pedagogical style designed to empower students. While the community college that Rhoads examines in his chapter is primarily monocultural in its approach to education, he does uncover a small "pocket" of multiculturalists within the culture of the college. In contrast, multiculturalism is the dominant culture in Trujillo and Diaz' por-trait of Palo Alto College. In this chapter, Bourdieu's theory of cultural capital is linked with Putnam's (1993) notion of social capital to explore the ways in which multiculturalism is operationalized in this college. The result is a student body which, although predominantly poor and Hispanic, nevertheless displays a consistently high transfer rate to four-year institutions.

McGrath and Buskirk also utilize Putnam's theory of social capital, or the role of social bonds in facilitating connection and shared norms, and label the resulting increase in students' self-esteem, engagement, and sense of hope "emotional capital." Both types of capital are seen in their comparison of two seemingly dissimilar support programs, as the authors uncover distinct simi-larities in the means through which each program engenders student connec-tion, self-esteem, and achievement.

Laden also focuses on formal elements of community college culture—specifically, curriculum, administrative practices, support services, and financial allocations—in her institutional-level analysis of two California community colleges. Drawing on Giroux's (1993) notion of "border knowledge," Laden points out the importance of "celebratory socialization" for diverse student groups, and explores the ways in which community colleges can create a "web" of affirmation and support that leads to empowerment and, ultimately, success.

Marilyn Amey's postmodern leadership study has important implications for the ways in which administrative culture can also reflect the larger institution's approach to diversity. Her chapter uses the life histories of two female community college administrators to explore issues of inclusion, power, and diversity within the administrative culture of these institutions, specifically with regard to gender. Kathleen Shaw also explores the intersection between institutional culture and diversity. She applies several strands of identity theory to the experiences of community college students to examine the ways in which institutional culture can both embrace and ignore the multifaceted nature of students' lives. Although the colleges in her study generally regard students as much less complex than they reveal themselves to be in their descriptions of their lives, Shaw's research suggests that some faculty and administrators do recognize and respond to the varying sources of identity that community college students articulate.

While the theoretical and substantive topics explored in these chapters are quite broad in scope, they are bound together with an important common thread: in some way, all pose the question of whether, and how, community colleges can confront the challenges of diversity within the context of providing real opportunities for upward mobility. Our readings of the cultural texts of these colleges are neither wholly encouraging nor largely discouraging. These chapters provide examples of both exciting and innovative approaches to education, and of practice which reflects neither a recognition nor acceptance of the challenges posed by diversity. Yet such variability is to be expected, since it confirms our suspicions that community colleges do not operate as a monolithic entity. When taken as a whole, this volume not only advances our understanding of the complexities of culture in community colleges; it also provides us with examples of progressive practice which can help move these colleges toward their full potential as empowering and democratizing institutions.

Below are brief summaries of the chapters which follow.

Chapter two by Dennis McGrath of the Community College of Philadelphia and Bill Van Buskirk of LaSalle University, explores cultures of support for at-risk students, and focuses upon the role of social and emotional capital in the educational experiences of women. The authors uncover elements of organizational culture that recognize and validate the experiences and knowledge that female students bring to the community college. Case studies of two community college-linked programs—a transition program for women wishing to enroll in an engineering program at a four-year institution, and a community-based women's education program that offers community college courses on site—form the basis of this analysis. Using the constructs of social and emotional capital, the chapter presents illustrations of the ways in which these programs recognize and confront issues of identity and membership in an attempt to create an inclusive culture that provides "bridging" experiences for participating women.

In chapter three, Stan Goto of Teachers College at Columbia University illustrates some dilemmas of implementing a democratic pedagogy in a diverse, basic writing course at a community college. Drawing on ethnographic data from classroom observations and interviews, he examines how three focal students from different cultural backgrounds interpret and respond to the classroom environment. The analysis shows how their differing expectations complicate the instructor's efforts to prepare them for the academic work while encouraging individual expression.

Goto focuses on the pedagogical practices of a Chicano male instructor that involve creating a contact zone where students are encouraged to express divergent views—a self-consciously democratic approach advocated by Harris (1995). The purpose of this chapter is not to criticize a particular teaching methodology, but to illustrate the difficulties of implementing any writing pedagogy (particularly a democratic one) when students have vastly differing views of literacy and college life.

In chapter four, "Navigating the Raging River: Reconciling Issues of Identity, Inclusion, and Administrative Practice," Marilyn Amey of Michigan State University describes how the bureaucratic and hierarchical organizational structures of community colleges often leave its members feeling disconnected and disenchanted with the institution. As she reveals in her research, the experiences of women and administrators of color are similar in many ways to those of students who lack the cultural capital of the white, middleclass, male-dominated society. Amey suggests that rather than viewing the struggles of women administrators in academe as a result of their own inadequacy, the emphasis on change and modification needs to be placed on the organization.

By detailing the work lives of two women, Amey identifies some of the structural and cultural barriers hindering women's performance in senior administrative ranks. She concludes her chapter with recommendations for redefining institutional climates by making them more conducive to a collective sense of power and leadership.

In chapter five, James R. Valadez of the University of Washington describes his study of a group of poor African-American women who enrolled in a work-preparation program in a rural southern community college. The purpose of the program was to prepare students to enter the world of work, sometimes for the first time in their lives. Most of those enrolled were high school dropouts and unskilled. The chapter describes the internal conflict the students have about schooling, and the influence of relationships with significant others in shaping their goals and aspirations.

Valadez also explores the impact of institutional structures on the aspirations of students. Despite the apparent good intentions of the instructors and administrators at the community college, their actions served to socialize students into becoming workers who would be pleasing to local businesses. Specifically, the college and the business community interacted in a way that preserved existing social and economic structures, and paved the way for students to accept low-wage, low-skilled jobs. Although students obtained employment and even escaped welfare in some instances, their longterm hopes and aspirations were ignored. The analysis in this study focuses on the complementary roles that social actors play in these complex scenes to enable us to understand the ways in which social and economic classes are reproduced through schooling.

Robert A. Rhoads of Michigan State University has entitled his chapter, "The Politics of Culture and Student Identity: Contrasting Images of Multiculturalism and Monoculturalism in a Community College." Chapter six discusses issues related to the politics of identity within the context of a community college setting. The chapter is based on a longitudinal case study and utilizes theories of culture and identity to highlight how visions that faculty have of education, pedagogy and students interact with assumptions they hold about the nature of social life. More specifically, monoculturalism and multiculturalism are presented as Weberian ideal types and are used to highlight essential differences between two groups of faculty.

Monoculturalism relates to the notion that a unified culture is needed to form a common sense of connection within a given society or organization. Because commonality is a driving force, identity differences tend to be suppressed. Multiculturalism highlights the heterogeneous nature of contemporary culture and the multiplicity of student identity. This chapter argues that because education and identity are linked, community colleges must rethink their organizational structures and practices based on an ethic of care in which a wide range of identities are embraced within the organizational context.

Research shows that community college students do not experience the same rate of success (in terms of retention or completion of baccalaureate degrees) as students who begin their studies at four-year institutions. In chapter seven, Armando L. Trujillo and Eusebio Diaz of the University of Texas, San Antonio, analyze student culture at a southwestern community college and examine the extent to which the institution accommodates the diversity of students' racial or ethnic, cultural and class backgrounds as a way of promoting student success and transfer. Through ethnographic methods, this chapter describes the multiple levels of interaction, nurturance and accommodation that take place among students, faculty and staff within various institutional contexts. The authors demonstrate that faculty and staff at the community college (a) recognize and value the cultural capital of the students and community culture in both the formal and informal curriculum; and (b) that this process in turn helps students develop the necessary social capital that enables them to succeed once they transfer to the university.

While many critical theorists posit identity as an effect of differential power structures connected to membership in a particular race, class or gender category, more recent theories point to fluid, multiple identit*ies* that are the result of a complex interplay among demographic positioning, individual agency and social structure (Bailey & Hall, 1992; Deleuze & Guattari, 1987). As Kathleen M. Shaw of Temple University illustrates in her chapter entitled, "Defining the Self: Construction of Identity in Community College Students," community college students seldom define themselves solely by membership in an oppressed category of race, class, gender, or sexual orientation. In addition to this type of identity membership, these students have often assumed familial, employment, and educational roles that create fractured, competing identities.

Chapter eight examines the subjective experience of identity as described by students, and the ways in which community colleges can embrace, as well as ignore, the lived experiences of students as they struggle with issues of identity. Since community colleges are increasingly the path through which oppressed groups attempt to overcome structural inequities, it is particularly important that these institutions recognize and embrace the cultures and lived experiences of their diverse student populations. In most instances, the formal and informal policies of community colleges reflect mainstream essentialist notions of identity as a stable set of innate characteristics. However, some have adopted pedagogical and organizational strategies designed to help students adjust to the fluidity and inherent contradictions of their multiple roles and identities. Ethnographic data from eight urban community colleges with high minority enrollment is used for this analysis. Organizational factors as well as individual, informal interactions between faculty, staff and students are analyzed.

Culture is a social sharing of cognitive codes and maps, norms of appropriate behavior, and assumptions about values and beliefs which profoundly influence our thoughts and actions (Delgado Gaitan and Trueba, 1991). Despite the diversity of the students they enroll, community colleges often do not respond appropriately to the academic and social needs of students from diverse cultures. Building on Van Maanen's (1984) notion of organizational socialization patterns and Rhoads and Valadez' (1996) work on celebratory socialization processes that embrace "border knowledge" (Giroux, 1995), chapter nine explores how two community colleges address the cultural knowledge and values that ethnically diverse students bring with them to the community college. Berta Vigil Laden of Vanderbilt University examines the effects that culturally-specific academic programs and support services can have on students' ability and willingness to become a part of the college community while maintaining their ethnic or racial identities.

An ethnographic case study methodology is adopted to compare the organizational practices of an urban community college with a majority population of ethnically diverse students, and a suburban community college with a low but rising enrollment of these students. The two case studies provide rich, descriptive analyses of events, interactions, and experiences of students involved in culturally-specific academic and support services programs. By using an ecological perspective of student life that considers the cultural context of their college experience, the author examines the ways in which connections to families, communities, and cultural practices affect students' experience in these programs. Findings suggest that the academic success of culturally diverse students hinges upon strong institutional commitment, leadership from both the faculty and the administration, allocation of resources, and the development and maintenance of culturally specific programs and services that affirm and celebrate students' rich cultural knowledge.

Laura Rendon of Arizona State University draws on both her experience as a former community college student and her expertise as a community college researcher to explore the implications of this book for community college research and practice. Comparing and contrasting monocultural and multicultural approaches to community college education, she argues that traditional models of leadership are ill-suited for leading community colleges into the next century. Rendon calls for a new generation of leaders, bound by a sense of social justice and democratic ideals, who will guide and prepare students to understand and pursue the full range of opportunities laid before them.

References

Bensimon, E. M. (Ed.). (1994). *Multicultural teaching and learning: Strategies for change in higher education.* University Park, PA: National Center on Postsecondary Teaching, Learning, & Assessment.

Bernstein, R. J. (1976). *The restructuring of social and political theory.* Philadelphia: University of Pennsylvania Press.

Brint, S., & Karabel, J. (1989). *The diverted dream: Community colleges and the promise of educational opportunity in America, 1900–1985.* New York: Oxford University Press.

Dougherty, K. J. (1994). *The contradictory college: The conflicting origins, impacts, and futures of the community college.* Albany: State University of New York Press.

Fay, B. (1987). *Critical social science.* Ithaca, NY: Cornell University Press.

Geertz, C. (1973). *The interpretation of cultures.* New York: Basic Books.

Giroux, Henry A. (1983). *Theory and resistance in education: A pedagogy for the opposition.* South Hadley, MA: Bergin & Garvey.

———. (1992). *Border crossings: Cultural workers and the politics of education.* New York: Routledge.

Grubb, W. N. (1991). "The decline of community college transfer rates." *Journal of Higher Education* 62:2, 194–217.

hooks, b. (1992). *Black looks: Race and representation.* Boston: South End Press.

Kincheloe, J. (1995). *Toil and trouble: Good work, smart workers, and the integration of academic and vocational education.* New York: Peter Lang.

Lincoln, Y. S., & Guba, E. G. (1985). *Naturalistic inquiry.* Beverly Hills, CA: Sage.

London, H. B. (1978). *The culture of a community college.* New York: Praeger.

McLaren, P. (1986). *Schooling as a ritual performance.* London: Routledge & Kegan Paul.

———. (1991). "Field relations and the discourse of the other: Collaboration in our own ruin." In W. B. Shaffir & Stebbins, R. A. (Eds.), *Experiencing fieldwork: An inside view of qualitative research* (pp. 149–63). Newbury Park, CA: Sage.

Mehan, H.; Villanueva I.; Hubbard, L.; & Lintz, A. (1996). *Constructing school success: The consequences of untracking low-achieving students.* Cambridge: Cambridge University Press.

Nora, A. (1993). "Two-year colleges and minority students' educational aspirations: Help or hindrance?" In J. C. Smart (Ed.), *Higher education: Handbook of theory and research* (212–47). New York: Agathon Press.

Putnam, R. (1993). *Making democracy work: Civic traditions in modern Italy.* Princeton, NJ: Princeton University Press.

Rhoads, R. A., & Valadez, J. R. (1996). *Democracy, multiculturalism, and the community college: A critical perspective.* New York: Garland.

Rhoads, R. A., & Solorzano, S. M. (1995). "Multiculturalism and the community college: A case study of an immigrant education program." *Community College Review,* 23(2), 3–16.

Richardson, R. C., & Bender, L. W. (1987). *Fostering minority access and achievement in higher education.* San Francisco: Jossey-Bass.

Shaw, K. M. (1997). "Remedial education as ideological battleground: Emerging remedial education policies in the community college." *Educational Evaluation and Policy Analysis* 19:3, p. 284–96.

Shaw, K., & London, H. (1995). "Negotiating boundaries and borders: Institutional and student cultures in high-transfer urban community colleges." Paper presented at the Assocation for the Study of Higher Education Annual Meeting. Orlando, Florida.

Tierney, W. G., & Rhoads, R. A. (1993). "Postmodernism and critical theory in higher education: Implications for research and practice." In J. C. Smart (Ed.), *Higher education: Handbook of theory and research* (pp. 308–43). New York: Agathon.

Tierney, W. G. (1993). *Building communities of difference: Higher education in the 21st century.* Westport, CT: Bergin & Garvey.

Weis, L. (1985). *Between two worlds.* Boston: Routledge.

West, C. (1993). *Race matters.* New York: Vintage Books.

CHAPTER 2

Cultures of Support for At-Risk Students: The Role of Social and Emotional Capital in the Educational Experiences of Women

DENNIS McGRATH AND WILLIAM VAN BUSKIRK

Introduction

Community colleges have long remained elusive institutions, much discussed, but still poorly understood. This illusive quality can be seen in the lengthy scholarly disagreement about the role of community colleges within the system of higher education and their impact on the lives of students. Some analysts see them as a major example of democratic higher education, "the people's colleges," providing access to groups long excluded from higher education (Griffith and Connor, 1994). Other scholars, though, argue that community colleges ultimately reinforce societal inequality by "cooling out" student aspiration and tracking talented students into limited vocational careers (Brint and Karabel, 1989; Zwerling, 1989). In the title of one recent study, these seemingly incompatible portraits of community colleges have lead them to be seen as "contradictory colleges" (Dougherty 1994).

It is a challenging task to bring community colleges into focus and resolve their contradictory qualities. To do so we must transcend longstanding debates by moving beyond conventional analyses of their administrative and structural features. We believe that a cultural framework is particularly fruitful, offering ways of exploring the distinctive academic and organizational cultures of these colleges. For understanding the contemporary community college requires learning to "read them as texts," examining how thirty years of open-access higher education has become inscribed in the habits, practices and discourses of faculty, students, and administrative staff.

15

This chapter contributes to this effort by examining the culture of social support for students and the features of exemplary programs. We believe that this is a critical issue for institutions that primarily serve nontraditional and underrepresented students. Unfamiliar with higher education and often having experienced limited success in their earlier schooling, nontraditional students are significantly at-risk when they enter college. If community colleges are to fulfill the democratic promise of open access higher education, they must develop exemplary practices capable of transforming students into active learners and empowered participants in the educational process (Shaw and London, 1995). However, while community colleges represent themselves as innovative institutions, typical student support programs are quite traditional and frequently ineffective.

Understanding Social Capital

Much has been learned in recent years about the factors that promote student persistence and performance. Astin (1985) and Tinto (1987) emphasize the importance of student involvement. They hold that college students are most likely to be successful if they are well integrated into the academic and social systems of a college campus, especially through informal, out-of-class interactions with peers and faculty, and participation in extracurricular activities.

This higher education research converges with current studies of effective secondary schools, particularly work emphasizing what Coleman (Coleman, 1993; Coleman and Hoffer, 1987) and Putnam (1993) term "social capital." The concept of social capital uses the economic metaphor of capital formation to focus on the ways in which social bonds "add value" to individual and organizational functioning. It calls attention to the critical role of social connections in facilitating effective collective effort. According to this framework, organizations are not purely instrumental, and they don't succeed on the basis of rational incentives alone. Rather, stocks of social capital, such as trust and shared norms, are vital in promoting effective collaboration and communication.

Studies of social capital in education find that student success is deeply affected by the social relationships within schools. Successful secondary schools, for example, function as "communal organizations." Such schools are characterized by a sense of shared purpose, and have practices that give life to these common beliefs, especially social relations centered around moral norms stressing responsibility and self-development (Bryk, Lee, and Holland, 1993). When these features join together, they promote engagement in students and commitment in teachers (Bryk, Lee, and Holland, 1993:275).

However, while the structural features of effective educational settings have begun to be mapped, much remains to be understood about the dynamics of student engagement. Research on student involvement in learning and the role of social capital needs to be complimented with a richer social psychology and cultural understanding of student experience. We need a better picture of how social capital, in the form of strong social bonds, networks of small groups, and norms of reciprocity, is translated into "emotional capital," which we define as the shared sense of trust, safety, and reciprocity that promotes involvement and commitment.

Understanding the role of emotional capital is especially important for today's increasingly diverse students, who are not well served by traditional institutional structures and practices. Research consistently finds that students most at-risk are least likely to get involved in the social and academic infrastructures of institutions, hence merely offering opportunities for involvement is not adequate (Nora, 1987; Rendon, 1994). The dynamics of engagement require more than providing programs. *What we do* with students has much more profound consequences than the resources that we offer. This is especially true with nontraditional students, who perceive involvement as someone taking an active role in assisting them rather than as taking the initiative themselves (Rendon, 1994). Effective intervention programs and educational reforms must be based on a detailed understanding of the interactive processes within schools. We need to understand how educational settings engage students and transform them into active participants by inducing emotions such as hope for the future, respect for others, enthusiasm about their studies and confidence in their ability to succeed.

Understanding Emotional Capital

We believe that current work in social psychology and organizational culture can provide useful perspectives on how social and emotional capital is formed. Recent findings in cognitive social psychology shed new light on how individuals become connected to organizations. The picture it offers of how people perceive and respond to social environments emphasizes that cognition is a complex, interpretive process. Thinking, feeling and acting in social settings involves the comprehension and interpretation of events. Cognition and emotional response are deeply intertwined as perceptions of the "situation," and are deeply affected by precognitive, especially affective factors.

We draw on this research to complement the concept of social capital with that of emotional capital. Emotional capital is *the capacity of an organization to evoke and hold in place over time, through its practices, symbols, and culture, positive appraisals of well-being in its membership.* In other words, emotional capital is the cultural and social psychological dimension of social capital. It is developed through the translation of the social bonds and shared norms created by social capital into emotions that shape the actions and perceptions of organizational members. In educational settings characterized by high levels of emotional capital, the environment as it is socially constructed will be experienced as benign or at least manageable within the stock of available coping resources. Under these conditions, students are able to concentrate on their studies and are not distracted by potential threats, worries or other preoccupations that might lurk on the periphery of awareness.

Our understanding of emotional capital draws on the concept of appraisal of well-being developed in social psychological studies of stress and emotion (Lazarus, 1991). Appraisals are evaluations that actors make about the significance of a situation for their well-being (Lazarus, 1981). Appraisals, and the emotions they trigger, are bound up with the generation of meaning, rooted in the individual's attempts to interpret ambiguous situations for threats and supports. For instance, the degree of stress a person experiences is determined by the individual's perception of both the stressful situation and of his or her ability to cope with events. It is the match between perceptions of threats in the environment and one's coping resources that generates positive or negative appraisals of well-being (Lazarus, 1991). However, most studies of appraisal and coping have been conducted in laboratory settings where individuals were asked to explicitly appraise experimentally fabricated situations. To be usefully applied to students' experience of school, we must add the dimension of organizational culture.

Theories of culture emphasize that the environment that is scanned for threats or opportunities is a social construction, an "enacted" rather than objective reality (Berger and Luckman, 1967). The events that actors perceive and respond to are shaped by the culture, which gives meaning to what would otherwise be an ambiguous situation. Organizational environments are constituted by the play of symbols and practices that organize experience for participants. The appraisal process, as it occurs in organizations, is culturally embedded (Van Buskirk and McGrath, 1992). Cultural symbols, myths, rituals and practices show one where to look, and what one can expect to find (Bourdieu, 1985). Organizational cultures also helps individuals formulate a "tool kit" of coping resources and generate strategies of action (Swidler, 1986).

The culture of schools is vital to educational success. It is through their symbols and practices that they evoke, transform and maintain appraisals of well-being that underlie students' ability to sustain their engagement in learning. Our studies of educational settings which are particularly successful in educating at-risk populations find that they contain a plethora of organizational and cultural practices which engender and maintain in students positive appraisals and hopeful images of themselves in the world (McGrath and Van Buskirk, 1993; 1994). This chapter examines two such programs: the Community Women's Education Project in Philadelphia and the Women in Engineering Initiative at the University of Washington. By looking at the "best practices" of successful programs we hope to make their lessons available to others. However, merely cataloguing program features is not enough. Rather, we believe a cultural analysis is essential to understand the transformations of meaning and feeling that go on in such successful programs. Students' response to educational settings is a complex, symbolic process, rooted in organizational communication. It is only through the interpretation of cultural practices that we can understand how emotional capital is engendered.

Methodology

This study utilizes a case study methodology, developing a comparative description of two successful educational support programs for women. The case studies were conducted over a two year period and involved a series of individual and focus group interviews with students and staff, along with observation of program activities. All interview sessions were audio tape-recorded and transcribed. Interview data were analyzed using a grounded theory approach, with coding procedures designed to identify emergent categories, themes, and patterns (Glaser and Strauss, 1967).

The Programs

At first glance, Philadelphia's Community Women's Education Program (CWEP) and the Women in Engineering Initiative (WIE) at the University of Washington seem to have little in common. CWEP is a community-based program serving low-income women in a poor section of Philadelphia, while WIE works with women students entering the School of Engineering at a distinguished public university. CWEP offers a range of programs from basic skills, GED, and job training through community college courses offered on-site through its connection with the Community College of Philadelphia. It has an annual operating budget of approximately seven hundred thousand dollars, from a mix of government contracts, foundation grants and corporate support. WIE provides an integrated set of programs for women engineering students, including tutoring, peer and professional mentoring, support groups, and a collaborative program with area community colleges. It has an annual budget of approximately $375,000. One-quarter of the budget is provided by the College of Engineering, with the rest coming from a wide range of corporate contributions and foundation grants.

Despite these surface differences, the two cases offer useful comparisons of the critical role of social and emotional capital in the educational experience of women students. Both serve women, although their clients have quite different demographic profiles and academic skill levels. At CWEP the typical student is a mother on public assistance in her mid- to late-20s who requires work on basic academic skills. WIE serves a more traditional student population, although its involvement in an area community-college alliance has increased the number of transfer students, including many nontraditional women students.

The programs are similar, though, in responding to significant challenges in the lives of their students that threaten to trigger discouragement and disengagement. The populations they serve both enter school lacking the social and emotional capital to persist in the long years of study necessary to accomplish their goals. CWEP's students have long struggled with the social and educational barriers that have locked them into low-paying jobs, and feel the growing societal hostility to women on welfare. Many dropped out of high school or graduated years ago, and are apprehensive about returning to school. They have to raise children by themselves and are often deeply in debt. Some have histories of alcohol or drug dependence. Many are discouraged from pursuing school by their families and communities.

The women students who apply to engineering programs must demonstrate outstanding academic performance. However, they too must struggle to succeed and are in need of support. Engineering remains a "hypermasculine" field strongly resistant to the entrance of women (Van Buskirk, Barrett, McGrath, Schor, 1995). Although women demonstrate a growing interest in engineering, approximately one-half drop their major by the junior year (Wilson, 1991). In short, the women served by both of these programs frequently experience their educational environments as uninviting and threatening. They must learn to cope with feelings of uncertainty, ambiguity and threat in order to concentrate on their studies. To be successful they must navigate demanding curricula as they also struggle with powerful negative emotions that challenge the new identities as they are attempting to develop.

Common Features: The Role of Social and Emotional Capital

Although there are many differences between WIE and CWEP, they develop social and emotional capital in similar ways. First, they transform students' images of the future from negative to positive. Second, they build a transformative culture by organizing their programs, processes and structures to reinforce positive appraisals of well-being. Third, each offers multiple pathways for involvement, which promotes engagement and stimulates volunteerism. Fourth, they provide support on many levels, including advice, information, emotional support and advocacy. Fifth, they encourage self-management skills that promote effective coping. Sixth, they provide a balance between support and letting go so that students do not become either alienated from or overly dependent on the programs. Finally, each attends to the outside environment which promotes their ability to expand services and advocate for students. These commonalities are discussed in more detail below.

Transmitting a Powerful Image of the Future. It is probably true for all students that a positive image of the future is necessary if they are to persist through years of study. However, because of their difficult circumstances, students at WIE and CWEP have a special need for an optimistic and believable image of their future. To succeed they must cope with uncertainty and ambiguity for long periods. To remain engaged in their studies, students must successfully manage powerful negative emotions such as anxiety, shame, and self-blame.

Both programs promote successful coping by providing students with "an image of the future" within which they can imagine a credible scenario of hope and success. The programs offer a picture of the world these women will someday enter that validates their current efforts. When this image is accepted by a student, it makes current day-to-day troubles less debilitating because they are placed into a context that is broader and more hopeful. With persistent worries put to the side, students can then concentrate on their studies. These images of the future function as shared "appraisal scenarios," helping students sustain positive appraisals by scripting emotional reactions to their situation and encouraging effective coping skills.

Generating an optimistic and believable future is an extremely empowering intervention. Even students in dire immediate circumstances can better cope when sustained by a sense that their future remains promising. However, at CWEP and WIE a positive sense of the future can never be taken for granted. Each program, through its own unique organizational culture, tries to inculcate such images in their students.

CWEP articulates a mission which states that the path to self-sufficiency for low-income, disadvantaged women lies in longterm education, rather than short-term training. WIE's mission is to increase the participation and retention of women students and to promote more positive learning environments in engineering programs. Both have organizational cultures that transmit their missions in powerful and sustained ways. Their organizational cultures encourage positive appraisals by students and help manage the anxieties, conflicts, fears and uncertainties that continually threaten to overwhelm them.

Storytelling is an important vehicle for transmitting organizational culture (Boje, 1991). Narratives shape perceptions of the environment that is experienced as real, as well as one's sense of self. In our interviews we probed for common stocks of stories that circulated throughout the organizations. In both programs, we discovered patterns of story telling that strengthened the supportive function of the programs and provided a positive and realizable image of the future for students.

At WIE the core narrative provides an image of what the life of a professional engineer is like, and how to become one. This is vital for women students who typically lack a clear sense of the field, worry about grades and frequently doubt their abilities. In tutoring sessions, support groups, individual counseling, and informal discussions, students are told stories of "women just like you" who through hard work and careful planning realized their goals. This narrative is crystallized in a slogan that serves as a kind of mantra for the students. In each interview, when asked about how they coped during a difficult time, the student would say something similar to, "and then I realized, you don't have to be a genius to be an engineer, you just have to do the work."

At CWEP the story focuses on how the women can break out of poverty through education. In a variety of settings, stories are told of "women just like you" who had been stuck in low-paying jobs, but came to CWEP and then went on to college or solid technical programs. This narrative is also crystallized in a slogan that students frequently recounted to us: "I don't just want a job, I want a career. I need an education, not just a training program."

These stories perform the classic functions of communal narratives, shaping the felt adequacy and worthiness of one's self, as well as the capacity to cope with what the environment presents. In both programs storytelling is a fundamental force shaping the emotional climate. These stories build emotional capital by helping students reframe their experience in common ways while evoking appropriate coping responses that encourage sustained effort. They promote academic involvement by validating the students as potentially successful and offering them an image of the future that is at least partly manageable.

Both programs also invoke a positive image of the future by engaging students in a dense network of social contacts. This is done in a variety of ways, most formally by making extensive use of mentors. WIE has large, formal programs of both peer and professional mentors, while CWEP makes heavy use of former students. WIE begins mentoring in the freshman year with the Big Sister's program, which serves approximately 150 students each year. Once a student has been accepted into an engineering department she is encouraged to become involved in the Professional Mentoring program, which utilizes over 120 professional women in engineering or related positions in the Seattle area. In this program, an upper-class undergraduate, or graduate student becomes a mentor to a freshman or sophomore. A student who returned to school after a number of years working in construction gives a sense of the impact of becoming involved with a professional mentor:

> I was so excited when I learned about the mentoring program . . . I didn't come from an engineering background. I got matched with someone in my area, environmental engineering . . . I talked to her a few times and just being able to look and see her is the next stage . . . She's actually a civil engineer and her company has jobs where you report to the EPA. Her company had a bid on a job in Honolulu and she's flying back and forth to Honolulu in December and January . . . Boy, I want to do that some day . . . now that's engineering.

By just telling the student about her own job, the mentor is transmitting a positive, vital image of the future. The student, who had worked on the Alaskan Pipeline, can now envision herself working in Hawaii. The mentor conveys a concrete conception of what an environmental engineer does, and can offer advice on the job market and the steps needed to prepare for a professional position.

Creating a Transformative Culture. The programs not only help manage the negative feelings that further debilitate students, but create cultural settings that transform those emotions. They perform this transformative function by managing the appraisal process at critical points in students' careers.

The programs carefully manage the student's initial contact with the institution. Further, they identify the predictable points in the students' career, where they are likely to experience disappointment, discouragement, uncertainty and anxiety. They offer both cognitive and affective support by providing setting and activities designed to help students interpret their experience in positive ways. By doing so they encourage students' continued engagement with their studies.

At CWEP most students begin in the basic skills program, "Workstart." Staff view communicating the agency's mission as a core function of Workstart, but recognize that it is a difficult task that must be carefully managed. Students and faculty typically begin with a very different sense of what they want to accomplish. Given their history, students usually expect another low-level training program and, at best, hope to sharpen some basic skills and perhaps get some leads on jobs. However, the program has structured a number of socializing experiences designed to help the students take on the mission of "longterm education" for their own. The first day of Workstart involves activities designed to challenge the students' assumptions about what school is like and what will go on in class. As one teacher notes, "we start out at orientation in small groups, talking to one another. It doesn't have to be about jobs; it could be describe your neighborhood."

The initial emphasis on discussion and student involvement is continued in the classes as well. The core courses break from the typical practices of training programs by placing heavy emphasis on reading and group discussion. Students present their own writing and react to the work of others. All the courses are characterized by lively discussion, with the teachers continually scanning the class to see if any of the students are hanging back and need encouragement to join the conversation.

The pedagogical emphasis on small group discussion and active learning promotes the acculturation process, and has a powerful effect on the students. As they become engaged in discussions in class, students learn about the other women, and begin to experience them as sources of support. Many of the negative appraisals that the women bring to the school experience begin to change as they learn of the struggles and successes of others.

> I felt comfortable there. A lot of the other students were in the same situation, single parent, not working at the time. We had a lot in common. Everybody communicated well with one another. I found that to be very reassuring.

The typical woman engineering student endures considerable confusion and uncertainty, especially at the beginning of her academic career. At the University of Washington, as at many universities, students begin as pre-engineering majors. They must complete a series of required science and math classes before they can petition for admission to the College of Engineering. As a student described it, "you have to take these giant classes . . . you don't know if you're going to be accepted . . . it's really stressful . . . you don't know what to do . . . how to find out anything."

It is even more stressful and confusing for students who begin at a community college and transfer to the university. They face a double transition, moving from pre-engineering to their major, and from the more supportive environment of the community college to a large, complex university.

> I came from a tiny community college. Now I'm surrounded by all these smart people who probably have a better background than me . . . I didn't have a sense of who I was and what my skill level was. I was afraid to tell somebody I wanted to go into engineering. They would probably say, "ha, ha, you want to go into engineering." When I transferred here there was no lifeline to hold on to.

WIE responds to these problems in several ways that help students cope with their feelings of uncertainty and anxiety and promote more positive appraisals of their situation. The Freshman Intervention Program identifies all entering women interested in science and engineering, and supports them through the pre-engineering coursework. This program involves a range of activities, including a special orientation session, peer mentoring and tutoring, counseling session, and the development of personalized academic plans.

The orientation, tutoring and counseling help new students with their entry into the university, while they explore their initial interest in engineering. The peer mentoring program further helps students develop positive appraisals of their prospects. The upper class student, who has already been accepted into her department, can offer an insider's view of departmental life and practical advice on coping with a demanding curriculum. But WIE designs peer mentoring to involve more than providing information. The Big

Sisters program offers beginning students social and academic relationships that they can draw upon for a wide range of help and encouragement. The peer mentors that we interviewed had a strong sense of responsibility for their "little sisters," and the relationship sometimes develops into a longterm friendship. Further, big sisters, through their frequent contact with mentees, quickly learn about their difficulties, so they are in a position to offer very specific advice and coaching.

The continual transformation of initially negative appraisals that take place in these programs has an effect far beyond the benefit to an individual student. In both programs, individual successes becomes the stuff of legend. As success stories are told throughout the organization the stories themselves become transformative, and the culture of support gains greater strength and coherence. For example, at CWEP a frequently reported story concerned "the first time I got an A." The story typically details early difficulties and initially low grades, but through the involvement of teachers and the help of other students, efforts end in success. The story is powerful since it embeds many positive appraisals of well being: students can develop competency, the program delivers on its promises, and teachers care for their students.

At WIE stories circulate about how to cope with the many difficulties encountered in the university. As narratives are repeated they become condensed into evocative symbols, and positive appraisals multiply. At WIE women talk about the enjoyment of seeing one of their peers get a research fellowship, "because that means that I'm closer to getting one myself." As stories and symbol help define the organization in the minds of its members, the program itself becomes a symbol with transformative powers. At the University of Washington, even women who seldom visit the center report that they are "glad that WIE is there in case I ever need it." Likewise, graduates of CWEP report that they are reassured by the organization's continued existence. "I never know when I'll need to go back." Both programs, by creating a strong organizational culture, provide an enhanced resource for the transformation of appraisals, and hence an enhanced sense of well being.

Providing Multiple Pathways for Involvement. The programs maximize the likelihood of student involvement by providing a range of formal programs and informal settings. Women come to WIE for a number of reasons. Most have received the organization's newsletter, and its reputation has spread around campus by word of mouth. But it is often not until a student encounters some difficulty that she seeks out the project. Students report that their initial contact is for a specific kind of assistance, such as tutoring, "brown bag" support-group discussions, or the desire to find a mentor.

But however students enter these programs, they soon discover that the setting offers a much wider range of support than they imagined. What is striking about both is how well the programs are structured to respond to the wide range of problems that emerge in the life of a student. For example, an undergraduate might come to a WIE luncheon discussion of large classes and get some helpful tips. In her sophomore year, she might seek advice on which department to enter. As she approaches graduate school, she discovers a whole new set of problems related to family issues, workload, relations with professors, and job hunting. At CWEP a woman who begins in Workstart may continue in Workstart II in order to continue working on her basic skills. She may make use of the on-site day care or the Parenting Program, while also talking with staff about job possibilities or financial aid to continue her schooling.

One result of the remarkable coherence between student needs and organizational structure is that there are multiple pathways through the programs. However a woman begins, she is likely to become involved in additional activities and services. This results in a rich and varied history of involvement with the organization.

The programs also enhance their stock of social capital by providing dense networks of interaction for students who would otherwise be isolated. In engineering, a student frequently finds that she is one of only two or three women in a class. This intensifies her feelings of isolation and doubts about whether she belongs in the field. However, the weekly support group discussions and informal study area lets women, who are isolated in their individual departments, form a critical mass of support. Also, WIE is the regional center for the national association of women in engineering programs, WEPAN, and hosts an annual conference. They encourage undergraduate and graduate students to attend, as well as community college students who are interested in the field. Students report that the conferences have a powerful impact on them. As one undergraduate put it, "you get over 200 women in one room and it's inspiring . . . it moves you." Rosabeth Moss Kanter has described the negative psychological dynamics created by the experience of being a token (Kanter, 1977). WIE provides settings where women, if only temporarily, can meet one another and feel that they are not alone, that others are pursuing the same path and finding ways to succeed.

By providing multiple pathways of involvement, the programs deepen students' sense of feeling supported as they develop an image of the organization as always "being there for them." The students involved in these programs have gone through many transformations. They increasingly experience themselves as able and competent. They receive support both for who they are and who they are becoming (Kegan, 1982). They have received a benefit far greater than an educational credential, for they have been transformed into the kinds of people who can take advantage of formal education. For many students this experience engenders a deep gratitude and a desire to "give something back" to the organization, and many become active volunteers. This blurs the distinction between clients, volunteers, and staff as many students become deeply involved and committed to doing the work of the organization.

This transformation from client to provider does not happen all at once. Indeed, in many cases it has been happening implicitly all along. However, at some point many student move beyond informal activities to help the organization in a more formal way, taking on roles as volunteers or as part time staff. At WIE students run the tutoring and mentoring services, coordinate support groups, and help organize citywide conferences on women and engineering. At CWEP student volunteers help with tutoring as well as communicating the mission of the organization to newcomers.

Volunteerism represents another increase in the organization's ability to engender positive appraisals and emotional capital. Significant numbers of students become committed to running the programs. They enhance the capacities of the programs and provide powerful symbols of students who are able to make a difference. Many report that seeing others volunteering gave them the idea to contribute their time. As one undergraduate engineering student noted, "from the first day I came here I knew I wanted to be like these women."

Providing Emotional Support, Advice, Information, and Advocacy. These programs offer many insights into how effective support works. They are particularly useful in identifying how support is communicated in emotionally powerful ways so that it is experienced as helpful by the client.

Perhaps most striking is the richness of the culture of support in these programs. They offer a sophisticated mix of emotional support, pragmatic advice, information, and advocacy tailored to the individual needs of the students. They are able to do this because the programs have developed organizational practices that permit staff to continually monitor the needs of students, identifying the times when they experience the greatest stress and most need help. As a result, the staffs of both programs have developed a fine-grained appreciation of the issues facing women students at all phases of their academic careers. This allows them to respond quickly and effectively to a wide range of specific student problems. Support is effectively communicated because staff make frequent, routine contact with students, and are able to respond to them during critical times when students feel in greatest need.

Such tailored responses are the intentional outcome of carefully designed organizational practices and program structures. Everyone who has contact with students—full time staff, part-time student workers, volunteers, tutors, peer and professional mentors—are trained to maximize their impact. Whatever the service, staff act to make cognitive changes in students by helping them interpret their experience in positive ways, while also offering tangible assistance. For example, at WIE the role of tutor is not limited to helping the student master the course material. The program has identified that women students seeking tutoring often suffer from a lack of self-confidence, which can be far more debilitating than any difficulty with course work. Self-confidence among the pre-engineering students is most typically undermined when women first experience the tough grading practices of the engineering and science programs. Students who have always performed well in their previous schooling now find themselves receiving far lower grades. This characteristically has a profound effect on women students, who tend to blame themselves for the problem, rather than seeing the lower grades as a typical experience of entering a rigorous curriculum. Unexpectedly low grades tend to trigger powerfully negative appraisals, strengthening feelings of uncertainty, and making women wonder whether they had made a mistake in entering the field.

> The guys, if they get a 2.3 they say that's okay. But the women, if they get a 2.9 they'll worry about being eliminated. Even if they do well they are hypercritical. If you get a 3.7 you should get a 3.9. I met somebody from a community college who thought a 3.5 was the lowest acceptable grade . . . think again I told her.

As WIE recognized this problem as a predictable crisis in a student's career, staff reshaped the role of the tutor, emphasizing the need to support and encourage students. Upper class students are recruited to provide tutoring services, and they go through formal screening, orientation, training and evaluation. Orientation and training sessions have expanded beyond how to answer student questions, stressing the need to help students interpret the university environment, and coaching them on how to deal with difficult situations. Since tutors have taken the same courses in which their younger colleagues are struggling, they are in a good position to help students identify positive ways to cope with stressful situations, and maintain a hopeful sense of their future.

The weekly support groups and peer mentoring, along with the informal opportunities for students to talk with one another provides many settings for women to share advice about how to handle difficult situations. The advice is typically quite concrete and pragmatic, but also helps students to reinterpret their experience in less threatening ways, and gain a greater feeling of control over their situation. This is captured well in a story told by one of the undergraduates about advice she was given before going to see a senior professor in her department.

> I had one professor, one of the reasons I could tolerate the man was that I was told by people at WIE, be prepared, when he thinks you're asking a stupid question he pushes his chair half-way across the room. And he does! You go to his office . . . he'll be telling you something and he gets really bristly. He pushes his chair back . . . But when you know that it is coming, and that it happens to everybody, it's not just you. You're not the only dummy in the

world . . . it's not a surprise and it's like a little boy doing the same thing over and over again.

This example shows the profound impact of stories shared by students. In this case a young woman, who might have been intimidated by a faculty member, has been informally coached to prepare for his expression of frustration. Rather than becoming frightened or feeling denigrated, the student can reinterpret the teacher's behavior in a way that permits her to continue the conversation until her questions were answered.

When advice or coaching are not adequate in resolving a student's problem, staff become advocates. The organization has worked hard to build a network of support within the university, and if a student has a serious complaint, the Director of WIE will contact the appropriate department head. Always taking a problemsolving, collaborative approach, the Director has helped the program develop a reputation for reasonableness which has increased its efficacy within the political environment of the university.

Staff also sometimes must act as advocates with families who are sometimes opposed to their daughter's pursuing engineering.

One woman came from the Philippines and was immersed in the Philippine culture. She battled with her father about wanting to be an engineer . . . She convinced him to come on campus and meet us. We talked a bit about what his concept of an engineer was, and the environment that an engineer worked in . . . He saw it as a hard core, coarse environment . . . he was concerned about his daughter working in those conditions. She was interested in an internship. He felt she should stay home and work with the family in the summer. We talked through those issues and about three weeks later. I got a letter from him . . . he agreed that she should pursue the internship.

Like WIE, CWEP has also developed a culture where many types of student contacts and support can flourish. Program staff are continually available to students so that they can identify and help resolve problems before they become overwhelming. Counselors "check in" regularly with students, averaging 80 contacts each month. The collaborative practices of the classroom and the extensive use of former students encourages discussion. This creates an emotional climate conducive to the open sharing of problems and group problem-solving of solutions.

Our teaching assistants are always former students . . . and the college students are past Workstart students and they're on site here. There are always times in the Workstart classes when former students come back to talk . . . there's a lot of formal and informal contact.

The classroom practices of active learning help the faculty come to know the students as individuals, permitting them to tailor their responses to the specific needs of the students.

> You have one-on-one contact, and they take the time . . . The teachers are very observant. They would see if you made a kind of face, little things . . . they would talk to you after class, do whatever.

The classes also help students form positive appraisals about their situation. Discussions among women help transmit common coping repertoires throughout the student group, as the women learn effective strategies from one another. Positive appraisals of their future are further supported as the ties that are formed among the students begin to extend beyond the classroom. Interviews with students disclose that the energy and good feeling of the classes promote positive relationships the student group. Despite their busy schedules, students stay in touch outside of class. As one student noted, "everybody exchanges phone numbers. You get home from class, you get on the phone and call somebody. The camaraderie is great."

Encouraging Self-Management Skills. A key resource in coping is what has been termed "self-efficacy," which includes the capacity to differentiate problems, generate plans, and act when confronted with threats (Bandura, 1977). A powerful dimension of the culture of support in these programs is the array of practices that promote self-efficacy. These programs help students reduce their sense of anxiety and uncertainty by enhancing their ability to manage difficult situations. Students become empowered as they gain coping skills that are effective, and begin to trust their own abilities. As students develop the sense that they have options and a plan of action for coping with events, their perception of threat and uncertainty is reduced.

This program impact is an important dimension of social and emotional capital. Program structures and practices, such as providing opportunities for frequent informal interaction and providing a mix of support, information, and advocacy, create a fund of social capital. This social capital, in the form of dense networks of relationships, maximizes the types of supportive interactions that promote self-management skills among the students. However, what makes these programs unusually effective is their ability to translate these supportive interactions into emotional capital which generates feelings of competence and self-control.

One of the major ways this is accomplished is through the positive cognitive impact of self-talk. Studies of "learned helplessness" and locus of control find that feelings of incompetence are associated with an individual's attribution of the source of their failure. This primarily occurs through the stories that people tell themselves, the internal narratives or "self-talk" they engage in. Research in health care finds that encouraging positive self-talk is a powerful cognitive coping strategy, effectively preparing patients for stressful medical procedures and encouraging self-management and adherence to health-related decisions (Holroyd, Andrasik, and Westbrook, 1977). Our interviews suggest that these programs have developed powerful ways to intervene in this self-talk, encouraging new internal narratives that encourage more positive appraisals.

A young Vietnamese woman who was finishing her second year of pre-engineering recounted the advice she was given by her peer mentor about speaking up in class. "My big sister said 'raise your hand, you're paying for it.' " A junior in electrical engineering who was struggling with the intensity of the workload said she was advised "don't look to the end, look at today." Another student told of how important she found the advice she gained from a support group. "They taught me to take a big problem and break it down . . . take care of the biggest problem first, put out the biggest fire."

These forms of advice have significance for the students because they presumably were engaging in negative streams of self-talk that had been generating a great deal of anxiety. This kind of self-talk amplifies negative appraisals which then restricts students' ability to cope with their problems. Another student's comments captures this dimension of supportive communication when she describes the impact of WIE by noting "they taught me how to think and to calm myself down."

Further, the many settings for informal interaction provide opportunities for new internal narratives to lead to new forms of behavior. A CWEP student who describes herself as having been painfully shy and unable to speak up in class recounts the benefits of the informal support groups. "You can talk about anything . . . it turned me around." The supportive culture of the programs act as a laboratory for exploring one's self and practicing new behaviors.

Perhaps the most important form of self-talk that these programs alter is the tendency toward self-blame. Mothers on welfare and women in engineering programs have a strong tendency to blame themselves for what happens to them. Their ability to develop successful coping skills depend on a cognitive reframing, so they can develop a more realistic understanding of their difficulties. As one undergraduate put it:

> Engineering is such an intense environment, that sometimes you need to go outside it for perspective, for a reality check . . . you lose your perspective in such a small fish-bowl . . . you go through an experience and you say, "am I blowing this out of proportion because I'm so exhausted?"

A graduate engineering student offered an incident that illustrates the importance of having someplace to go to get a "reality check" so you can sort out what has happened and who is at fault.

I was given an interview for a fellowship . . . The interviewer wanted to meet in his hotel room. He was really hostile and started asking me questions like "are you going on a diet?" It was really awful and I got really flustered and couldn't get up enough guts to walk out. I just fell apart in front of him. I didn't have anybody in my department to go to for advice . . . I wanted to write a letter to the organization, but it was the chairman of the organization who did the interview . . . I didn't know what to do . . . I came to WIE for help . . . people here helped me break it down into what was wrong. I was so shocked.

The staff at CWEP see one of their most important tasks as helping the students understand why they are on welfare and why they've remained locked into a series of low-paying jobs. The director of CWEP describes their work with students:

We try to shape a sense of assertiveness and entitlement . . . as a person I'm entitled and I can negotiate what's going on . . . Workstart gets women talking about what they can have control over and what's been taken away from them. We give them an overview of the welfare system to counteract the sense of personal failure . . . we introduce the idea that there are systemic failures instead of personal failures . . . that everything is not your fault.

Balancing Support with "Letting Go." Support at CWEP and WIE is much more than a series of discrete interactions. Instead, they serve as "safe places" for students to try out new identities and new ways of behaving while structuring out anxiety-producing considerations. A critical dimension of emotional capital is the ability of an organization to reduce anxiety and threat so that individuals can focus on their developmental tasks. In doing so, organizations engender strong feelings in their members and shape how they imagine their present and their future.

These programs function as "holding environments" (Kegan, 1982), providing safe places for students to try out new identities and new ways of behaving while structuring out anxiety-producing considerations. By helping students reinterpret their experiences in ways that build a sense of competence, they allow them to concentrate on the task at hand. As their sense of threat and uncertainty is reduced, the women engineering students are able to focus their efforts on mastering an intense and demanding curriculum. The low-income women at CWEP are helped to block out the demands of their difficult lives so that they are able to become engrossed in their school work. Students in both settings describe this enhanced capacity to concentrate as a critical aspect the programs.

At the same time that these programs "hold" students in a safe and supportive environment they also encourage independence so that they can move on. As students develop new competencies they must shift their attention to the future and move on to new educational or professional settings.

The programs must shift their orientation from immediate support to promoting a sense that the organization will still "be around for them." Both programs do this in a variety of ways, ranging from letting individuals go their own way to providing transitional supports and opportunities for former students to return as volunteers.

This balance of "holding on" and letting go" that Kegan describes as essential to adult development (Kegan, 1982) produces graduates who are neither alienated from the organization nor overly dependent on it. Most students we interviewed stated that they were glad that the program was there even if they didn't rely on it for help any more. All said that they felt confident that the programs "would be there for them" in the future if they ever needed assistance. A former student who is completing her associate's degree at a community college described her relation to CWEP in these terms:

> I participate in the Parenting Project. There's Parent Support Group, Headstart, there's a lot of other things I still go there for. I have two girlfriends I'm getting into GED. I tell my girlfriends, go ahead, they can help you out.

Attending to the External Environment. As these programs create strong organizational cultures that do much of the work of transforming appraisals of well-being, they free up the time and energy of some paid staff to look outward. This capacity to focus externally is critical to the effectiveness and continued existence of these relatively small programs. At WIE, the executive director spends considerable time building relationships with the dean and department heads in the School of Engineering, as well as other administrators in the university. These relationships allow her to be effective in advocating for women students. This advocacy in turn is a powerful symbol of the program to students, who frequently refer to WIE as "the big gun" that can be used to protect them. The executive director has also worked to promote the national reputation of WIE through her involvement in WEPAN, the national organization of women in engineering programs, and by sponsoring citywide and regional conferences on issues related to women in science and engineering. It is this national reputation which contributes to the ability to raise funds to expand programs and further strengthen its image with university administrators.

CWEP also sustains an outward focus. During a critical fundraising period the executive director worked with the board chair to attract new board members from the corporate sector which brought critical new skills to the organization. CWEP has also been active in city and state-level discussions of welfare reform and the role of education in work to welfare programs.

Both programs have also had a considerable impact on the community colleges with which they are associated. CWEP draws on community college faculty who teach the college courses that are offered on-site. These faculty members have been deeply influenced by the CWEP culture of support, and over time have become a cohesive and highly committed group. They have drawn on their experience at CWEP in advocating for curricular and student support changes at their institution. WIE has also had a disproportionate impact on area community colleges. Staff work with a coalition of Seattle-area community colleges to identify potential engineering students and assist them in transferring to the university. Through this connection WIE has worked to improve the teaching of math and science by bringing university and community college faculty together in discipline groups to discuss pedagogical issues. WIE has also worked with staff at the women's programs that exist at each of the area community colleges to develop creative ways in interest women students in science and engineering, and support them through the transfer process.

Conclusion: The Links Between Emotional Capital and Educational Success

Researchers such as Coleman (1993) and Bryck, Lee and Holland (1993) have demonstrated the efficacy of social capital in improving the effectiveness of schools. This work has important implications for community colleges that serve large at-risk, nontraditional populations of students. However, the way in which social capital has been theoretically formulated leaves difficult but important questions unaddressed.

We have attempted to show that the concept of emotional capital i[a useful extension of the literature on social capital. Viewing emotional capital as the capacity of an organizational culture to hold in place positive appraisals of well-being directs attention to how programmatic and cultural factors intertwine and mutually strengthen one another. The analysis of emotional capital clarifies how educational settings can respond to the needs of culturally diverse, at-risk students whose practical difficulties are aggravated by cultures in which negative and dispiriting interpretations of reality predominate.

We believe that the concept of emotional capital has much to offer community colleges. Most community colleges have large student service divisions and pride themselves on being "student-centered." However, typical student service programs continually struggle to improve student retention and academic performance, especially among students who are most at-risk. As our institutions face increasingly diverse student populations with a wide range of needs, support programs need to identify the best practices and programmatic features that have the greatest impact on students.

It is the achievement of both WIE and CWEP that in very different settings, and with minimal resources, they resolve so many problems for their students. These programs are emotionally charged and cognitively powerful.

They shape student responses by developing cultural practices and organizational forms that sustain high levels of positive appraisals. These programs demonstrate that effective social support helps students acquire adequate coping skills. In addition, they enhance the likelihood that those skills will be used by promoting a high degree of hope and self-confidence in students about their ability to surmount whatever difficulties they may face. The programs do this by providing dense networks of support that offer students a mix of information, pragmatic advice, emotional support and advocacy. These networks of support offer numerous settings where students can have close contact with mentors, see effective behavior modeled for them, practice defining problems and generating plans, and try out new behavior and new identities. Also, they provide multiple pathways for involvement, enhancing the likelihood of student involvement and commitment.

By developing powerful cultures of support these programs leverage their resources in ways they permit them to have a disproportionate impact on students and other institutions. They do this by continually drawing in resources and building commitment among students, staff, and volunteers. Both programs offer powerful models of ways to transform students and support them through their academic careers. The major question they pose is whether the development of such high levels of social and emotional capital is possible only in special programs or whether key features of these programs can be transferred throughout community colleges.

References

Astin, A. 1985. *Achieving educational excellence: A critical assessment of priorities and practices in higher education.* San Francisco: Jossey-Bass.

Bandura, A. 1977. "Self-efficacy: Toward a unifying theory of behavioral change." *Psychological Review*, 84: 191–215.

Berger, P., & Luckman, T. 1967. *The social construction of reality.* Garden City, New York: Anchor.

Boje, D. M. 1991. "The storytelling organization: A study of story performance in an office-supply firm." *Administrative Science Quarterly*, 36: 106–26.

Bourdieu, P. 1985. "Social space and the genesis of groups." *Theory and Society*, 14: 723–44.

Brint, S., & Karabel, J. 1989. *The diverted dream: Community colleges and the promise of educational opportunity in America, 1900–1985.* New York: Oxford University Press.

Bryk, A.; Lee, V. E.; & Holland, P. B. 1993. *Catholic schools and the common good.* Cambridge: Harvard University Press.

Coleman, J. 1993. "Social capital in the creation of human capital." *American Journal of Sociology*, 94, Supplement (February): S95–S120.

Coleman, J., & Hoffer, T. 1987. *Public and private high schools: The impact of communities*. New York: Basic Books.

Dougherty, K. J. 1994. *The contradictory college: The conflicting origins, impacts, and futures of the community college*. Albany: SUNY Press.

Glaser, B., & Strauss, A. L. 1967. *Discovery of grounded theory: Strategies for qualitative research*. Chicago: Aldine.

Griffith, M., & Connor, A. 1995. *Democracy's open door: The community college in America's future*. Portsmouth, NH: Boynton/Cook Publishers.

Kanter, R.M. 1977. *Men and women of the corporation*. New York: Basic Books.

Kegan, R. 1982. *The evolving self*. Cambridge, Mass.: Harvard University Press.

Lazarus, R. 1981. "The stress and coping paradigm." in C. Eisdorfer (ed.) *Models for Clinical Psychopathology*. New York: Spectrum.

Lazarus, R. 1991. *Emotion and adaptation*. New York: Oxford University Press.

Lazarus, R., & Folkman, S. 1984. *Stress, appraisal, and coping*. New York: Springer.

McGrath, D., & Van Buskirk, W. 1993. *Crafting a culture of success for women engineers*. Philadelphia: Nonprofit Management Development Center, La Salle University.

McGrath, D., & Van Buskirk, W. 1994. *Voice, participation, and empowerment: The community women's education project*. Philadelphia: Nonprofit Management Development Center, La Salle University.

Nora, A. 1987. "Determinants of retention among Chicano students." *Research in Higher Education*, 26(1): 31–59.

Pascarella, E., & Terenzini, P. 1991. *How college affects students: Findings and insights from twenty years of research*. San Francisco: Jossey-Bass.

Putnam, R. 1993. *Making democracy work: Civic traditions in modern Italy*. Princeton, N.J.: Princeton University Press.

Rendon, L. 1994. "Validating culturally diverse students: Toward a new model of learning and students development." *Innovative Higher Education*, 19 (Fall): 33–51.

Shaw, K., & London, H. 1995. "Negotiating boundaries and borders: Institutional and student cultures in high-transfer urban community colleges." Paper presented at the Association for the Study of Higher Education Annual Meeting, Orlando, Florida.

Swidler, A. 1986. "Culture in action: Symbols and strategies." *American Sociological Review*, 51: 273–86.

Tinto, V. 1987. *Leaving college*. Chicago: University of Chicago Press.

Van Buskirk, W., & McGrath, D. 1992. "Organizational stories as a window on affect in organizations." *Journal of Organizational Change Management* 5.

Van Buskirk, W.; Barrett, F.; McGrath, D.; & Schor, S. 1994. "Coping with hypermasculine tradition in organizational cultures." Paper presented at the annual meeting, Academy of Management, August 6–9, Vancouver, British Columbia.

Wilson, R. 1991. "Colleges start programs to encourage women who are interested in engineering careers." *The Chronicle of Higher Education*, June 12.

Zwerling, L. S. (ed.) 1986. *The community college and its critics.* In *New Directions for Community Colleges,* 54 (June), San Francisco: Jossey-Bass.

CHAPTER 3

The Struggle for Mobility in the Contact Zone of Basic Writing

STANFORD T. GOTO

Introduction

The willingness of community colleges to pursue multiple goals is both an admirable strength and an Achilles heel. Embedded in the institutional mission are explicit or implicit goals of maintaining academic rigor, facilitating access, and encouraging diversity. It would be difficult to contest the merits of any of these individual objectives. However, the issues become murky when these goals are pursued together. Observers point out that conflicts might arise, particularly when the need to maintain open access is balanced against the need to preserve academic status (see Roueche & Baker, 1987).

These conflicts are particularly visible in the area of basic writing.[1] As one of the chief mechanisms for facilitating access to higher education, basic writing programs must welcome virtually any student, regardless of his or her ability. At the same time, as an academic discipline, composition instruction must sort students by ability, advancing only those who are deemed "proficient." Basic writing's actual record in promoting these goals has often been called into question. Critics (e.g., Traub, 1994) claim that the proliferation of remediation in the last several decades has not allowed significant numbers of underprepared students to move in into the academic mainstream. Furthermore, some contend that the spread of remediation has undermined standards in regular academic courses. Bruno Manno, former U.S. Assistant Secretary of Education for Policy and Planning, concludes that these developments have resulted in a general "dumbing down" of the curriculum (1995).

These serious allegations have emerged in an area which has received surprisingly little attention from researchers. Most studies of community-college-based composition are in-house evaluations of programs in single institutions or college districts. National studies of remediation (e.g., Mansfield and Farris, 1991; Piland and Pierce, 1989) have tended to focus on program characteristics and total enrollment. Providing a broad overview of remedial education, studies like these have been the principle sources of ammunition for critics. Educator have generally assumed in interpreting the research that desirable outcomes, such as high exit test scores or low attrition rates, are the result of effective teaching and good program design. Conversely, undesirable outcomes are usually attributed to ineffective institutional practice. These conclusions, I would argue, are not as self-evident as they may seem. Even the more detailed studies leave a great deal unanswered about why certain outcomes occur. Questions persist because researchers have focused on program-level issues, as opposed to classroom-level issues. A common concern has been the overall effectiveness of basic writing instruction at given institutions. To assess program effectiveness, researchers (e.g., Slark, 1989) have relied on survey instruments, institutional records, and/or writing tests. Typically, baseline data are gathered at the beginning of the semester, and outcome data are collected near the end. What happens between the first and last weeks of the semester remains a mystery. Presumably, instruction has a strong bearing on student outcomes. In addition, there may be any number of other relevant influences such as student preparation, family and work commitments, interpersonal dynamics in the classroom, and so on. Largescale survey studies have not been able to tease out how such factors come into play.

I believe that, to understand why students succeed or fail in basic writing, we must examine teaching and learning as they occur in the classroom. We must look closely at what happens to students over time and why. Particularly suited for this type of inquiry are fine-grained, qualitative approaches which focus on the classroom or the individual as the unit of analysis. I conducted a year-long study along these lines in basic writing classes at a small community college. Using ethnographic and socio-linguistic methods, I studied how individual students and instructors grappled with differing ideas about academic literacy. This chapter illustrates how conflicting student interests complicate one instructor's efforts to promote academic mobility and maintain academic rigor. I focus on a brief event in one class to provide a detailed view of learning and teaching on the individual level. This work draws on Mary Louise Pratt's notion of a "contact zone" (1991) to explain how misunderstandings might arise when the instructor and students approach an assignment with different agendas. While findings from this micro-analysis are considerably less generalizable than those which might emerge from the study of multiple events or multiple sites, I have opted in this chapter to pursue depth of detail, rather than breadth of scope, in order to illustrate a point which has not come to light in traditional research—that the diversity of student intentions in basic writing might make it necessary for the instructor to pursue potentially conflicting goals. This point, I believe, complicates current notions of institutional mobility and "cooling out."

Remediation as Conduit or Diversion?

Tensions between the various and often competing goals of the community college came to a head in the era of open admissions. By the early 1970s, community colleges had shed almost all admissions criteria, opening institutional doors to an unprecedented heterogeneity of students. Dramatic increases in the size and diversity of student bodies might have been hailed as an egalitarian triumph if it were not for alarmingly high dropout rates, which prompted some cynics to refer to open-door policies as the "revolving door" (see Cohen & Brawer, 1989). Clark (1960) foreshadowed this problem when he argued that high attrition is a symptom of fundamental tensions in community colleges. In his view, community colleges are obligated to invite all people to attend—as if social mobility were universally possible. At the same time, limited opportunities in society force community colleges to allow only a portion of the student body to advance to higher levels. In Clark's view, these circumstances make it inevitable that community colleges will enroll and "cool out" large numbers of ambitious students who are not prepared academically to move through higher education.

It was in the early days of open admissions that remediation gained prominence as a possible means to promote access while maintaining academic standards. Prior to the 1960s, junior college leaders were not terribly concerned that institutions might divert underprepared students[2] away from transfer-oriented education. While educators (e.g., Bogue, 1950) felt obligated to provide second chances, they considered it their duty only to re-administer basic content in remedial classes, which differed little from high school English classes. The assumption was that students were ultimately responsible for grasping what they should have learned earlier in life. This Darwinistic view began to change as proportions of underprepared students rose sharply through the late 1960s and early 1970s (see Donovan, 1991). Educators realized it was morally indefensible and fiscally unwise to allow large portions of the student body to succumb to attrition. Simply allowing students to enroll in classes was not sufficient. For access to be genuine, students had to have real opportunities for upward mobility. Educators began to consider how basic writing instruction might function proactively to keep students moving toward transfer. If basic writing could act as a conduit, taking in underprepared students and allowing them to be successful in regular academic work, the institution would live up to the promise of open access without having to change standards of academic excellence.

Critics often claim that basic writing instruction in community colleges fails on the whole to move students through the academic pipeline because the field is plagued with ineffective teaching. McGrath and Spear (1991) claim that writing instructors confound cognitive and affective goals. The diluted curriculum allegedly deprives students of opportunities to practice literacy in ways which would allow them to advance in mainstream academics. Richardson, Fisk and Okun (1983) reach a similar conclusion in their naturalistic study of literacy in community colleges. They argue that basic writing instructors focus more on socialization goals than on academic competencies. In failing to prepare students academically, basic writing instruction presumably inhibits social mobility by denying students the education they need to earn university degrees and secure better jobs. This claim is consistent with Marxist-influenced theories of social reproduction in community colleges (see Karabel, 1972; Pincus, 1994; Zwerling, 1976). Emphasizing how institutional structures influence student mobility, these so-called structural theories hold that community colleges divert working-class students away from transfer education into semi-professional areas, effectively strengthening the class hierarchy (Brint and Karabel, 1989).

Two factors which remedial doomsayers tend to overlook are student efficacy and student diversity. Structuralist critics generally assume that instructors control the social world of the basic writing classroom. Presumably, whether students fail or succeed in entering the academic mainstream depends primarily on the instructor's effectiveness in preparing them. This perspective fails to take into account the extent to which students control their own educational trajectories and the extent to which the students' intentions differ from those of the instructor. A central assumption of the cooling out argument is that students initially enroll in basic writing because they see the class as a necessary step in their transfer-oriented goals. This is not necessarily true. Basic writing classes are often prerequisites or precursors to English prerequisites, not only for transfer, but also for a variety of non-transfer programs. Consequently, these courses tend to enroll a broad cross-section of individuals from the general student body. In his analysis of national data, Grubb (1991, p. 195) reports that 18 percent of community college students in 1986 sought a university degree, while 48 percent wanted an A.A. and 11 percent wanted a certificate. Moreover, Grubb suggests that, among those who wanted to transfer, some were only marginally committed to this goal. Presumably, these "experimenters" came to college without a clear idea of what they wanted to achieve in higher education. If these findings apply to the subset of basic writing students, they would tend to suggest that only a minority of students are committed to pursuing transfer-oriented, liberal arts education—the *raison d'être* of basic writing. This possibility complicates the claim that the institution cools out the ambitions of students in basic writing classes.

I would argue that, to better understand student outcomes in basic writing, we must consider how educators and students influence each other. Weis (1985) uses this approach in her ethnography of African American students at an urban community college. The author presents this work as a response to theories which portray students as passive victims of institutional conspiracies. She describes how the African American students in her study resisted instructors' efforts to impose institutional norms on them. Encountering defiance, the instructors lowered their teaching expectations, which made the students intensify their resistance. The cycle of resistance and retreat allegedly perpetuated the marginal status of African Americans at this college. Weis' analysis adds another dimension to structural theories of student attrition. Cooling out is seen as the result, not simply of institutional action, but of the interaction of educators and students. One limitation of Weis' analysis lies in her characterization of this interaction. Resistance and compliance are portrayed as collective actions of one group in response to another. I believe that student actions and perceptions are less unified, particularly within a diverse group of students. I would argue that students in heterogeneous basic writing classes are more likely to act on their own initiative, rather than in consort with their peers. To observe these phenomena, one must examine learning processes on the individual level. This approach is used by McCarthy (1987) in a sociolinguistic case study of a novice academic writer. The author examines how the student makes sense of writing assignments which do not seem entirely consistent. Because her study design does not require her to make generalizations about multiple research subjects, McCarthy is able to analyze learning processes at a level of detail which is unattainable in studies of large groups. The author, however, does not discuss how instructors responded to this student. In my view, the dynamics of teaching and learning in basic writing might be understood best by analyzing how the instructor and individual students influence each other dialectically.

Remedial Writing and the Contact Zone

Composition theory has led to some promising developments along these lines. In recent years, educators have drawn on Bakhtin and other theorists to explain how social roles in the composition classroom are constructed through language, rather than dictated by socioeconomic structure. Responding to the determinism of structuralism, these poststructural discourse theories have been used to examine ideological conflict between students and instructors without presuming that differences necessarily lead to social reproduction. Educators have found Pratt's notion of the "contact zone" (1991) to be particularly useful for these purposes. Pratt questions the assumption that the language classroom is a "speech community" where linguistic outsiders (i.e., students) are indoctrinated into a "unified and homogeneous social world in which language exists as a shared patrimony" (p. 38). She argues that students come to class with their own notions of language and that they selectively interpret or challenge conventions which differ from their own. In this sense, the classroom might be described as a contact zone—a social space where individuals grapple with conflicting ideas. This characterization of classroom interaction implies that the process of meaning negotiation is not unilateral (instructor influencing students) or bilateral (the instructor influencing students and visa versa) but multilateral (any individual potentially influencing any other). A further implication is that the instructor cannot control or predict with total certainty how students will progress through a class session, much less through a semester.

Some researchers have begun using the metaphor of the contact zone to guide their studies of basic writing classes. Mutnick (1996) draws on Pratt and other theorists to conduct a semiotic analysis of how basic writers and adjunct faculty make sense of writing tasks. She argues that students and instructors continually "construct" their respective roles as they transact through spoken and written language in the classroom. This claim challenges the distinction between instructors as academic insiders and basic writers as outsiders. Another work in this vein is DiPardo's 1993 ethnography of students and tutors in an adjunct writing program. Although the author does not refer specifically to the contact-zone literature, she proceeds in the spirit of Pratt to analyze how ethnically diverse basic writers negotiate the demands of academic life in a predominantly white university. Like Weis, both Mutnick and Pratt use naturalistic, contextually-bound research methods to explain why students progress or fail in their coursework. However, unlike Weis, the other two researchers focus on micro-relationships between individuals rather than on macro-relationships between groups. It is significant to note that, like almost all other qualitative research on basic writing, the Mutnick (1996) and Dipardo (1993) studies were conducted in university writing programs.

I believe that similar research can be useful in the study of community-college-based remediation. A qualitative micro-study of relationships in the classroom might address the persistent question of how basic writing instruction promotes or hinders student mobility in community colleges. Unlike studies which approach the mobility question by tracking where students go (see Dougherty, 1991, 1994), a micro-study might analyze how teaching and learning mutually influence each other. An inquiry of this sort could test the claim that remedial writing instruction fails to provide students with literacy skills necessary for personal advancement (see McGrath and Spear, 1991). The research approach would differ from that of Richardson et al. (1983), who examine instruction as if it were an independent variable causing students to learn in certain ways. A study based on the contact zone metaphor would consider, not only how students perceive and respond to their instructors, but also how instructors adjust their teaching in response to students. This approach might shed light on how the negotiation of diverse interests influences student progress in basic writing.

Research Site, Classroom, and Teaching

In the remainder of this chapter, I will draw on observation and interview data to highlight some pedagogical dilemmas which arise as an instructor tries to address multiple needs in a remedial writing class. First, I will provide a general overview of the site. Then, drawing on the contact zone metaphor, I will examine how one instructor and three students respond to a brief series of events during a class period. This micro-analysis will show how the instructor makes moment-to-moment decisions to encourage students and/or enforce academic standards. The analysis, furthermore, will show how these efforts are complicated by the students' personal agendas.

My research was conducted at a community college located in a small city in an area with both agricultural and industrial businesses. Historically, the institution served a predominantly white population engaged in farming and food processing. Regional demographics were changing, however. A boom in affordable housing and an expansion of retail employment attracted a variety of newcomers in the 1980s including commuters, refugees, and a new generation of immigrant farm workers (Department of Commerce, 1993). Changes in the general population brought new diversity to the student body. The trend was particularly evident in the writing program, which (like many remedial programs) enrolled a disproportionately large number of minorities.

Data were gathered in writing classes and around campus. Initially, I observed composition courses taught by four instructors. I also administered surveys to get a general sense of how students were progressing. In the following semester, I worked with two instructors, who allowed me to observe classes and tutor students. The out-of-class tutoring sessions gave me opportunities to interview students about events in class. I also gathering data by collecting student writing samples, interviewing instructors and administrators, observing campus events, and reviewing departmental documents.

My analysis of teaching-related data suggests that composition instructors at this college held two types of pedagogical goals. For the most part, they agreed on a set of text-related goals, which were documented by the department. It was commonly understood that students in remedial classes should learn to write simple essays using conventional grammar and organizational structures. In addition to these officially-recognized goals, instructors maintained numerous unofficial course goals which were not documented by the department. These aims, which varied from one instructor to the next, generally had to do with helping academic newcomers become successful college students. The division between official and unofficial goals indicates that instructors were aware of the need to enforce academic standards and to welcome non-traditional students to higher education.

These issues were prominent in the basic writing class of Ignacio Sanchez, a popular Chicano instructor. Like his colleagues, Sanchez felt strongly that he was responsible for preparing students to write "at the college level." In addition, he believed that, as one of the few minority faculty members, he should make students feel comfortable with college—particularly when minority students came to him for guidance. His success in both of these areas was evident in his enrollment, which tended to be more diverse than in other sections. The class which I observed had 15 Latinos, three Asians, two African American, and two whites. About half of the students were recent high school graduates, and the rest were in their early twenties to mid-thirties.

The following narrative is an excerpt from an observation in Sanchez's class. The five-minute segment illustrates a common daily activity—clarifying instructions for an assignment. This segment, however, does not represent the usual tone of the class or the range of pedagogical approaches used by the instructor. Typically, interaction in class was casual and friendly. On this particular day, there were more tensions than usual. The observation took place in the tenth week of the fall semester. Seventeen students were present. They had rearranged the desks into uneven clusters so they could sit with their friends. Cesar and Haum sat together near center of the room, with Helen and Terry seated directly behind them. Cheleen sat with her three friends to left of Cesar and Haum. Two more pairs were against right and left walls, and several students sat in the back. Sanchez was walking desk to desk, picking up students' essays and explaining the procedures for "work-shopping" papers:

Instructor: I'm going to take these (papers) to the printers and you guys are going to be famous. I'm going to hand these out and we're going to read them in class. If you don't want anyone to know it's yours—

Haum: Oh, I forgot about that.

Instructor: —make sure you give me a little note that says "take my name off" and I'll make sure your name is off.
(Haum, Cheleen, and other students look through their binders and notes in search of their essays. Some pull out laser-printed pages. Others tear out handwritten pages from spiral notebooks. Cesar, who is staring at the wall, did not do the assignment.)

Helen: You're not talking about the rough draft, right?

Instructor: Yeah, we're talking about the rough draft. We're going to read it, workshop it, make it better as a class. We're going to learn how to do that. If you have a real problem with it, talk to me after class. And for those of you who didn't turn it in today, well, you don't get to workshop anyway, so I wouldn't worry about it.

Cesar: I didn't know.

Instructor: (teasing Cesar) And that's not Cesar's fault. Huh, Cesar? It isn't your fault if someone else's papers are late?

Terry: It's Mother Nature's fault!
(Haum and others laugh. Cheleen is writing something in a binder. She does not respond to the activity around her.)

Cesar: (looking at the instructor, speaking under his breath) Don't kid around.

Terry: Can we turn our papers in late?

Instructor: You can, but it's not going to be workshopped.

Terry: (feigning surprise, playing on the word "workshopped") It's not even WORTH IT?

Instructor: (enunciating) It's not going to get WORKSHOPPED.
(Students laugh again. Cesar slumps in his chair. Cheleen stops writing and lays hear head on her desk.)

Instructor: (addressing Cesar directly) Cesar, if you have a real hard life story, you can talk to me after class, OK? (No response. Instructor addresses class.) Anyone who has a hard life story, I'm willing to listen.

The instructor conducts this lesson with two general objectives in mind. Outside of class, he explains, "The most immediate goal is to get (students) ready for the next level" which is the next writing course in the sequence leading to regular first-year composition. One of his approaches is to call attention to the ways in which skilled writers go about writing: "If there's one thing I try to get the students to realize . . . is that writing is a process of trial and refinement. They need to do multiple drafts." One step in the process involves workshopping papers—having the class collectively edit each individual's draft. Sanchez believes that this sort of critique should be handled carefully. Basic writers, in his view, are not convinced that they can be successful writers and students. Consequently, they are easily discouraged by criticism. To address this issue, Sanchez pursues a secondary goal "to give (students) self-confidence as writers." He points out, however, that this affective goal should not replace critical guidance. To balance these objectives, he tries to give students a good deal of encouragement at the beginning of the semester and gradually he moves toward more critical evaluation of their writing: "The first part of the class is just writing—writing and reading their writing. We look at the good things . . . Once they're comfortable with that, we spend three or four weeks on form and voice. And then the last part which we just started this week is editing."

The classroom narrative further reveals a behavioral dimension to the instructor's goal of preparing students for "the next level." By repeatedly explaining the rules of the assignment, Sanchez attempts to socialize students to what he believes is the ethos of higher education. Initially, he explains that late papers will not be included in the packet of essays to be workshopped. Embedded in his instructions are implicit messages about classroom norms: Deadlines are inflexible (unless one has a "hard life story"); students must pay attention to the syllabus; students must do everything in their power to complete assignments by the due dates; failing to complete one assignment makes it difficult for students to complete future work. These messages emerge again when the instructor says jokingly to Cesar, "It isn't your fault if someone else's papers are late?" Here, the mini-lesson is that each person is responsible for getting his or her assignments in on time. This didactic teasing appears to be an attempt to engage Cesar—to challenge him in a friendly way to think about timeliness and personal responsibility.

"I'm Not Hyped Up"

Cesar is no stranger to challenges. In an essay he writes about surviving in a small town in Mexico: "My first day in kindergarten I got jumped by a couple of fat kids. In school some students didn't listen to the teachers. I hated teachers in school. If you got in trouble or if someone set you up, the teacher would hit you with a ruler or a wooden stick. I got jumped in school and in my neighborhood a lot! For about five and a half years. My dad showed me how to fight and he told me not to give up easy or take shit from people." When he and his family moved to California, Cesar hoped he could get away from the violence which plagued his life. Trouble seemed to follow him, however. He got into fights at his high school until he was transferred after being labeled a "troublemaker." The situation worsened in the new school, which was a regional rival of his old high school. Cesar eventually dropped out.

Now, at age 20 after earning his GED, Cesar sees his first semester of college as a chance to change his life for the better. Here, no one knows his reputation for getting into fights. He hopes he can create a new image as a hard-working student. His goal is to go into law enforcement and become an undercover policeman. He hopes that a year in the administration of justice program will allow him to take the entrance test for the police academy.

This opportunity has come with a new set of challenges, however. Cesar is the first among his family and friends to pursue higher education, and he is finding the experience to be alienating. "I'm a friendly person," he comments. "I used to be the class clown. Everyone knew me. But now I'm in college. I feel like a stranger here. There are a lot of races. I see people raising their hand in class. I think I know the answer, too, but I don't say nothing. People might think I'm stupid." The unfamiliar faces, the diversity of the student body, the arcane rules of behavior, the unfamiliar subject matter—all confirm Cesar's impression that he is outside of his element and that he does not belong here. The problem is compounded by what Cesar sees as a lack of adequate guidance from counselors and instructors: "Counselors try to help you, but they don't take the time to know what you want . . . . I want someone to be a 'hype-up'—someone to encourage you, be proud of you. I feel like at (this college) there's no one here to help you. I feel uncomfortable." The perceived shortcomings of the system are of great concern to Cesar, who is reminded by skeptical family members that he is losing money by studying and not working: "My parents are proud of me that I'm going to college. But then people tell me that college is a waste of time—that I need to get a job." In weighing the monetary and opportunity costs against the expected benefits of college education, he finds little tangible evidence to justify a prolonged commitment.

To some extent, basic writing has been a bright spot in an otherwise rocky semester for Cesar. He says he feels more relaxed in this class, in part, because the instructor and most of the class are Chicano. He particularly appreciates the casual rapport which Sanchez maintains with students. This makes Cesar feel comfortable enough to "clown around" occasionally in class. In one tongue-in-cheek presentation he says that the instructor "(keeps) it cool like a Chicano teacher should." Encouraged by the friendly atmosphere, Cesar tries to remain optimistic about college.

At times, however, he feels overwhelmed, particularly when he finds little support elsewhere within or outside of the institution. He observes somewhat bitterly, "I made it to college myself, and now there are so many problems stopping me." Preoccupied with the challenges of staying in college, Cesar finds little energy to write and edit essays. This has led to a vicious cycle in which Cesar's feelings of doubt and confusion have caused him to fall behind in his studies, generating more doubt and confusion. He admits, "I have problems understanding Mr. Sanchez when he gives us homework. He talks too fast."

The classroom narrative shows the outcome of a particular misunderstanding between Cesar and the instructor. Cesar becomes agitated after he learns that the assignment is due: "I guess I didn't hear it when Mr. Sanchez told us when the drafts were due. That pisses me off. He should let me turn in my paper late." Usually, Cesar accepts responsibility for not doing assignments on time, but in this case his anger is aroused when the instructor teases him, saying "It isn't your fault if someone else's papers are late." Joking between Cesar and Sanchez is common, and typically Cesar takes the teasing in stride. In this instance, however, the particular wording touches a raw nerve. He explains that earlier in the week he was in a different class quietly doing his work when some other students became rowdy: "All of a sudden, the teacher yelled at us, telling a bunch of us to get out. I didn't come to college to be labeled for anyone else's faults. I never expected to feel anger toward my teachers. I feel ashamed, embarrassed." This incident raised bad memories of high school, when teachers identified him as a "troublemaker." A few days later, the subject comes up again by coincidence when Sanchez makes the comment about turning in late papers. Cesar feels that, once again, he is blamed unfairly.

"I Want to Improve My Writing Skill and Reading"

Haum does not remember much from his early life. He was born in a refugee camp in Thailand, where his parents and older siblings spoke their native Hmong. The family immigrated to the United States when Haum was a child. They lived in Montana for a short time and later moved to the West Coast. "School was strange," comments Haum as he recalls some of the language problems he encountered in grammar school. Eventually, he adapted to the surroundings. He made friends and did reasonably well in academics.

Now, the 18-year-old enjoys being in college—a sentiment influenced strongly by the positive experiences of his siblings. When he was in high school, Haum regularly visited a sister who was a biology student at Stanford and an older brother who was an engineering major living in a university dorm. This exposure made Haum more than passingly familiar with the conventions college life. As a first-year community college student, Haum knows which prerequisites he needed to fulfill in order to transfer to a state university as a computer-science major. He particularly looks forward to the required courses in math, his favorite subject.

Haum is not excited about English classes, however. "I never been interesting in writing," he writes. "For me is hard because the words just don't flow. Reading it gets boring and it's hard to concentrate for hours reading. Sometime I get confused. I'm taking (basic writing) to prepare for the next level. I need (freshman composition) for transfer." He recalls that he got passing grades in high school English by closely following his teachers' instructions. This strategy, he believes, will serve him well in college. "I do what Mr. Sanchez says," he comments. "I should do okay in this class."

Despite his misgivings about English as a subject, Haum has come to enjoy Sanchez's class. One thing he likes is that students are encouraged to interact in class. Haum explains that in most classes he remains aloof so he can learn without interruption: "Me, I want less people and quieter—you know, not so much noise. For me, I don't like sitting in groups that much, anyway, because you want to do the work and someone's bugging you. You can't really do your work if you do that." It came as somewhat of a surprise to Haum when he found he could benefit from class discussions following lectures in basic writing: "Actually, I like both—I mean lectures and talk about (the readings). Students talk. I enjoy doing this. You get to express how you (think), so you see different sides of people."

In the classroom narrative, Haum seems to be at least moderately engaged in classroom activities. He is seen following directions regarding the workshop assignment. His comment, "Oh, I forgot about that," implies that he is trying to understand what the instructor is saying. He also interacts in ways which the instructor encourages. While he does not join in the verbal bantering, he watches the action and laughs at people's jokes. It appears that he is attuned to some of the instructor's behavioral objectives. What we cannot determine from his comments is whether or not Haum has grasped an important subtlety of the workshop assignment—that editing is part of what the instructor calls a "process of trial and refinement." Implicit in the assignment is the assumption that the writer must move beyond the stated instructions to explore unfamiliar creative territory through trial and perhaps error. It remains to be seen whether Haum's insistence on "do(ing) what Mr. Sanchez says" would allow him to view writing as the instructor does—as a creative process in which it is desirable to probe tentative ideas, run into stylistic dead ends, throw out weak text, and start over.

"If I Could Take My Little Group"

At 22, Cheleen is determined to make her second try at college a success. "The first time was just too crazy," she recalls. "I just couldn't handle the pressure." The dissolution of her marriage and problems in her family made it too difficult for her to study. She dropped out in the first semester. Her financial situation became increasingly more dire during the next few years, when she developed a substance addiction and became pregnant. She recalls, "After I had my son, I decided I wanted to provide a better life for him and be a good example. I told myself I'd get off drugs, get off AFDC, and go back to college." Her situation is better now. Cheleen is in a recovery program and she has a part-time job at Burger King, which helps her pay bills. "I think I'm going to make it this time," she says with a smile.

Cheleen finds it takes all the determination she can muster to stay focused on her school work. She says she has trouble concentrating, even when there are no external distractions. "I can't remember details," she claims. "I don't have a good imagination." Part of the problem, she suspects, is that she has been away from school for three years. In addition, her baby recently started walking, so Cheleen rarely has uninterrupted stretches of time to do her school work. She prefers to leave the toddler with her mother or brother when she studies or goes to class. Frequently, however, they are not available, so she must take him with her. When her son is with a sitter, Cheleen tries to use her time as efficiently as possible. One of her strategies is to work with other students whom she thinks are serious about school. Cheleen, a white student, says she does not think about race when she picks study partners. Instead, she gravitates toward individuals who are "more mature"—usually returning female students, like herself. She explains, "I need a friend in every class. Like in English, I really relate to Susan. She has kids, too. So we get together and talk about school work and children. We sit near the front of the room, and she helps me out. It helps me stay awake."

Cheleen finds it particularly difficult to concentrate in composition class. Part of the problem is that, in her view, writing objectives are too nebulous. "In high school I dreaded English," she recalls. "I didn't know what the teacher wanted. I don't like interpretive writing. I don't like imaginative writing." A more immediate problem in the present class is that certain students are "immature" and "loud," according to Cheleen. "Those people in the back—they're constantly screwing around," she complains. "It's like you're in high school. I can't stand it! And then there's Terry. I have a problem with her. I feel like she's trying to take over the class—that she wants to be the instructor. . . . I think there's a time for this and there's a time to be quiet and go back to your seat. And she doesn't know the difference." The result of Cheleen's frustration is seen in the classroom narrative. Earlier in class Terry had dominated the classroom discussion, making Cheleen increasingly angry. Eventually, Cheleen gives up all pretense of doing school work and lays her head on the desk in quiet protest.

All in all, Cheleen has mixed feelings about how the instructor conducts the basic writing class. In her view, Sanchez lets students get away with too much socializing. "He needs to be mean," she comments. "I think that would straighten up a lot of us—even me . . . I mean, if you get kicked out for a couple of days, it might dawn on (those students): 'Hey, I've been kicked out.'" Aside from the discipline issue, Cheleen thinks the instructor is doing a good job. She particularly likes how he analyzes the reading assignments and encourages students to think about how essays are composed: "He breaks it down and shows us what he feels, and then, you know, we can form our own opinions on it—why it was written that way. Or he points out, 'This is a good sentence—the way it's structured, the way it's described.' I like discussions. It brings out different people's views of how they see it." It appears that classroom talk is fine, in Cheleen's opinion, as long as the focus remains on academic subject matter. She implies that the responsibility for maintaining this focus rests partly with the instructor but mostly with students: "I think if we didn't have a head-strong person and chit-chatters, we would actually have a real class. . . . If I could take my little group (of 'mature' students)—if you could multiply us by four times—things would be fine."

In many ways, Cheleen is progressing as Sanchez hopes. Her comments suggest that she has a good understanding of his pedagogical aim to "get students to realize . . . that writing is a process of trial and refinement." As she puts it, the instructor "breaks down" the readings so "we can form our own opinions on it—why it was written that way." Moreover, she demonstrates some of the affective and behavioral characteristics which Sanchez encourages in students. She shows academic self-confidence, which is evident in her assertion that she and her "little group" are exemplary students. She also is self-motivated to pursue success in college, and she takes responsibility for her work.

While Cheleen appears to be well on her way to moving into the academic mainstream, she still faces many hazards. Certain external factors must remain constant: Financial aid must continue; child care must be available; work hours must remain flexible; bills must be paid. Changes could easily endanger her enrollment status. In addition, Cheleen still must face the personal challenge of coping with students whom she finds annoying. She becomes tense even thinking about Terry: "If I have that woman in a class next semester, I swear I'll drop that class."

The Intersection of Mobility, Diversity, and Pedagogy

This study calls into question the capacity of basic writing instruction to promote or hinder student mobility. In the past, both supporters and critics have considered instruction to be the pivotal factor determining academic success. I would suggest that effective instruction is a necessary condition for student progress but not a sufficient one. My findings suggest that what students learn in class depends, not only on the instructor's teaching, but also on any number of personal and environmental factors. It is possible for motivated students like Cheleen to fail academically for reasons unrelated to instructors or teaching. Conversely, it may be possible for adaptable students like Haum to succeed in classes which do not cater to their styles of learning.

These findings do not support the claims of early critics (e.g., Karabel, 1972; Pincus, 1980) that community college educators deliberately divert students away from transfer education. The students in this basic writing class are not passive bodies herded in a common direction by the instructor. They follow their own agendas, and they sometimes act in ways which the instructor does not predict. Moreover, some individuals resist the instructor when they disagree with what he is doing. Resistance takes the form of non-compliance in at least two instances in the classroom narrative—when Cheleen stops working and when Cesar tells the instructor not to "kid around." In some ways these actions resemble the oppositional behaviors described by Weis (1985). As with Weis's African American students, Cheleen and Cesar act out of frustration and, perhaps, resignation. It is not a foregone conclusion, however, that their behavior is part of a downward spiral leading to drop out, as Weis observed. In Cesar's case the instructor sees the immediate problem and tries to make corrections. This action contradicts the argument that educators deliberately conspire against students.

It is less clear from these findings whether or not basic writing instructors inadvertently contribute to students' academic failure. The existence of official and unofficial pedagogical goals supports McGrath and Spear's argument (1991) that basic writing educators have broadened the instructional focus well beyond training in academic essay writing. Also, the classroom narrative illustrates McGrath and Spear's contention that cognitive and affective goals may confound each other. Within the five minutes, Sanchez adjusts his teaching several times. Initially, he addresses the class, clarifying the directions for the workshop exercise. When he sees that Cesar does not have his paper, he shifts to a more casual mode, chiding Cesar publicly to make a point about turning papers in on time. He shifts his pedagogical focus, however, when he sees that Cesar is not responding positively to teasing as he usually does. At this point, the instructor addresses Cesar privately, implying he might reconsider the deadline in light of a "hard-life story." Then he makes the same offer to the class. Here, the instructor reassures those who are not prepared that they still have hope for success—a central theme in the instructor's longterm goal to build students' self-confidence as writers. Yet students might easily become confused as the instructor attempts to address different needs. The longterm influence on students cannot be determined from this brief snapshot. Longitudinal data are needed.

The events in the classroom narrative described here reveal some extenuating circumstances to the problem of conflicting pedagogical objectives. In this instance, the instructor pursues cognitive and affective goals simultaneously, not out of disregard for pedagogical history as McGrath and Spear argue (1991), but in response to fluctuating circumstances in the classroom. The sheer diversity of student needs may compel basic writing instructors to pursue diverse pedagogical goals which may conflict. One implication of these findings is that improving academic preparation in basic writing is not simply a matter of increasing academic rigor or employing the "right" teaching techniques.

This research suggests that we must reconsider linear views of remediation in community colleges. The predominant model of instruction was once described by Cross (1979) as a "superhighway." Like automobiles, students move along a centralized route toward a common destination. They enter via designated on-ramps, and they presumably obey traffic laws which keep the flow moving uniformly. Basic writing is one of the main on-ramps to the superhighway. The slow vehicles coming up the on-ramp are supposed to accelerate so that they are moving at highway speed by the time they merge with the main stream of traffic. However, a number of conditions must exist for students to achieve this kind of linear, mass mobility. Among other things, they must want to move into the academic express lane, and they must have the resources and ability to keep up with traffic for extended periods of time. In addition, they must understand the institutional rules of the road—the formal and informal conventions which dictate how students should progress. In the writing classroom, the students and instructor must have some common conceptions of academic language and personal goals. In short, there must be a "speech community" as described by Pratt (1991).

However, the classroom narrative in this study illustrates that basic writing is by no means a "unified and homogeneous social world" (p. 38). It would appear that, while students have the same general goal to improve their lives through education, they are much less unified in the specifics of what this means or how this will occur. The remedial writing classroom might be more accurately characterized as a contact zone of differing agendas, rather than a section of highway with unidirectional traffic.

Viewing basic writing as a contact zone, as opposed to a highway or conduit, would require educators to reorient their notions of what basic writing should accomplish. Historically, those who embrace the highway model of education have regarded unconventional orientations to college, affective needs, and work and family commitments as potential distractions which might impede students' learning of academic content. Indeed, critics have argued that addressing these issues in class necessarily dilutes the academic curriculum. Even educators like Cross (1981), who have championed the needs of "non-traditional" community college students, ultimately call for linear forms of instruction. Intended to accommodate diverse learners, many alternative modes of instruction—such as self-paced courses, computerized instruction, and distance learning—have proven to be repackaged versions of regular coursework. A more productive approach might be to view diverse perspectives and circumstances, not as problems to overcome in basic writing, but as pedagogical opportunities. As Harris (1995) observes, composition instructors should help students rise above the cacophony of the contact zone to negotiate their own understandings of literacy. Lu (1994) sees this exchange as a desirable form of multicultural education. She believes that, as students and instructors juxtapose their differing conceptions of literacy, they will come to see how notions of error are embedded in culture and power relationships. By experiencing how academicians use language to contest ideas, students might equip themselves to enter the mainstream of academic discourse. Perhaps a pluralistic and flexible curriculum such as this can meet the diverse needs of students while accommodating the multiple directives of the community college.

Notes

1. Educators use a number of terms (e.g., basic, remedial, developmental, compensatory) to describe college writing classes which are below "freshman composition." Each of these terms carries strong connotations. For additional explanation, see Fox (1990) and Bartholomae (1993). I will use the term "basic writing" in reference to composition courses and pedagogy. "Remedial" and "remediation" will be used to describe pre-transfer level instruction in writing, reading, or math.

2. I will use the term "underprepared" to describe students who, for whatever reasons, cannot or will not follow conventions of academic literacy.

References

Bartholomae, D. (1993). "The tidy house: Basic writing in the American curriculum." *Journal of Basic Writing,* 12(1), 4–21.

Bogue, J. P. (1950). *The community college.* New York: McGraw-Hill.

Brint, S., & Karabel, J. (1989). *The diverted dream: Community colleges and the promise of educational opportunity in America, 1900–1985.* New York: Oxford University Press.

Clark, B. R. (1960). *The open door college: A case study.* New York, McGraw-Hill.

Cohen, A., & Brawer, F. (1989). *The American community college* (2nd ed.). San Francisco: Jossey-Bass.

Cross, K. P. (1979). "Education as a superhighway." *Journal of Developmental and Remedial Education,* 3(2), 2–4.

Cross, K. P. (1981). *Adults as learners.* San Francisco: Jossey-Bass.

Department of Commerce. (1993). *1990 census of population and housing: Population and housing characteristics for census tracks and block numbering areas.* (Publication No. 1990 CPH-3-234). Washington, DC: U.S. Government Printing Office.

DiPardo, A. (1993). *A kind of passport: A basic writing adjunct program and the challenge of student diversity.* Urbana, Ill.: National Council of Teachers of English.

Donovan, R. (1991). "Creating effective programs for developmental education." In W. Deegan & D. Tillery, (Eds.), *Renewing the American community college.* (pp. 103–28). San Francisco: Jossey-Bass Publishers.

Dougherty, K. J. (1991). "The community college at the crossroads: The need for structural reform." *Harvard Educational Review,* 61(3), 311–36.

Dougherty, K. J. (1994). *The contradictory college: The conflicting origins, impacts, and futures of the community college.* Albany: State University of New York Press.

Fox, T. (1990). "Basic writing as cultural conflict." *Journal of Education,* 172(1), 65–83.

Grubb, W. N. (1991). "The decline of community college transfer rates: Evidence from national longitudinal surveys." *Journal of Higher Education,* 62(2), 194–224.

Harris, J. (1995). "Negotiating the contact zone." *Journal of Basic Writing,* 14(1), 27–42.

Karabel, J. (1972). "Community colleges and social stratification." *Harvard Education Review,* 42(4), 521–59.

Lu, M-Z. (1994). "Professing multiculturalism: The politics of style in the contact zone." *College Composition and Communication,* 45(4), 442–58.

Manno, B. V. (1995). "Remedial education: Replacing the double standard with real standards." *Change,* 27(3), 47–50.

Mansfield, W., & Farris, E. (1991). *College–level remedial education in the fall of 1989.* (Office of Educational Research and Improvement report No. NCES 91-191). Washington: U.S. Department of Education.

McCarthy, L. P. (1987). "A stranger in strange lands: A college student writing across the curriculum." *Research in the Teaching of English,* 21(3), 233–65.

McGrath, D., & Spear, M. (1991). *The academic crisis of the community college.* Albany, NY: State University of New York Press.

Mutnick, D. (1996). *Writing in an alien world: Basic writing and the struggle for equality in higher education.* Portsmouth, NH: Boyton/Cook Publishers.

Piland, W. E., & Pierce, D. (1989). "Remedial education in the states." *Community College Review,* 12(3), 16–20.

Pincus, F. L. (1980). "The false promise of community colleges: Class conflict and vocational education." *Harvard Educational Review,* 50(3), 332–61.

———. (1994). "How critics view the community college's role in the twenty-first century." In G. A. Baker, (Ed.), *A handbook on the community college in America: Its history, mission, and management.* (pp. 624–36). Westport: Greenwood Press.

Pratt, M. L. (1991). "Arts of the contact zone." *Profession,* 91, 33–40.

Richardson, R. C.; Fisk, E. C.; & Okun, M. A. (1983). *Literacy in the open-access college.* San Francisco: Jossey-Bass.

Roueche, J. E.. & Baker, G. A. (1987). *Access and excellence: The open-door college.* Washington: AACJC, Community College Press.

Slark, J. (1989). *Student outcomes study: Fall 1988 follow-up study of students enrolled in remedial writing courses in fall 1986 and remedial reading courses in fall 1987.* Sacramento, CA: Learning Assessment Retention Consortium.

Traub, J. (1994). *City on a hill: Testing the American dream at city college.* Reading, MA: Addison-Wesley Publishing Company.

Weis, L. (1985). *Between two worlds: Black students in an urban community college.* Boston: Routledge & Kegan Paul.

Zwerling, L. S. (1976). *Second best.* New York: McGraw-Hill.

CHAPTER 4

Navigating the Raging River: Reconciling Issues of Identity, Inclusion, and Administrative Practice

MARILYN J. AMEY

Introduction

Christine Latimer[1] spent the last 15 years at Henley Community College, working her way slowly up the organizational hierarchy from hourly employee to senior administrator. Although she said overall "This has been a good place for me," and doesn't want to work elsewhere, something about her career has always gnawed at her in ways that, until recently, she has been unable to articulate. "My place [at Henley] hasn't come easy," Christine said slowly. "For instance, it was an interesting challenge for me to get this position. There were four people who really didn't want me to be hired. They thought I'd be a yes person for my supervisor and weren't sure I'd be strong enough for the job. It was a personal challenge for me . . . an ugly time." The four oppositional voices were all long-standing male administrators at Henley.

When the president of Madison Community College asked Delores Watkins to design a particular program for his institution similar to one she had developed at a nearby college, she was honored by the proposition and looked forward to being part of the president's team. What started as a one-year appointment grew into a long career at Madison, marked with several advancements and exciting challenges. Delores was now a senior administrator, and technically part of Madison's leadership team, but the acceptance and connection she hoped for when originally hired had yet to fully materialize. A sense of instability and tenuousness was reflected in the fact that after five

59

years in her current position, Delores said, "I haven't completely moved into my office yet. I'm still in boxes." In hindsight, Delores believed she "came in under hostile circumstances. I worked in the building before taking the job. But there were a couple of others who thought they should have gotten the job. It hasn't been easy." The unresolved conflict was clear when Delores said, "I like the job, but some days, well, I got sick when I first got the position and lost 30 pounds. The worst part about the job is that I still have to focus the most on those people who still resent me." "Those people" were mostly senior male administrators.

The stories of Delores and Christine will be used throughout this chapter to highlight issues related to identity, inclusion, and administrative practice. Through their educational and professional histories, I hope to shed light on some broad administrative concerns and bring greater light to some of the cultural challenges faced by contemporary community colleges.

Community colleges are believed to be places relatively welcoming to students with diverse educational backgrounds and abilities. They have been heralded as a model for providing greater access than any other type of postsecondary institution for students and for administrators. For example, more than 50 percent of the students attending community colleges are women, as are nearly 50 percent of the faculty, and over 10 percent of the presidents (Townsend, 1995a). Community colleges have been dubbed the "people's colleges" (Brint & Karabel, 1989), and are seen as providing sound educational opportunities for first-generation college students (Valadez, 1996). They have historically been less exclusive and inbred than research universities (Moore, Salimbene, Marlier, & Bragg, 1983), and their faculty and administrators have more varied and often less prestigious backgrounds than those at other institutions (Moore et al., 1983; Townsend, 1995b). The perception is that community colleges are a place where virtually anyone can succeed, regardless of race, ethnicity, gender, socioeconomic status, or cultural capital.

At the same time, the leadership and organizational behavior in community colleges has often been characterized as bureaucratic and hierarchical (Birnbaum, 1988; Vaughan, 1989), dominated by male and elite imagery (Amey & Twombly, 1992; Twombly & Amey, 1994), and often leaving employees feeling disconnected (Cross & Ravekas, 1990). In many ways, this creates for women and administrators of color (particularly women of color) a similar dilemma of cultural capital that exists for many students in this environment: they may be forced to adopt dominant values to work and succeed in the organization, and in the process, lose touch with the unique qualities they bring as women or as women of color. This dilemma may be analytically ameliorated if one assumes that the power to succeed in the organization and administer effectively is vested in the organizational structure itself rather than in the person (Townsend, 1995a, 1995b). Hence, focusing on the shortcomings of organizational structure, rather than those of individuals, offers new possibilities for creating change.

For example, instead of simply blaming the struggles of women administrators in academe on their own inadequacies, we can examine instead the ways in which the structure and culture of the organization present barriers to their success. Such an approach can suggest new administrative models that will be more enabling for women. This approach is particularly important when considering the experiences of female community college administrators. Nationally, the number of women in senior administrative positions continues to grow. Yet despite this seeming advancement, research suggests that these women are still facing systemic challenges and personal conflicts similar to those experienced by their predecessors. Life for women administrators in community colleges does not seem to be changing dramatically in spite of greater numeric representation.

It is through the lives of Delores Watkins and Christine Latimer that I identify some of the structural and cultural barriers in community colleges that hinder women's performance and their role in senior administration. As a number of recent scholars have noted, there is much that can be learned from the narratives of underrepresented minority leaders as well as women. In what follows, I call upon some of this literature as I explore the background of the study upon which this chapter is based.

Background and Methodology

Increasingly over recent years, scholars have been turning to general life histories, professional life histories and the use of narrative to explore the cultural experiences of those involved in educational settings, including college students (Carson, 1996; Whitt, 1994), faculty (Boice, 1992; Weiland, 1994) and administrative leadership (Ideta, 1996; Tedrow, 1996; Zenger, 1996). Marshall and Rossman (1995) suggest that life histories are "particularly useful for giving the reader an insider's view of a culture" (p. 87). Denzin (1989) points out that the story may cover an entire life, or a part of a life, and that the part may be topical or edited, focusing only on a particular set of experiences deemed to be of importance. Regardless, the opportunity for women to share their stories in their own words, apart from the constructions of traditionally defined norms and beliefs about what is of value, is central to the use of narratives (Heilbrun, 1988).

This chapter focuses on the narratives of two women community college administrators. The data are from a larger multi-state study undertaken by several researchers. Two research teams and a single principal investigator conducted interviews with leaders from a variety of higher education organizations. Believing that leadership is in large part socially constructed (Amey & Zenger, 1994; Morgan, 1987; Tierney, 1993), and therefore, a function of the beliefs and values of those within the organization (as opposed to primarily a function of position), the researchers chose to interview persons who seemed not to fit the stereotypic mold of their position and/or institution. Approximately 35 interviews were conducted with leaders across different institutional settings. The data were compiled separately by each research team and then compared within and across teams for themes and patterns. The specific data upon which I draw in this chapter are based on two interviews conducted as part of this larger project. In choosing to focus on the experience of two women, rather than providing less depth across more cases, I hope to give the reader a more detailed and rich sense of the ways in which organizational culture affects women community college administrators.

Interviews with Delores and Christine were audio recorded and supplemented by field notes. The purpose of the interviews was to allow the participants to discuss in detail their views of leadership, their own leadership roles, and to examine the ways in which their life circumstances contributed to their beliefs about leadership within their organizations. Each interview ended with a discussion of organizational metaphors and the drawing of cognitive maps. From their responses, the researchers sought to understand how these women saw themselves, as leaders, and how they experienced life within their organizations and in relation to others (Sheppard, 1992).

Qualitative data analyses were ongoing throughout the data collection, focusing on the interview transcripts, field notes, and cognitive maps. Adhering to the tenets of Patton (1990), Lincoln and Guba (1985), and Manning (1992), data analyses involved discovering patterns and themes shared by Christine and Delores, and took the form of unitizing and categorizing. As the data were originally collected by a research team, they were analyzed individually, then collaboratively in order to develop confidence with the emergent themes. Christine and Delores reviewed the transcripts of their interviews, providing input and feedback into their stories as we had recorded them. Not only did their input adhere to Lincoln and Guba's (1985) notion of member checking, the process through which one provides a means for continued participant involvement in the production of research findings, but it allowed for a more complete transformative learning process for both the leaders and the researchers (Connelly & Clandinin, 1990).

As with any case study research, generalizations from the data are made with appropriate caution. Nonetheless, the patterns and themes that emerged from the telling of the stories of Christine and Delores illuminate commonalties shared by many others who may have similar work environments, similar background characteristics or life experiences. This sharing of experiences allows for generalized "lessons to be learned" from the case study (Merriam, 1989) and increases the utility of this form of research.

The Women and Their Colleges

Christine is a white administrator at large, predominately white, male-dominated Henley Community College. Henley's student population makes it the largest single-campus community college in the geographic region, and the socioeconomic level of most of its students makes it one of the wealthiest. Most of the students at Henley are white, and administrators describe diversity at the college in terms of age rather than race or ethnicity. A significant portion of the students are first-generation, although not as high a proportion as at other community colleges in the state, and while Henley provides transfer, vocational, and community education, the majority of students identify the transfer function as their primary reason for attending. Henley has a close working relationship with four-year institutions in the area, and many of its students are enrolled for only one course that would transfer into degree programs elsewhere. Henley's physical facilities reflect the tax base which supports its activities: students have the opportunity to use classroom, cultural, library and computer resources that are state-of-the-art. Members of the Henley community speak of being part of a "college on the move." This sense is supported by several examples of reorganization, continuous quality improvement strategies, and a most recent self-examination leading to the label of "Henley Community College—A Learning Organization." The initial impression one receives is of a place of excitement, opportunity and growth. However, the existence of a newly formed women's group and the development of a campus Ombudsperson suggests that not every member of the Henley community necessarily feels an equal sense of excitement or opportunity.

It was in this environment that I met Christine, an administrator with a long history at the college. Her current position in the organization was considered upper administration, although she is not a member of the president's senior cabinet. She had been a first-generation college student, while many of her administrative colleagues had not. She was also a recent doctoral recipient, something Christine pursued not only for personal edification but for its perceived effect on her professional options and credibility at her institution. Christine is frequently reminded of the fact that she worked in a climate of longstanding male administrators from more prestigious academic institutions and higher socioeconomic backgrounds.

Delores is an African American administrator at large, culturally diverse, male dominated Madison Community College. In many respects, Madison resembles Henley Community College. Madison is of similar size, similar mission, and also has a strong working relationship with nearby four-year institutions to which it feeds students and student transfer credit hours. Members of the Madison community also consider themselves part of a college on the move, and speak of growth in program offerings, grant awards, and recent physical plant acquisitions as evidence of their increasing status. The economic base of Madison reflects a county that has experienced growth and decline in cycles common to many urban areas. As a result, the physical plant of the college is splattered with an odd combination of new and old buildings. In many ways, these buildings mirror the faculty and staff within them. As Delores notes, "There are two groups here. I'm part of the old group who's been around for a long time, forever. Then there are the new folks. They're different from us oldtimers." The students are as varied as the faculty and staff, reflecting the spectrum of diversity in backgrounds and educational goals. Many are from lower socioeconomic backgrounds or have not met with initial success at a four-year college and thus are pursuing work at Madison and utilizing its many support services.

When I first met Delores, what was most striking was her role as student advocate at Madison. She had worked at Madison Community College for many years, but also had lengthy prior work experience in other educational environments. For the last four years, she held a senior-level position as dean of a unit, with several vice-presidents reporting to her. The position made her a member of the president's cabinet. Delores, as Christine, was a first-generation college student, and is the most senior woman administrator at her institution and the only person of color in the upper echelon. She is a single parent, twice divorced (a fact she said symbolically represented her equality with men and the belief that men do not appreciate a strong woman partner), and has pursued, but not completed, her terminal degree. These characteristics are among those that set Delores apart from others with whom she presently works, even though the academic and socioeconomic backgrounds of Delores' counterparts are more varied than Christine's. Both women are approximately the same chronological and professional career age.

The Streams

Three primary themes, or "streams", emerge from the data analyses of the women's stories: "Cross-Cultural Currents," "Rowing Upstream," and "Shooting the Rapids." All of these streams describe experiences that contradict the notion of the community college as a welcoming, inclusive environment often presented in the literature. Christine and Delores both chose to work in community colleges because of certain beliefs they held about themselves, postsecondary education, and administration. These beliefs, while maintained throughout their careers, are continually challenged by the community college system and are often in conflict with systemic values required to achieve full membership in the cohort. Below, I utilize the voices of Christine and Delores to flesh out the three major challenges that they confront as they navigate the "river" of community college administration.

Cross-Cultural Currents

In selecting to interview Christine and Delores, I knew that each was among only a few female senior administrators at their respective institutions. What I did not know, but what became clear during the course of these interviews, was the frequency with which they found themselves to be the only female, or only minority, in an educational or administrative setting (what I have called "cross-cultural currents"). These experiences strongly influenced their development as administrators and their commitment to the community college environment.

Educational Experiences. In many respects, Christine and Delores began facing challenges of standing out from the group early in their educational experiences. Both chose academic pursuits that were not well supported by the public school systems of their day (mid-1960s). Christine always wanted to be a math teacher, recounting, "I always loved math and thought it should be more fun. Even then, I thought they didn't encourage women to be good at and enjoy math." Delores' goal was to get a college education: "My high school counselor said I wouldn't make it in college so I should go to secretarial school. She thought she was doing me a favor. It was a real negative." At the same time, both Christine and Delores found pockets of support for pursuing their educational goals. Family members, clergy, and some teachers were often supportive even if they were not always in agreement with the educational decisions. Delores remembered a sixth grade teacher as a reason for her academic confidence: "She was the greatest influence. She's the first one who told me I was bright and should be doing better in school. I thought I was capable but never knew anybody else thought so, too." Christine remembered elements of support this way:

> No one in my family had completed college before me. There wasn't much money for college. I had a grandfather who was very bright but had not gone past the fourth grade. His saying to me was, "Christine, you can do whatever you want" . . . and he expected you to. I believed him. My dissertation is dedicated to him.

Each was the first member of her respective family to attend college and complete a baccalaureate degree, although neither attended a community college as a student. Both eventually pursued advanced degree work, Christine completing her doctoral studies shortly before the time of the interview, and Delores saying that her dream was to finish her terminal degree. In each woman's life history, this pursuit of postsecondary education was important in shaping her beliefs about herself and her abilities; the women established goals and accomplished them often against substantial odds. But the pursuit also set them apart from others in their families and communities, disconnecting them in a way with which neither woman seemed entirely comfortable. As Christine explained, "My parents still aren't sure why I put myself through all of this (the terminal degree) . . . why it was necessary . . . it's hard to explain to them." In relating their own educational desires to the subsequent employment choices they made, each woman asserted that she was drawn to career opportunities within community colleges as a result of her own struggle to achieve academically. Both women began their professional careers working with low socioeconomic, at-risk high school students in programs intended to ease transition to college in ways they had not personally experienced.

Cultural Heritage and Identity Issues. Although neither Delores nor Christine should be seen as representative of her racial, ethnic or gender group, both are in situations where such characteristics influence their beliefs about themselves as administrators. In the organizational contexts in which they work, each woman came to understand the strengths drawn from one's cultural heritage and identity, and the difficulties in confronting institutional monoculturalism as an outsider. Their experiences mirror those of other organizational outsiders such as the women studied by Kanter (1977), Lyons (1988), Sheppard (1992), and Cross and Ravekas (1990).

Delores speaks with passion of the impact of moving from undergraduate study at a historically black institution to a predominately white institution where she was the only female African American female graduate student on campus.

That was CULTURE SHOCK! I got a job on campus working with another minority group. That gave me a whole different perspective on life. You need to understand this took place at a time that was significant—during the 1960s. There were only 50 black men on campus. They were going to be radicals and I got caught up in that. I learned so much from it, grew so much from it.

The "radical" attitudes of her graduate days remain with Delores as she speaks of breaking down barriers for students in her current administrative capacity. As I listened to her speak, I heard the passion of a fighter for justice, of one who struggles on behalf of the underdog, and for those who must fight to be recognized and found worthy. This passion echoes the way Delores speaks of trying to gain a place for herself in her graduate studies. The need to serve in this advocacy role seems also to have led Delores initially to her work in the community college setting where she could serve students of color and those from lower socioeconomic backgrounds. She speaks of understanding where students come from and of what they need to survive in the system, often relating back to her own graduate struggles.

Christine's rural upbringing did not afford much contact with people of color prior and even during her postsecondary education experiences. However, upon graduation from her undergraduate institution and seeking fulltime employment, this situation changed. In describing significant influences on her beliefs about administration, Christine speaks of having been mentored by a woman of color in her earliest professional position. At the time, she was working in a predominately black school district through a special grant to assist low socioeconomic, at-risk students under the supervision of a woman she affectionately described in this way:

> She was a large black woman with her wig always askew. There was nothing feminine looking about her but she never lost her femininity. She was a great role model for women, a great leader. She was competent, caring, concerned, able to see the big picture yet never forgot about the individuals involved. I always thought she'd be a great first black female president.

In describing the experience of being a racial minority, Christine focuses on the relationship with her supervisor and the ways in which this woman nurtured and developed those within the work unit, created a professional environment, and drew others to her. These leadership behaviors are paramount to Christine's definition of leadership today. Yet in reflecting on a period of time when she was a "minority," her remembrances are far more positive than when speaking of the present circumstances in which she finds herself as one of only a few women working in senior administration at Henley.

Woven throughout Christine's comments about leadership and her early experiences working with her mentor is a clear sense of the role that inclusion played in creating a positive work experience in the predominately black school district. In contrast, Christine expresses great concern about the lack of inclusion and connectedness she experiences in her current environment as a white female administrator in a white, predominately male community college administration. Delores' need for inclusion is expressed less overtly than Christine's but is nonetheless significant. Throughout her depiction of her life and work, Delores mediates between descriptions of herself as a single agent and her need for connection.

For both Delores and Christine, race, ethnicity, and socioeconomic status all influence their beliefs and have at times caused them to stand apart from the group. Yet in sharing their stories with the research team, gender issues emerge most frequently when they speak of their administrative roles in the community college. Even though they have often experienced a lack of cultural capital in various situations in their lives, the perceived impact of gender in male-dominated organizations is seen as most prevalent, most isolating, and most difficult to overcome. It may be that Delores and Christine speak so passionately about their gendered experiences because of their current professional roles and organizational contexts; the concerns with childhood and early professional experiences may long ago have been reconciled through memory and rationalization. At the same time, both women sought and have maintained employment at community colleges because of their belief in the inclusivity of the environment for the broad spectrum of students and staff, including women. That this belief has not been borne out without significant personal cost to Delores and Christine seems to justify the level of conflict they articulated. It may also be that, in Delores' case, her statements are reflections of the interactions with me, a white woman, and my research colleague, a white male; she may not have felt any more comfortable sharing cross-cultural conflicts with us than she did with her white professional peers.

Rowing Upstream

The complex interactions between individuals and organizational structures, referred to throughout this volume as "cultural texts," are as apparent in the lives of administrators as they work and advance within the college hierarchy as they are in students as they attend college. Socialization has long implied the adoption of established norms, practices, and beliefs by those who wish to be members of the organization, and those who are not appropriately socialized are often seen as deviants, outcasts, outsiders, or even troublemakers (Blackmore, 1989; Kanter, 1979; Simeone, 1987; Theodore, 1986). Community colleges have been criticized recently for failing to provide a venue that nurtures the diversity of their student populations (Rhoads & Valadez, 1996), and similarly can be criticized for having failed to provide an administrative culture inclusive enough for the diversity of their administrative staffs (Amey & Twombly, 1992; Cross & Revekas, 1990; DiCroce, 1995; Winship & Amey, 1992). As Mittlestet (1994) suggests, "one of the interesting ironies regarding community colleges is that all too often, they lack . . . community" (p. 549).

A second theme emerging from the stories told by Christine and Delores is that as senior women interacting with a dominantly male administrative culture, they do not feel accepted as competent administrators in their institution. Unlike the women in Kanter's (1977) research, these women have not figuratively "become men" to get to senior administration, nor are they experiencing the rewards associated with having been promoted in the system, such as increased administrative confidence, professional self-esteem, and status. The "welcoming nature" of the community college for students does not transcend to administration, at least not for Delores and Christine, and they describe a need to continually prove themselves in order to "make the grade," to carve a niche within their respective institutions, and to arrive at a culturally appropriate definition of success (Blackmore, 1989). I call this struggle "rowing upstream."

Neither woman describes the culture of her institution as a coherent whole, but rather each describes elements of it on numerous occasions in terms of how she is not adhering to it, does not fit in, or is not part of the inner circle. As a means of gathering richer perceptions about their understandings of their role within the organization, Delores and Christine were asked to draw cognitive maps of their organization, locating themselves within the map. The maps provide a kind of context in which leadership takes place and a more complete depiction of where the leader finds herself on a daily basis (Amey & Zenger, 1994).

Delores' organizational map (see Figure 4.1) is fairly functionalist-structuralist. That is, her first version, by her own account, is a functional map that focuses on students, depicting various services affecting students' lives (Delores was not a Student Services Administrator). "It's a functional map—why we're here," she stated. In this map, Delores says, "I'm in a peripheral role—not a major part but I have a major influence on their (students') lives." However, she does not locate herself on this functional map. Making the distinction between a functional and psychological map, Delores drew a second version (Figure 4.2), where students are no longer the focal point. Whereas in the functional map services emanate from the students in equal fashion like spokes from a center sphere, size becomes important in the psychological map; some spaces are bigger than others, indicating their degree of importance. Delores drew the psychological map from a faculty perspective, even though she is an administrator. She put herself into the map this time, in a small box slightly overlapping with a larger box labeled, "administration." "The faculty see me as their conscience . . . I overlap with administration but have more trust. If I stayed where I am right now (in my present position), I would move more into administration."

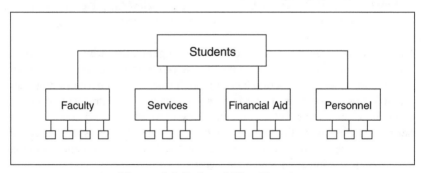

Figure 4.1 Delores' First Drawing

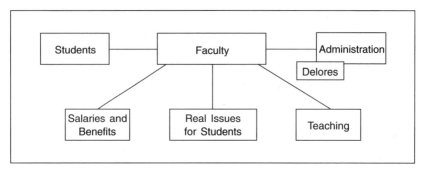

Figure 4.2 Delores' Second Drawing

Both of Delores' maps suggest a strong commitment to students, as do most of her interview responses. Apart from her advocacy for students, Delores' maps do not illustrate a sense of strong connection to the organization or to other faculty or staff; at the same time, the maps are hierarchical with power relationships present in each. Her stories tell of struggles for control and to balance her own place in the organization with her relationships to others. For instance, she says, "I thought the higher up you go, the less you have to do 'grunt work.' I've seen it work for others. But I'm still doing grunt work because I don't have enough people to delegate to. I just get more to do." She goes on to add:

> In terms of employees, I may be old-fashioned but I think the supervisor should have more control over work time than employees do . . . I share information with my staff. At the same time, I feel and insist upon respect as head of this department and what goes with that. I don't expect you to say "I don't agree"— I am the head of this department and I approve some things and not you . . . I want to have the knowledge and confidence in my area, the trust of my employees. Yet there is some degree of paranoia that I wish I could get over. Even in the areas where I need improvement, but no one will tell me [in what areas and how to improve]. Above [me], they don't know; below [me], they are afraid because I am the one who approves them for merit salary.

Delores seems somewhat isolated from the organization while at the same time very embedded in it. She strives for self-determination and power over her circumstances, and struggles with inclusion and with reconciling her relationships with others. There is a need to appear in control and strong as a senior administrator, yet a continued lack of validation and confidence in her own leadership ability that resonates throughout her stories. It is as if she remains unable to fully integrate her personal and professional beliefs into the administrative context in which she works.

    Christine's organizational map began much the same way as Delores'— with a common core. After a failed attempt, Christine said, "I started by saying we are all going towards quality instruction and well maybe that is our utmost goal and sometimes we just forget that because we have all the road-blocks of the political maneuverings." She then drew a map of the power structure she perceives at her institution. As can be seen in Figure 4.3, Christine's map looks much more like a ladder than Delores' collection of spheres, with the identified rungs being position, personal power, connections or networks, political roadblocks, and the inner-circle set at the top of the ladder.

> I could give you a route to this organization . . . Right up here, the first road-block at the very top is the political roadblock and if you can't pass that then you can never get into the inner circle, whatever that is . . . I'm sort of thinking to get into this whole organization, wherever it is, you have the position which gives you a certain amount of clout to get to that inner circle, but then more than that, you have some personal power that has to take you beyond—it's who you are, who you know and then can you play that political game well enough to get into the inner circle. I think this inner circle changes—sometimes it's small, sometimes it's large, sometimes it's real small . . . We have the board, they're always in the inner circle, but then you have the president and the executive council . . . and the other people who sort of go in and out, in and out.

In reflecting on the visual image she drew, Christine explains the map further:

> You know, the other things about seeing this visually is that once you get in here (the inner circle) it's sort of like these circles are putting up blinders to everything else that's happening out here so the reality of what's going on out here is becoming more and more skewed. So it's harder for people to see what happens out here.

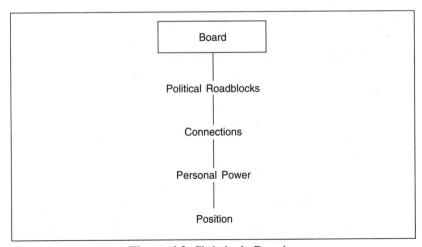

Figure 4.3 Christine's Drawing

Christine talks about ways people at Henley move towards the inner circle, detours that are taken based on personal power and connections, of ways in which members help each other, and about how those in the inner circle have "built some pretty good walls around that keep them in." Christine sees herself as a traveler along the road to the inner circle, going in and out but never to "the inner-inner" circle. At one time, getting into the inner circle was a goal but at present, she says, "I don't know anymore . . . I think I move in and out of that a bit more . . . based on more information, based on reality, based on my own needs and aspirations, and satisfaction."

Even though she identifies herself as a traveler along the road to the inner circle, it is evident that there are many unresolved power and inclusion issues for Christine as a leader in Henley Community College. As with Delores, the conflict of balancing personal and professional beliefs with organizational press remains unresolved, or perhaps continually evolving, and the administrative identity is not fully developed.

Shooting the Rapids

Perhaps the most illustrative aspect of Delores and Christine's stories came in their descriptions of their relationships to the institution. Each was asked to select a leadership metaphor that represents the institution as they experience it and themselves as a leader. Imagery such as "great man," "pioneer," and "commander" has permeated community-college literature over time, focusing on a single person for guiding, manipulating, and dominating the academic organization (Amey & Twombly, 1992). With its focus on a singular visionary figurehead, the traditional imagery has not allowed for the use of more connected and inclusive forms of leadership, such as teams, collaborative leadership, or leaders who are not organizational titleholders. The traditional metaphors also tend to exclude women and people of color from relating to and seeing themselves in these leadership roles where, traditionally, function and position rather than process are the defining parameters of leadership. It is important to hear the ways in which Delores and Christine describe themselves metaphorically within their organizations to know more fully how they understand their roles and the college's functioning (Sheppard, 1992). Given their earlier responses to questions, I was only somewhat surprised that Christine and Delores both use turbulent imagery to describe their organizations (which I have labeled, "shooting the rapids").

> Right now, it's like wild horses running away. What I'm seeing is a stagecoach and it's without a driver. It's running . . . .the horses are out of control. And the driver is trying to hold them back . . . We have this little man that's in front of the stagecoach who is trying to stop the horses, and then you have the driver who is trying to stop the horses, and it's almost like there's some conflict there.

And then you have the riders there in the stagecoach—they don't know which direction they're going. [Christine]

It's a raging river—constantly changing, in motion. It varies in width in different places and depth. It is a strong force, very powerful. It can be destructive but it can also be nourishing, with a lot of life. There are some road blocks but some things are more positive. [Delores]

In both metaphors, issues of power, domination and self-determination arise. They suggest institutions out of control, or at least moving at a rapid pace, and perhaps a leader (Delores and Christine) who perceives she has limited control or power over the organization and limited self-determination within the organization. By looking more closely at the meanings Delores and Christine assign to their experiences in their organizations, I began to see the messages reflected by the metaphors differently. For example, in positioning herself within the metaphor, Christine explains:

Right now, I'm in the stagecoach but at times, I think some of the people in the stagecoach . . . are pulled out to try to make a difference, to stop the stagecoach, or to give some direction. But then I think they're pushed back into the stagecoach where it's so bumpy . . . I think I would see myself as one of about five other people that would be called out (of the stagecoach) . . . and we are called out from time to time to try to make change. We are always in the stagecoach in the front but it's how people choose to let you out or how you're pushed out to what role you take . . . I think sometimes I choose to try to make a change; I volunteer a lot to committees for different things . . . By the nature of the length of time I've been here and the kind of job I've done, I think some people do respect me on campus and that I would be called out as a person who they saw as having some information or ability or a willingness to try to make change.

From the description Christine provides, it seems that there are periodic elements of control and self-determination that Christine or others can capitalize on to create change for the organization. Although a sense of chaos is evident, at the same time, for those in the stagecoach, there is shared opportunity to make a difference, set direction, and provide leadership for the organization. Christine explains in some detail the various members of the stagecoach and ways in which each is affected by the bumpy ride; it is clear she values the presence and role of other organizational members. Colleagueship *per se* is not necessarily a part of her metaphorical discussion, although it is evident that Christine sees an interconnectedness with others; what remains unclear from the metaphor is whether she finds these relationships to be empowering, stifling, derailing, or supportive. Christine presents a fairly fluid depiction of leadership at her institution, while at the same time, she acknowledges that the "inner circle" has some longstanding consistent members. Making it to the front of the stagecoach seems to represent acquiring sufficient cultural capital to be recognized as an institutional leader and change agent, at least in certain circumstances. Christine still speaks of a "they," the nature of which is ill-defined; she maintains a sense of disconnection from the "other" while still, at times, being part of it.

Delores' metaphor describes an institution rapidly moving and changing, perhaps due to the growth it has experienced during the last ten years. Her description mirrors many of her other comments, attempting to provide a balance between change and stasis, strength and nurturance. In elaborating on her description, Delores says:

> I am trying to navigate it (the raging river). Like Huck Finn. Some days are easy; some are hard. Some days you have to get off. I am just one of the leaders trying to navigate it. Other leaders are the campus movers and shakers, policymakers like the board, the president, and faculty . . . .a couple institutional deans are leaders—insightful, with vision. Others hold us back more than they lead us.

Although her metaphor connotes a level of chaos similar to Christine's, Delores seems to perceive the voyage as less bumpy, more a matter of course. In depicting her life experiences, Delores articulates the many ways she has exercised high levels of control over her internal and external environments that may affect her feelings of instability, insecurity, or isolation. She mentions other leaders at her institution but provides less understanding of her relationship to and with them. Delores does not communicate a sense of collaboration with her unit or the larger organization, even though she characterizes herself as being, "one of the most known (leaders) on campus because I'm friendly." She speaks more often of others in the third person, even those persons within her own unit with whom she works most closely. Delores navigates the raging river seemingly on her own; she talks little about ways in which persons ferry the river together.

Again, as throughout her in-depth interview, Delores presents a leadership mosaic with some pieces more connected to others and some placed awkwardly alone within the organizational backdrop. The balancing act she wages between connection and independence, individual strength and organizational interdependence is clear. In her assessment, status as institutional leader has not yet afforded Delores the luxury of full membership, or perhaps as the only female of color in senior administration, she does not feel free to exercise that option. In any case, even after many years of administrative success in their respective community colleges, both Delores and Christine continued to express a sense of identity confusion. This same phenomenon has been noted in studies of other community-college women leaders (Gillett-

Karam, 1989; Winship, 1991) but is rarely noted in similar studies of male counterparts (Roueche, Baker, & Rose, 1989; Winship & Amey, 1992).

Lessons About Community-College Structure and Culture

The stories of Delores Walker and Christine Latimer portray conflict between personal and professional beliefs held by each woman and the institutional administrative culture in which they work. The result is a continued sense of conflict in relation to professional identity. The challenge for Delores and Christine is to reconcile the desire for connection and inclusion with issues of power, authority and independence. Both women look for ways to compensate for the lack of connection: Delores through her relationships with students, and Christine through her involvement in a new women's group on her campus. Neither of these outlets has a particular institutional power base associated with it, so the women often rely on personal power and influence in decision-making processes rather than tapping into the organization's power structure. Each also works in her own way to negotiate issues of inclusion — to determine the degree to which interdependence is allowed before one is viewed as a weak leader. The women sit on the doorstep, but they do not seem to gain real admission to the club.

In many respects, Christine's and Delores' accounts are not different from other administrative stories. It is hardly surprising to find that women are not well represented in the inner circles of collegiate administration, for instance, or that each feels a certain need to prove competence over time. What makes Christine's and Delores' situations perhaps more complex is that they detail the nature of the struggle related to professional performance. Both women are perceived to be effective administrators on the rise in their institutions, as evidenced by their nomination for inclusion in the original research study; yet to take the "final step" requires compromises they are not sure can be reconciled with their belief systems. There is no evidence in either case that the institution is holding them back from continued promotion, but rather that the women themselves are reluctant because of perceived choices they may be forced to make between institutional values and their own.

So often when we look to see whether leadership is changing in collegiate organizations (and infer from this that the culture is also changing), we focus on the senior ranks and count the number of male and female presidents or top administrators. We believe that this number represents individual competence, since traditional bureaucracies theoretically promote the most able for the task (Bolman & Deal, 1991); therefore, lack of women in the inner circle must mean lack of competence, be that a function of skill level, emotional stability, childrearing responsibilities, or other mythical rationalizations that have been constructed over time to account for the void (Blackmore, 1989). The conflicts faced by Delores and Christine suggest a systemic problem apart from individual competence; the question is not "are the women qualified and able to be community college leaders?" (a focus on the person as a problem to be solved) but rather, "is the community college the kind of environment in which these women choose to exercise leadership?" (a focus on the system as the problem to be solved).

The clash of professional and personal values may in fact cause women not to pursue advancement to the organizational inner circle, or may encourage the creation of a type of counter-circle as a means of acquiring leadership rewards without the same cost involved, as with Christine's women's group. Blackmore (1989) addresses this issue in part when she suggests that adherence to the culture of corporate managerialism that is so dominant in educational organizations, including community colleges, offers little that is attractive to or of value to women. Sheppard (1992) reinforces this assertion, in suggesting that the dissonance inherent between institutional or managerial press and women's values and definitions of self will continue to be problematic until we change the nature of the organization itself.

Another unique aspect of their stories is that the initial reason Delores and Christine chose the community college work environment was because they believed it offered a strong possibility of success for diverse persons, including presumably their own leadership opportunities. Each has succeeded, if success is defined as promotion. But interpreting their lives from each woman's cultural perspective (Codd, 1989) suggests otherwise. In terms of reconciling conflict between institutional values (those held in a male dominated administrative hierarchy) and their personal values (belonging, connection and inclusion), success has yet to be accomplished. Neither speaks of leaving, nor suggests a desire to work elsewhere or in another kind of institution. But as illustrated in their metaphors and cognitive maps, Christine and Delores remain both attached to and isolated from their administrative cultures. Factors such as organizational press and others' beliefs about acceptable behavior and appropriate leadership force Christine and Delores to regularly re-evaluate their stance, their futures, and their sense of membership in the organization.

These women face the same challenges of other academic women documented so many times before (Blackmore, 1989; Moore & Sagaria, 1991; Simeone, 1986; Theodore, 1987). Unlike women at elite research universities who are often the subjects of such studies, however, Christine and Delores work at the "people's college," intended to be more adaptive to the needs and orientation of its clientele. It seems that both women would welcome working in institutions with a more multicultural administrative culture, where various approaches to management and leadership are accepted, where inclusion and interdependence are more prevalent, and where the relational view of judgment serves more as the basis for decisionmaking (Blackmore, 1989; Gilligan, 1982; Lyons, 1988). Were Delores and Christine working in colleges with team orientations rather than traditional hierarchies or in systems where diverse persons, administrative styles and cultural interpretations were welcomed, they might now feel less as outsiders. As it is, their perception of what is required to succeed in their organization runs often in opposition to their own value orientation causing frustration and role conflict. The narrow band of acceptable behavior (Morrison, *et al.,* 1987) they encountered does not squeeze them entirely out of administration, but nonetheless creates a constraining and awkward fit.

Considering the fact that community colleges will face substantial faculty and staff labor market shortfalls in the next twenty years (Educational Policies Committee, 1991), and given the numbers of women and people of color already in the pipeline and in need of recruitment, it would seem an important time for current administrators to reconsider their world view and leadership beliefs. If the community college is truly an "open-door" institution where diversity can be heralded, differences celebrated, and multiculturalism woven into the daily fabric of the college experience for students, then the same must occur in the lives of its faculty and administrators. Rather than reinforcing a hierarchical or more autocratic form of leadership that rewards only the elite few, community colleges could adopt a more humanistic approach to governance where leadership enables the individual and the group, where information is more widely shared and authority diffused throughout the system (Blackmore, 1989; Watkins, 1989).

Recent work on community college administration calls for just such cultural changes. Participative management, flattening the hierarchy, quality circles, and leadership teams are all part of the changing rhetoric in and research landscape of community colleges today (Acebo, 1994; Alfred, 1994; Fryer & Lovas, 1991; Rhoads & Valadez, 1996; Twombly & Amey, 1994). Although systematic studies of these organizational shifts and their impact on outcomes and community members are only in their infancy, there seems a recognition of the need to do something different in order to move community colleges into the 21st century. As community colleges seek ways to accomplish their missions in an increasingly diverse environment, the vestiges of organizational monoculturalism must be dismantled.

In her chapter on "Women and the Community College Presidency," DiCroce (1995) suggests a framework for action to be enacted by presidents. Reframing some of her ideas from a focus on individual adaptation to one of systemic changes that might lead to multiculturalism in the community college, I offer two primary suggestions that also reflect lessons learned in the stories of Delores and Christine recounted here. The first suggestion is that community colleges should reconstruct and redefine institutional power structures in order to create institutional climates conducive to a collective sense of power. The second suggestion is a critical review of institutional policies and practices for their cultural appropriateness in order to unpack the power bases embedded within and perpetuated by them. Neither suggestion is particularly radical; each is also not an easy task. But as demonstrated in the shared experiences of Delores and Christine, without a better understanding of the cultural texts of administrative lives, it is likely not possible to change the culture of the community college in ways that allow women and people of color to find success. Traditional lenses uncover only those structures perpetuated through them, and in the case of Henley and Madison Community Colleges, these lenses reveal women on the administrative rise, rather than the monocultural organization that they have had difficulty navigating.

That Delores Watkins and Christine Latimer have committed themselves to careers in the community college environment in spite of the conflict they experience is a good thing; what needs to change is the price exacted by the system for that commitment. The tenets exist in the most recent literature; they just need to be embraced and enacted. Perhaps by their example, Delores and Christine are fostering a generation of women and people of color who will in fact be able to shape and redefine the institution in ways that empower more diverse leaders and where a "one-size-fits-all" culture of administration is a thing of the past.

Notes

1. The names of informants and their institutions are pseudonyms.

References

Acebo, S. C. (1994). "A paradigm shift to team leadership in the community college." In G. A. Baker, III (Ed.), *A handbook on the community college in America: Its history, mission, and management.* (pp. 580–88). Westport, CT: Greenwood Press.

Alfred, R. L. (1994). "Research and practice on shared governance and participatory decision making." In George A. Baker, III (Ed.), *A handbook on the community college in America: Its history, mission, and management.* (pp. 245–58). Westport, CT: Greenwood Press.

Amey, M. J., & Twombly, S. B. (1992). "Re-Visioning leadership in community colleges." *The Review of Higher Education*, 15:125–50.

Amey, M. J., & Zenger, S. (1994, November). "Follow the yellow brick road: Describing the leadership journey through metaphors and maps." Paper presented at the meeting of the Association for the Study of Higher Education Annual, Tucson, AZ.

Belenky, D. F.; Clinchy, B. McV.; Goldberger, N. R., & Tarule, J. M. (1986). *Women's ways of knowing: The development of self, voice, and mind.* New York: Basic Books.

Birnbaum, R. (1988). *How colleges work: The cybernetics of academic organization and leadership.* San Francisco: Jossey-Bass.

Blackmore, J. (1989). "Educational leadership: A feminist critique and reconstruction." In J. Smyth (Ed.), *Critical Perspectives on educational leadership.* (pp. 93–130). Philadelphia: The Falmer Press.

Boice, R. (1992). *New faculty.* San Francisco: Jossey-Bass.

Bolman, L. G., & Deal, T. E. (19891). *Reframing organizations: Artistry, choice, and leadership.* San Francisco: Jossey-Bass.

Brint, S., & Karabel, J. (1989). *The diverted dream: Community colleges and the promise of education opportunity in America, 1900–1985.* New York: Oxford University Press.

Carson, B. H. (1996). "Thirty years of stories: The professor's place in student memories." *Change,* 28 (6), 11–17.

Codd, J. (1989). "Educational leadership as reflective action." In J. Smyth (Ed.), *Critical perspectives on educational leadership.* (pp. 157–78). Philadelphia: The Falmer Press.

Connelly, F. M., & Clandinin, D. J. (1990). "Stories of experience and narrative inquiry." *Educational Researcher,* 19, 2–14.

Cross, C., & Revekas, J. E. (1990). "Leadership in a different voice." *AAWCJC Journal,* 7–14.

Denzin, N. K. (1989). *Interpretive biography.* Newbury Park, CA: Sage Publications.

DiCroce, D. M. (1995). "Women and the community college presidency: Challenges and possibilities." In B. K. Townsend (Ed.), *Gender and power in the community college.* New Directions for Community Colleges, No. 89. (pp. 79–88). San Francisco: Jossey-Bass, Inc.

Educational Policies Committee. (1991). "Hiring effective faculty: An introduction." Sacramento, CA: California Community Colleges. (ERIC Document Reproduction Services No. ED 364 278).

Fryer, Jr., T. W., & Lovas, J. C. (1991). *Leadership in governance: Creating coalitions for successful decision making in the community college.* San Francisco: Jossey-Bass.

Gilligan, C. (1988). "Remapping the moral domain: New images of self in relationship." In Gilligan, C., Ward, J. V., & Taylor, J. McL. (Eds.), (1988). *Mapping the moral domain.* (pp. 3–20). Cambridge, MA: Harvard University Press.

Gilligan, C. (1982). *In a different voice.* Cambridge, MA: Harvard University Press.

Gillett–Karam, R. (1989). "Women in leadership roles." In J. E. Roueche, G. A. Baker, & R. R. Rose (Eds.), *Shared vision: Transformational leader-*

ship in American community colleges. (pp. 235–63). Washington, DC: The Community College Press and the American Association of Community and Junior Colleges.

Heilbrun, C. G. (1988). *Writing a woman's life.* New York: W.W. Norton and Company.

Ideta, L. M. (1996, November). "Asian women leaders of higher education: Inclusionary empowerment in pursuit of excellence." Paper presented at the meeting of the Association for the Study of Higher Education, Memphis, TN.

Kanter, R. M. (1977). *Men and women of the corporation.* Basic Books, Inc.: New York.

Lincoln, Y. S., & Guba, E. G. (1985). *Naturalistic inquiry.* Beverly Hills: Sage.

Lyons, N. P. (1988). "Two perspectives: On self, relationships, and morality." In G. Carol, J. V. Ward, & J. McL. Taylor (Eds.), (1988). *Mapping the moral domain.* (pp. 21–48). Cambridge, MA: Harvard University Press.

Manning, K. (1992). "The case study approach." In Francis K. Stage (Ed.), *Diverse methods for research and assessment of college students.* (pp. 45–56.) Alexandria, VA: The American College Personnel Association.

Marshall, C., & Rossman, G. B. (1995). *Designing qualitative research.* (2nd ed.). Thousand Oaks, CA: Sage Publications.

Merriam, S. B. (1989). *Case study research in education: A qualitative approach.* San Francisco: Jossey-Bass.

Mittlestet, S. K. (1994). "A synthesis of the literature on understanding the new vision for community college culture: The concept of building community." In G. A. Baker, III (Ed.), *A handbook on the community college in America: Its history, mission, and management.* (pp. 549–65). Westport, CT: Greenwood Press.

Moore, K. M.; Salimbene, A.; Marlier, J.; & Bragg, S. (1983). "The structure of presidents and deans careers." *Journal of higher education,* 54, 501–15.

Moore, K. M., & Sagaria, D. A. D. (1991). "The situation of women in research universities in the United States: Within the inner circles of academic power." In G.P. Kelly & S. Slaughter (Eds.), *Women.* (pp. 185–200). Boston: Kluwer Publishers.

Morgan, G. (1987). *Images of organizations.* Beverly Hills: Sage Publications.

Morrison, A. W.; White, R. P.; Van Velsor, E., & The Center for Creative Leadership. (1987). *Breaking the glass ceiling: Can women reach the top of America's largest corporations?* Reading, MA: Addison-Wesley.

Patton, M. Q. (1990). *Qualitative Evaluation and Research Methods.* Beverly Hills: Sage Publications.

Rhoads, R. A., & Valadez, J. R. (1996). *Democracy, multiculturalism. and the community college: A critical perspective.* New York: Garland.

Roueche, J. E., Baker, G. A., & Rose, R. R. (1989). *Shared vision: Transformational leadership in American community colleges.* Washington, DC: The Community College Press & the American Association of Community & Junior Colleges.

Sheppard, D. (1992). "Women managers' perceptions of gender and organizational life." In A. J. Mills & P. Tancred (Eds.), *Gendering Organizational Analysis.* (pp. 133–50). Newbury Park, CA: Sage.

Simeone, A. (1987). *Academic women: Working towards equality.* South Hadley, MA: Bergin & Garvey.

Tedrow, B. M. (1996). "Senior women community college administrators: Life in higher education's inner circle." Unpublished doctoral dissertation proposal. Michigan State University, East Lansing.

Theodore, A. (1986). *The campus troublemakers: Academic women in protest.* Houston: Cap & Gown Press.

Tierney, W. G. (1993). *Building communities of difference: Higher education in the twenty-first century.* Westport, CT: Bergin & Garvey.

Townsend, B. K. (1995a). "Editor's notes." In Barbara K. Townsend (Ed.), *Gender and power in the community college.* New Directions for Community Colleges, No. 89 (pp. 1–5). San Francisco: Jossey-Bass.

Townsend, B. K. (1995b). "Women community college faculty: On the margins or in the mainstream?" In *Gender and power in the community college.* New Directions for Community Colleges, No. 89. (pp. 39–46). San Francisco: Jossey-Bass.

Twombly, S. B., & Amey, M. J. (1994). "Leadership skills for participative governance." In G. A. Baker (Ed.), *A handbook on community colleges in America.* (pp. 268–83). Westport, CT: Greenwood Publishing Group.

Valadez, J. R. (1996). "Educational access and social mobility in a rural community college." *The Review of Higher Education, 19,* 391–409.

Vaughan, G. B. (1989). *Leadership in transition: The community college presidency.* New York: ACE/Macmillan.

Watkins, P. (1989). "Leadership, power and symbols in educational administration." In J. Smyth (Ed.), *Critical perspectives on educational leadership.* (pp. 9–38). Philadelphia: The Falmer Press.

Weiland, S. (1994). "Writing the academic life: Faculty careers in narrative perspectives." *The Review of Higher Education, 17,* 395–422.

Whitt, E. J. (1994). "I can be anything!": Student leadership in three women's colleges." *Journal of College Student Development, 35,* 198–207.

Winship, S. (1991). *An analysis of gender differences in position paths of community college presidents.* Unpublished doctoral dissertation. University of Kansas, Lawrence, KS.

Winship, S. W., & Amey, M. J. (1992). "Gender differences in the position pathing of community college presidents." *American Association of Women in Community and Junior Colleges Journal*, 21–25.

Zenger, S. J. (1996). *Interim leadership: The professional life history of Dr. Delbert M. Shankel*. Unpublished doctoral dissertation. The University of Kansas, Lawrence, KS.

CHAPTER 5

Preparing for Work in a Post-Industrial World: Resistance and Compliance to the Ideological Messages of a Community College

JAMES R. VALADEZ

Introduction

Myra[1] is a 29-year-old student at Prescott Community College struggling to make a better life for herself and her two children. She talks about the challenges she faces and what it means to be a participant in a work-preparation program:

> I worked at the shoe factory for years after I left high school then had my baby and I had to quit. I wanted to go back there to work but it shut down and now there ain't too many jobs that pay that good. I didn't finish high school so the jobs that I can do don't pay what I got at the factory. I been getting assistance but now I want to get something better. I can't work no minimum wage jobs because that's not going to pay the rent and feed my family. I came to this program because I need to better myself to get some skills, learn something to get a good job. There's some jobs that pay good money but I got to get my GED [Graduate Equivalency Diploma] and go on to get more education.

Myra's path through life resembles that of many of her friends and relatives. She did not do well in high school and dropped out in the eleventh grade. She took a job at the shoe factory, and though it was hard work and not particularly well-paying, she managed to pay her bills and put food on the table for her children. Losing her job made her life more complicated, and she struggled with decisions about what to do with her future.

Myra's struggle coincides with the expansive social and economic changes throughout the U.S. over the past two decades. Bell (1973) describes these changes as a postindustrial shift, characterized by a move from the production of material goods as the primary source of capital and exchange, to a highly technical and service-oriented economy. Several significant changes have paralleled this postindustrial era. Among them have been the growth and rising prestige of a new professional class, and the greater importance of technical knowledge. Computer skills, for example, are now highly prized if not essential for workers in this new economy. The deindustrialization of society has also resulted in the shutdown of many factories and the movement of these concerns overseas. Factory shutdowns have had serious consequences for Prescott County. Many workers lost jobs, and with few marketable skills have had difficulty finding work for comparable wages. The loss of jobs has also contributed to income inequities among race, gender, and social class groups, and the loss of a tax base for schools, libraries, youth programs and other community agencies in the county.

Nationally, educational institutions are responding to changes in the postindustrial economy by emphasizing the preparation of students to enter more highly technical jobs. Schools and colleges are also sensitive to reports that current graduates not only lack the knowledge to fill highly technical jobs, but that students lack the work ethic and knowledge of the workplace that employers want. Responding to pressure from the media and politicians, schools and colleges look toward strengthening their graduates by tying classroom work more closely with the skills students need to be successful in the workplace, emphasizing workplace values and teaching on–the–job behaviors that employers find desirable.

Previous studies on work education (Hull, 1993; Kincheloe, 1995; Schultz, 1995) maintain that work education programs are promoted as vehicles for equality, but in reality prepare students for low–level, unskilled, entry–level work. Kincheloe's critique focuses on the idea that educational institutions present themselves as value–free, neutral sites but in fact promote the status quo by indoctrinating students to incorporate values and attitudes pleasing to employers and subvert attempts by students to showcase any individuality or independent thinking. In this respect work (and the education that prepares one for it) is not perceived as a moral pursuit, but rather as an instrumental process that conditions students to become compliant and passive workers. Yet critical educators argue that vocational education must strive for a moral and civic rationale. Kincheloe (1995) and Rhoads & Valadez (1996) call for work education that prepares students to become "good workers," or those who strive to reshape their workplaces into democratic organizations.

In a democratic workplace, workers engage in dignified work because they have a voice in the organization. Good workers expect to contribute and participate in the decisions made by their organizations. In good workplaces, workers are not mistreated or exploited because their active participation and monitoring of activities discourages any abuse of workers. As Kincheloe (1995) points out, vocational classrooms will need to be reshaped to prepare workers to become active participants in democratic workplaces.

In this chapter, I describe the experiences of a group of rural African American women who entered a community-college work-program to seek the skills they needed to escape the welfare rolls, by preparing them for jobs in their community. I studied how these women oriented themselves for finding jobs, and report their experiences in a program designed to prepare them for the world of work.

Boudieu's Concept of Habitus

I turn to Pierre Bourdieu's (1990) concept of "habitus" to help explain the contradictions and complexities in the daily lives of these women as they struggle to overcome their difficult situations, and face decisions about their future in a rural community offering few options for longterm secure employment. Bourdieu (1990) explains:

> The habitus, a product of history, produces individual and collective practices—more history—in accordance with the schemes generated by history. It ensures the active presence of past experiences, which when deposited in each organism in the form of schemes of perception, thought and action, tend to guarantee the "correctness" of practices and their constancy over time, more reliable than all formal rules and explicit norms (pp. 54–55).

Habitus creates a system of preferences and perceptions of the world that allows an individual to assess situations and to make decisions. Bourdieu defines it as a strategy-generating principle that drives all thoughts, perceptions, expressions, and actions, enabling individuals to decide about diverse tasks in their daily lives. An individual's habitus is formed through socialization experiences determined by the person's position in society. The stratified nature of society exposes an individual to varying experiences, and to resources that are unevenly distributed throughout the social structure. Individuals at the upper end of the social ladder have certain advantages over those at the lower end because their experiences allow them to accumulate cultural capital that can be exchanged in social situations, such as school or work, for preferential treatment by teachers or supervisors (Bourdieu, 1977; Bourdieu & Passeron, 1977). Differential treatment, particularly in the schools, gives students with more cultural capital greater access to more desirable positions, and contributes to the reproduction of the social order.

An individual's habitus also acts as a filter for examining external stimuli and making day-to-day decisions. In school settings, working-class individuals often view course offerings from a different perspective than middle- or upper-class students. For example, working-class students may pursue vocational courses that seem practical and lead directly to employment and may discount more academic courses as irrelevant. As an example, Saundra, a 33-year-old woman, provides some insight concerning the applicability of Bourdieu's notion of habitus. She says: "I want to learn something to get me a good job. I only got so much time and I need a job and I don't need to be going to school forever." Gloria, a 36-year-old ex-factory worker, also offers helpful comments for making sense of the role of habitus: "I was in speech class and I asked the teacher why I needed to be in this class because I don't need to be making speeches when I get on the job. Show me how to get a better job, not make speeches."

What does habitus mean for the group of African American women that I describe here? Habitus is a useful construct in exploring the students' understandings of their futures, and how the community-college program and the world of work fit into their understanding. It helps explain the complex and often ironic responses that the women give when pondering their futures. The students have expectations and aspirations for finding jobs that they hope will carry them out of poverty. They also express hope that their children will have comfortable lives and secure futures. However, when faced with the range of job options in their community, their enthusiasm is tempered with the realism that their choices are limited to low-wage, dead-end jobs.

The concept of habitus also helps me to understand the social relations in the community college and the rural south. As I argue in this chapter, the decisions made by the women to enter the job market, ostensibly to escape poverty, are shaped by the social and cultural influences of the institution and their community. This account of social and cultural reproduction is not complete however, without exploring the students' own role in the reproduction of society. In what follows I outline a theoretical framework that acknowledges the place of social structure in social reproduction, but also implicates the students' own participation in the reproduction of society. Specifically I examine the contributions of critical educators (Giroux, 1983; Willis, 1977; MacLeod, 1995; Schultz, 1995) who infuse the role of resistance into understanding the relations between oppressed groups and the schools.

Social Reproduction and Resistance Theory

The ways in which students make academic and career decisions have often perplexed educational researchers. As Paul Willis (1977) writes, "the difficult thing to understand about why middle-class kids get middle-class jobs is why others let them. The difficult thing to understand about why working class kids get working class jobs is why they let themselves (p. 1)." Althusser (1971) and other structuralists explain that students' decisions are channeled by the external conditions of society that result from their location in the social structure. In other words, the organization of schooling differentially educates upper-, middle-, and working-class students, training students from the upper classes to assume positions at the top of the social ladder, while socializing working-class students to accept positions at the lower end of the economic structure. This perspective has been widely criticized because it views the students' own wishes and aspirations as irrelevant. In this structural model the external conditions of society overwhelm the desires of the students, and choices are based on the students' exposure to class-based conditions.

Willis and other critical ethnographers have countered such structuralist explanations by infusing cultural interpretations of the reproduction of society. Willis (1977) claims that:

> For a proper treatment of these questions we must go to the cultural milieu and accept a certain autonomy of the process at this level which defeats any single notion of mechanistic causation and gives the social agents involved some meaningful scope for viewing, inhabiting, and constructing their own world in a way which is recognizably human and not theoretically reductive (p.155).

Willis does not however, deny the importance of structural influences. His insights are distinct from Marxist traditions that implicated students' background characteristics, geographical location, local opportunity structures, and education attainments on their eventual job choices. Willis's work attempts to move beyond the important but limited theoretical advances that characterize social and cultural reproduction theories.

Giroux (1983) advances this work by refining a theory of resistance. Giroux considers resistance as a response to the educational system rooted in "moral and political indignation," not a psychological dysfunction. Student resistance represents a fertile area for study because it considers the ongoing active experiences of individuals while simultaneously perceiving in oppositional attitudes and practices a response to structures of constraint and domination. Oppositional behavior is not always straightforward, but as I attempt to explain in this study, it is linked to the individual's own explanations of their behavior, and contextualized within the nexus of peer, family, and work relations out of which resistance emerges.

This case study highlights the conflict present in these students' lives as they consider the alternatives laid before them. Do they follow and accept the rhetoric of the institution that claims that the path out poverty can be found through hard work and sheer determination? How realistic is that message to these women, given their histories of encountering racism and neglect by society? To make sense of the decisions made by these women it is necessary to look at the cultural milieu of the students and to investigate the processes involved in constructing their views. Bourdieu's concept of habitus is relevant here because students must choose a course of action from a range of alternatives, but their decisions are based on the individual's perceptions and taken-for-granted cultural assumptions.

Using a cultural perspective, students' views are theorized to be formed by an interaction of individual experiences and background. Willis's "lads," for instance, reject the ideology of academic achievement, subvert the authority of teachers, and disrupt classes. Willis claims that the lads' resistance is the result of their analysis of the economics of their social class conditions under capitalism. The lads make a choice to join their brothers and fathers on the shop floor, and apparently do it willingly and without coercion. In the end, this acceptance of class and male culture ensures their economic fate and the reproduction of class structure.

In related work, Ogbu (1978) theorizes that the lack of achievement by so-called "castelike" minorities is the result of their perception of a job ceiling. Young Blacks do not see the sense of achieving in school, because academic credentials do not lead to economic success for members of their caste. MacLeod's (1990) "hallway hangers" also reject mainstream values and are blind to the connection between schooling and social mobility. Even though the outcome of these studies could be explained by structuralist theories, a cultural analysis as provided by Willis and MacLeod shows how students view, inhabit and help construct their social world. This cultural rendition of the reproduction of society shows the role of agency in making real decisions about life. Accounting for human agency, rather than relying on structural theories, forces us to include cultural elements, such as ethnicity, community life, family histories, and peers in studies of class relations.

The work that I present here differs from previous cultural analyses on the transition from school to work (MacLeod, 1994; Valli, 1990; Weis, 1990; Willis, 1977) on several significant fronts. Except for Weis, these ethnographies chart the relationship between school and an industrial society. Weis considers the experiences of students moving from high school into a postindustrial economy, but her work concentrates on white working-class youth in the urban northeast. The study reported here explores the experiences of African American adult women within the context of a rural community in a rapidly changing postindustrial society.

The rural aspect of this study has further significance considering the impact of the closing down of the major industries in this community. While the textile mills and manufacturing plants have historically provided jobs to the working class, the work conditions were often bleak. Additionally, the longstanding anti-labor, anti-union sentiment of the south kept wages low and has done little to improve the shameful work conditions. Closing down the shoe factory and the local textile mill ended a familiar pattern for the young people of Prescott County. Many youngsters had counted on moving from high school to the shop floor for a lifetime of employment. As the factories closed, working-class youth, as well as displaced laborers, have faced unfamiliar decisions about their futures. In all likelihood these individuals have few skills to qualify for technical jobs in the emergent computer industry in the urban centers of the state. Their options are limited to making a living in the low wage service sector of their community or to look toward the community college to find the skills they need for decent jobs.

Thus, a central aim of this chapter is to examine the path students take as they move from a work-preparation program into the work force. My purpose is not merely to take the side of the critical educators (Fine, 1990; Freire, 1985; Giroux, 1983; McLaren, 1994) or critics of the community college (Brint & Karabel, 1989; Karabel, 1976; Pincus, 1980) who have implicated the role of educational institutions in derailing the ambitions of poor students. My goal is to let my arguments be informed by the people who are seeking new opportunities through the work-preparation program. The views of these students inform and temper my opinions regarding community-college work-training programs. As Gloria, a participant in the program said: "I've been on welfare and I know these checks aren't going to be coming forever. I need to find a job, for my sake and the sake of my children."

Method

I set out to study how people experience work-education programs. I was interested in how these programs influence the type of work these students could get, given the type of training they received. Much of the previous work on vocational education and training has focused on the outcomes of these programs with attention to retention and job placement rates (Grubb, 1991; Hull, 1989). In contrast, this study focuses on the participants of the program and their processes for making decisions about their lives.

To understand the decisionmaking processes of the individuals in this study, I used an ethnographic approach and employed multiple methods for collecting data (Bogdan & Biklen, 1995; Patton, 1990). Multiple methods also encourage the triangulation of the data, providing a means of checking and verifying the findings (Wolcott, 1994; Yin, 1994). In previous work (Rhoads & Valadez, 1996) I examined Prescott Community College and its efforts to help working-class students develop careers that served to reinforce their socioeconomic status. In this study I take a specific program at the same community college and explore it through the lives of 13 women. Thus while some theoretical discussion builds upon my previous work, the data collection is much more rooted in the educational histories of these women.

For one year I collected data at Prescott College, focusing on the college's work-preparation program. I collected life histories of the students, centering on their previous education and jobs, and their views on their future employment. I also conducted follow-up interviews with most of the participants after they had been placed in jobs or enrolled in the community college. In addition, I conducted extensive interviews with the administrators of the community college (president; vice-presidents for student affairs, academics, and administration; deans of arts and sciences, and vocational education, and the director of developmental education), the director of the work-preparation program, and the instructors of the work-preparation program. Mr. Vance, the director of the work preparation program, was supportive of this study and introduced me to the instructors and the students. Mr. Vance felt that his program lacked the support of the administrators of the college and welcomed my interest in the program. He used this opportunity to express his beliefs about the importance of what he and the instructors were doing.

Twice a week I attended class during which I gathered data about the program by taking field notes of class activities. Occasionally during class I was called upon by the instructors to offer my opinion on a topic related to the class discussion or lecture. I also took the opportunity to talk to the students and instructors informally in the hallways or in the cafeteria over coffee during break times.

An additional source of information was the prospective employers. I conducted extensive interviews with the director of a temporary employment agency and the personnel director of a local hospital. These two individuals represented a primary avenue of employment for the students in the program.

Finally, I reviewed the relevant documents related to the work-preparation program. I examined course materials, including handouts, questionnaires, assessments, and assignments. Institutional documents make available to me included statistical data, news releases, and institutional reports.

I used several guiding questions to search for grounded explanations concerning contributing factors for social and cultural reproduction and possible student resistance at Prescott Community College. The questions I asked included: How did these students perceive their place and role in society? What were their perceptions of the occupations and careers that lay ahead of them? What were their perceptions of the community college and its role in shaping their futures? Finally, what response did the students have when they recognized the potential limitations and low expectations that society had placed on them?

Context of the Study

Currently there are 2400 students at Prescott Community College taking courses in a variety of programs including one-year or shorter vocational courses, two-year technical programs, and college transfer programs. The student body is typical of many rural community colleges in this southern state. Most of the students are white (67 percent), but a sizable proportion of the students are African American (29 percent). The remaining 4 percent of the students are Latino, American Indian, and Asian. These proportions are comparable to the surrounding community, which is 66 percent white, 32 percent African American, and 2 percent Latino, Asian, and Native American.

Most of the faculty and administrators are white; only 8 percent are African American. At the senior administrative level (dean, vice presidents, president), the situation is similar. Six of the eight (75 percent) are white and two (25 percent) are African American. Only one woman is a member of the senior administrative team.

Prescott's community has not experienced the explosive growth that has been common to the urban centers of the state. As a result, the population has remained stable with 104,000 residents. There is a large disparity in income and educational attainment between the African American and white residents. White families have a median income of $26,000, compared with the African American family income of $17,160 (Bureau of the Census, 1990). In terms of educational attainment, 75 percent of the whites in the county over the age of 25 have achieved at least a high-school diploma, compared with 65 percent of the African Americans.

This picture of the Prescott community is not unlike that of other rural areas in the state. In the midst of unprecedented growth and prosperity in the urban areas, many rural communities have been left behind economically. Consequently, Prescott Community College, and other rural community colleges in the state, are faced with many pressing problems. As a center of educational and cultural activities, Prescott is seen as a vital community resource. The college is expected to provide not only education and job training, but also to serve as a catalyst for economic development.

The Work-Preparation Program

Most of the students in the work-preparation program are women. In the group that I describe here, all thirteen are African American women. When I meet them, some women are in their late twenties and have never worked. They have been out of school for five or more years and are hoping this program will give them the skills to find a job. Three women in their early to mid-thirties are "displaced workers." They had been employed at the shoe factory that closed down several months before. Three women are in their late teens and are high school dropouts. All the women are single parents of young children and were hoping this program would lead them on a path toward the working world, get them off public assistance, and help them to make a better life for their children. Clara said:

> I've had a difficult life. I have three kids. I'm on welfare and I need something better. I came to this program because I heard that it will get you a job. I know two ladies that came here and they got jobs in the hospital. I'm looking to better myself. I hope this program will help.

Mr. Vance is firm in his belief that his program offers opportunity. He states that "some of these people needed a "kick in the butt" and he feels that his program is designed to give students the motivation to "get on track." In his opinion, a real attraction of the program is its history of being able to place students into jobs after graduation:

> We're required to follow up on the students. The need to have some kind of placement, a job or they must be enrolled in school, GED, vocational program, something. We follow them for a year to find out what they are doing. We have connections with the hospital, so if they want to work we can help them get jobs.

The work preparation course meets Monday through Thursday for four hours a day for ten weeks, and includes followup activities consisting of phone interviews throughout the academic year. Mr. Vance and the two instructors, Mr. Buchanan and Mr. Tyler, lead the discussions, provide demonstrations, and give lectures. Mr. Vance limits his participation to the first week of the course, where he contributes what he calls the "motivational piece." It is in this section of the course that Mr. Vance attempts to "change the students' lives around." He says:

> We're here to get the students on the right track. These students have low self esteem, they don't believe in themselves. We try to build up their confidence, get them to thinking about their futures. We have different exercises that we use and we give them support to help them get ready for work.

In Mr. Vance's view, his portion of the course is the most critical information to be imparted to the students. He sees his motivational lectures as his opportunity to reshape the students into a new image. Mr. Vance hopes that his message will make a permanent mark on the students and help them to become self-sufficient individuals. He is also direct about his objective of constructing an image that the business leaders of the community will find pleasing. Here is an excerpt from a lecture:

I tell you ladies that I never see a lady look better than one who knows how to wear makeup and dress to impress. Remember you are in a selling position and you've got to sell yourself to your employer. Package yourself. Walk in with confidence and walk straight in there and sit up straight when you go in for that interview. Look the interviewer in the eye and don't mumble. Speak clearly and confidently and let them know you are the right person for the job.

Throughout the week Mr. Vance emphasizes the theme of presenting a positive image to employers. He states that he wanted the women to "leave behind old habits" and to affect new ways of thinking to prepare themselves for the job market. The fact that the jobs they are being prepared for are minimum-wage jobs in hospital, restaurants, and department stores is not mentioned by Mr. Vance.

In the ensuing weeks the course material rarely strays from the initial messages laid out during the first week of the course. Much of the instruction relates to learning the behaviors students need to make themselves pleasing to employers. On one day students learn to apply makeup. On another day a representative from a local department store instructs them on proper business attire. On another occasion an instructor from the college's cosmetology department gives a lecture on hair and nail care. All of the speakers stress the importance of a "businesslike appearance" and "not sticking out" as important in finding a job.

In the session on interviewing, the instructors also place value on the students' appearances and behaviors. Mr. Buchanan emphasizes:

You will be competing with others for the job. What's going to make the difference and make you stand out from the rest is how you present yourself. How about a smile. I'm a big black guy and sometime people are afraid of me for no other reason than I'm big and black. I always have a smile on my face and it works. You have to get folks to get rid of their fear and if I smile a lot and it helps, then why not.

Later in the term Mr. Buchanan and Mr. Tyler cover on-the-job behavior. The instructors stress behaviors and attitudes that tie in with the first week's messages of "fitting in" or "becoming successful." The virtues of timeliness, orderliness, attention to detail and giving "eight hours work for eight hours pay" becomes a mantra for the students. Mr. Tyler is forceful when he speaks about job attitudes and behaviors. He provides anecdotes from his own job experiences and emphasizes what he believes the students need to know about getting along with coworkers.

I try to bring a positive attitude to work. That may mean smiling or giving compliments. It may be a bad day, but when I get to work I don't bring my problems with me. You've got to watch your attitude because that's the first thing others notice about you. You don't want to be a complainer and you've got to watch who you hang out with. You don't want to be around a bunch of losers. How can you fly with eagles when you hang around with turkeys. Remember you become the kind of people you hang around with.

The instructors place strong emphasis on relationships with supervisors on the job. Mr. Buchanan recalls "that there are many brilliant folks out there who can't hang onto a job because they can't get along with their boss." He reminds students that they will be entering situations where they need to follow instructions and to do tasks as instructed. For example, he explains to the students that they should not argue on the job. The students listen attentively while Mr. Tyler and Mr. Buchanan lecture. Discussion periods are active with most students participating willingly. Gloria, however, frequently sits in the back of the room with her head down or appears to be staring out the window. She is an infrequent contributor to the discussions, but participates in the demonstrations and simulations. I ask Gloria what she thinks about the class. She says: " I don't buy all of it. Some of it just isn't me. I want to find a job and maybe some of this information might help."

Resistance to the Ideological Message

Like Gloria, Elizabeth shows open defiance to the message being delivered. Although Gloria is the most frequent resister, on one occasion Elizabeth turns her desk completely around, lays her head on the desk, and appears to go to sleep. I ask Mr. Buchanan if the behavior disturbs him. He says that "it did at first, but I just let it slide now." Mr. Buchanan goes on to say that what they are teaching is not going to "hit all the students as important," but that some day they would realize the significance of the message.

I ask Gloria about her future and how this program is helping her decide what she wants to do with her life. Gloria is unsure about her future, but she knows that she "wouldn't be on welfare for the rest of [her] life." She goes on to say:

I know a lot of white folks think that we just want to be having babies and collecting money from the government. It ain't like that. They need to be in my shoes for a day. It ain't easy being poor and waiting for that check every month. They talk about wanting to cut or take away money and I just don't see how I can do it. I know I got to work. I want to work and do better, but it ain't that easy. I got kids. Who's going to take care of them if I go to work? I got to earn enough money to pay the bills and pay for childcare if somebody can't take care of them.

Gloria values school and says she "did well in school when [she] was young." She recognizes that going to the community college is what she needs for training and education. She says: "I always wanted to go back to school. I just never had the time or money." Yet Gloria is not convinced that this program is right for her. She resents Mr. Buchanan's attitude and "[doesn't] like the way he says we got to do this and that and that's all there is to it. He don't know what it's like. He's got a wife to take care of his kids and he doesn't know what it is to come home tired and have to cook and do all those other things."

Several of the other women have similar feelings about Mr. Buchanan's attitude. Myra says "Mr. Buchanan is too full of himself." Elizabeth says that "there were some days I could scream" because she [is] "tired of being preached to." Saundra does not have anything negative to say about Mr. Buchanan, but she is disturbed that "they made it sound so easy. Like all you got to do is say OK now I'm going to go get a job and my problems are over. It don't go that way."

Clearly, Gloria can see through the rhetoric and myth-making presented in the work-preparation program. She wants to be trained for work, but the training she is getting in this program is not the answer to her problems. Her response is to reject the message through her resistant behavior.

As Giroux (1983) has pointed out, not all hostile or discordant behavior in the classroom is resistance. But in Gloria's case there is sufficient evidence to suggest that her resistance has genuine sociopolitical grounding. Her analysis of the welfare system, and the possibilities presented to her in the work preparation class, lead her to conclude that the educational system is failing her again. She is not being trained for anything that is going to improve her situation in life, so she refuses to participate in her own undoing. Unfortunately, the consequences of resistance are that she will contribute to her own undoing. By refusing to be trained, she thereby loses any chance for entry into the world of work. The irony of course is that if she complied with the messages delivered by the institution, she would enter the workforce with a minimum-wage job, but she would not be better off economically than she was when she started the program.

Getting a Job

If the point behind the job preparation program is to place students into jobs and to get them off public assistance, there seems to be little thought given to the possibility that such movement will not necessarily lift them out of poverty. Once the students are placed into jobs, the followup of their activities consists of phone calls to ask whether they are employed or enrolled in school. I ask Mr. Vance if the program provides any career counseling for the women. He replies:

No we don't do that but if they need that kind of help we refer them to the counseling center here on campus. We're responsible for following the students for a year to make sure they are employed and if they aren't working then they're supposed to enroll in school. We really don't have the resources to give them that kind of guidance. We really just want to make sure they got a job or they're in school.

There is no question that the students have longterm aspirations to achieve positions beyond minimum-wage employment. They come to the program because they are dissatisfied with their economic conditions, and they look upon the work preparation program as their avenue for getting a foothold on the world of work. The following is an excerpt from a conversation with Myra:

Interviewer: What kind of plans do you have after you finish this program?

Myra: I want to do something with my life. I've had a difficult back-ground. I have three kids and get public assistance but I'm hoping to get my high school diploma and then I want to enter the medical field. I want to start with my diploma and go on to be an R.N.

Interviewer: How do you think this program will help?

Myra: This program will help me get on track. Right now I need to get my life together and find a job.

Interviewer: Do you know what kind of job?

Myra: Just about any kind of job, but like I said I'm interested in the medical field. They have a nurse's assistant program. I may do that.

I wonder if Mr. Vance is concerned that these jobs are not fulfilling the students' ambitions for a better life. He says he is concerned about the low wages, but that it is his responsibility to motivate the students, and that the students have to "take responsibility for their own lives." He goes on to say: "Some of these people have some real problems, things we can't do anything about here like drugs, but if they listen, we'll change their lives." Mr. Vance empathizes with the students and is concerned for them, but also recognizes that his program is about getting students employed.

I want them to know that they can do it if they want. I tell them about my own experience. I started out working in the hospital and wiping butts just like some of them will. That doesn't mean you're going to do that for the rest of your life.

I didn't want to wipe butts any more so I came to school here and then I transferred and got my degree. They got to realize they need to motivate themselves, they got to aim high if they want to move in this world.

Aiming high proves to be difficult for the students in the course. Since the shoe factory and the textile mill shut down, many workers in the community have left town, seeking work elsewhere. Those who have stayed have tried to find jobs in the local restaurants, banks, and other remaining businesses. Unfortunately for the workers, none of these jobs pay as much as their old ones, and other amenities such as benefits are inferior to those they were accustomed to. Nevertheless, these are the only jobs available to this group of students, and representatives from several of these businesses come to speak with them. Ms. Turner from the temporary employment agency lectured:

> We are looking for people with can-do attitudes. If you want a job, we can get you one. These are ideal jobs for those of you who don't want to work forty hours a week and need flexible hours because of your children or school. We will work with you to accommodate your schedule.

Later, I ask Ms. Turner whether there is a chance for advancement for the students. She replies that "talented individuals could be successful." I asked her if she knows of people who have advanced and she replies:

> There are lots of people who got fulltime jobs. I don't have any records because we don't really track that kind of information, but I've heard from companies and from people we've refered that they are now working full-time. You know that the whole point of the company is to meet the needs of the businesses in the community and the people who come to us for work. Many women come to us who don't want to work fulltime. This is the perfect situation for them. They choose when to work and we try to work with their schedules. If they are good, we can find work for them.

I continued to think about what Mr. Vance said about giving the students a start but several things troubled me. The short-term nature of the course and the focus on preparation for specific jobs in the local economy does not seem to broaden the students' options in life. It does give them entree into a job, but it does not necessarily place them on a path that will help them recognize their educational problems, or even give them a hint at finding a path out of poverty through meaningful employment. As Gloria states: " What I want is to be able to pay the rent and to buy my daughter shoes when she needs them." The jobs these students step into when they leave the program provide no such assurances.

The Aftermath

Later that year I attempted to follow up on the women who had attended the course. I was able to get in touch with ten of the thirteen participants. The three women I could not contact had moved out of the area and left no forwarding address. Of the ten women I interviewed, the three teenaged women had enrolled in the community college GED program. Two of them were still enrolled, and the one who dropped out said she was going back to school the next fall. Of the remaining seven women, Myra went on to find a job at a chicken processing plant, one of the few remaining industries in the area, making $6.25 an hour. Three had registered at the temporary job agency, Gloria found a minimum wage job at a local department store but later quit, and Saundra worked for six weeks for minimum wage at a local fast-food restaurant. Elizabeth had not found work because her four-year old "son was having health problems" and she said she needed to stay home with him. She thought she would be looking for a job soon because her son's health had improved.

Myra was the only student from the course who was still employed when I followed up on their activities. I asked Myra how she felt about working at the chicken processing plant:

> It's a hard job. It's smelly and my back hurts and I'm tired when I get home. I'm too tired to even talk and I got to think about cooking dinner for my kids. It's something though, and I needed something. It's tough. I barely got enough money to make it to the next pay day. This ain't something I want to do the rest of my life but right now I got to have something.

Myra originally had aspirations for entering the medical field. I wanted to know if she still believed she could become a nurse. She said: "I still got that in the back of my mind. I want to go back and get my GED and further my education and eventually become a nurse."

Besides Myra, other women from the program entered the work force with varying results. Saundra worked at MacDonald's for six weeks, but transportation problems forced her to quit. She explained: "There ain't no bus. I had to get rides and that got to be a big hassle." Gloria worked at the Walmart, but she said the cost for day care was more than she could afford. Patricia, Clara, and Cecilia registered with the temporary job agency but with limited success. They found that their lack of a high school diploma limited their options. They wanted to work in offices or banks, but their qualifications limited them to janitorial or other manual-labor jobs.

Discussion: Making Sense of the Students' Struggle to Escape Poverty

There are several contradictions involved in the preparation of students at Prescott for entering the world of work. There is the unrelenting ideological message that the students are being prepared to become contributing members of society. There are consistent reminders that welfare recipients are losers and are somehow less than those who work for a living. What the students are not told, however, is that the jobs they are being prepared for will not pull them out of poverty, but will assure them of entering the class of the working poor.

Ultimately, the students are not convinced that working but remaining poor puts them in a better position than receiving public assistance. Mr. Vance and the instructors attempted to inculcate the students into the belief that entry into the workforce will lead to better things, but as students analyze and experience the local economy, that message seems unrealistic. Gloria says:

> It got to be ridiculous. I was trying to get to work and have someone watch my kids. My mother would do it sometimes, but when she couldn't I didn't have any choice but to stay home with them. The little check they gave me wasn't going to cover what I needed. No way. It wasn't going to work with what they were paying me.

Toward the end of my time at Prescott I ask Mr. Vance about what needs to be done to improve the work-preparation program. He unhesitingly states that there has to be better "than $4.25 an hour" jobs for these students to look forward to. Mr. Vance admits that these jobs are unsatisfactory, and that finding students better jobs would improve the program and help the community. He qualifies his statement by saying that his program is meant to be a start, and is not the solution to their problems. He says:

> They've got to recognize that cleaning bedpans is not the answer. They've got to be able to see that it doesn't end there. Some of these people get on the job and they think the work is too hard for too little money and that's true. I've been there, but I didn't stay there. They got to see this as the start. They got to look at it as a series of steps and this is the first step. They are not going to instantly go from no skills and being on welfare to getting a top-paying job. It's not going to happen.

Where does the solution lie? Kincheloe (1995) and Hull (1993) have argued that a postindustrial world requires a postindustrial classroom. Vocational classrooms modeled on Fordist assembly line principles are hardly relevant in today's society. According to Bell (1973), postindustrial workplaces are not the hierarchical, rule-dominated, bureaucratic entities that dominated industrial America, but are workplaces where decisionmaking is more cooperative and where there is a need for creative, analytical thinkers to participate in collaborative problemsolving. Kincheloe suggests that vocational programs need to emphasize ideals that give students the knowledge they need to make decisions about their education and careers. Hull writes that education that emphasizes democratic principles enable students to acquire "the modes of critical analysis, theoretical ability and moral incentive to transform society rather than serving the dominant order (p. 145)." Unfortunately, vocational classrooms have not made the shift to the postindustrial era. Rather, as is illustrated in the work-preparation program described in this study, they emphasize workplace hierarchy and attention to rules, preach compliance and passivity, and pay little attention to the critical thinking skills needed to prepare students for workplaces that require individuality and creativity.

How might this work-preparation program be transformed into one that prepared students for the postindustrial world? We can imagine a curriculum that would not just teach students how to get a job in a restaurant, but would lead them to inquire why so many of the prospective employers have only minimum-wage jobs to offer. They would also wonder why so many of the minimum-wage jobs are being filled by African American women. This would lead students to question why the jobs seem to be divided along race, class, and gender lines. The work-preparation program would become more than a place where students would dream of advancement and high-paying jobs. Instead, they would take the opportunity to research the companies that were recruiting them and learn about the possibilities of advancement in their new places of employment. In short, the work-preparation program would become a site where the students would not passively accept their fate in low-wage, dead-end jobs, but where they would learn to critique their positions in society and discuss opportunities to collaborate with other members of the program.

Conclusion: Where Do We Go From Here?

As was true in Hull's (1993) work, my study focuses on how a group of poor women enter the work preparation program with high hopes for employment. In considering their desperate situations, I describe the ways in which the instructors, the community college, and the local employers all interact to create the conditions that sustain a work preparation program that sends students toward low-level, short-term, dead-end jobs. My analysis reveals the complex ways in which students make decisions to go into particular lines of work. The women in the work-preparation program are presented with a range of job options. Nevertheless, their choices are limited by what the institution provides for them, and how their ideas are shaped by instructors, their families, and the economic conditions of the community. One must recognize that individuals are active in determining their own fate, just as Willis's (1977) lads marched obligingly to the shop floor; but we must simultaneously acknowledge that access to knowledge about careers is determined by a variety of institutional, social, and cultural factors. In analyzing the students' decisions to follow a career path, learning what affects the women's perceptions of the choices laid before them is important. It is also crucial to consider these women's own perception of reality. These percpetions are driven by their notion of what jobs are available, what skills are valued by employers, what their skill levels are, and what they need to do to help their families. These beliefs are forged by their daily experiences and are reinforced by the work preparation program that clearly steers them toward certain jobs. They know what the world is like and what the possibilities are, and use their experiences or habitus as a filter through which any message is tested, confirmed, rejected, challenged, or reinterpreted. Changing their habitus would mean changing their life, cultural, and social experiences, rather than providing them with motivating messages about hard work, commitment, and achieving the good life.

Note

1. All of the names used in this chapter are pseudonyms.

References

Althusser, L. (1977) *For Marx*, translated by Ben Brewster. London: NLF.

Bell, D. (1973). *The coming of postindustrial society*. New York, NY: Basic Books.

Bourdieu, Pierre. (1977). *Outline of a theory of practice*. Cambridge: Cambridge University Press.

———. (1984). *Distinction: A social critique of the judgement of taste*. Cambridge, MA: Harvard University Press.

———. (1990). *Logic of practice*. Stanford, CA: Stanford University Press.

Bourdieu, P., & Passeron, J.-C. (1977). *Reproduction in education, society and culture*. Newbury Park, CA: Sage.

Brint, St., & Karabel, J. (1989). *The diverted dream*. Cambridge: Cambridge University Press.

Fine, M. (1990). *Framing dropouts: Notes on the politics of an urban public high school*. Albany: SUNY Press.

Freire, P. (1985). *Pedagogy of the oppressed*. New York: Continuum.

Grubb, N. (1992). Postsecondary vocational education and the sub-baccalaureate market: New evidence on economic returns. *Economics of Education Review*, 11 (3), 225–48.

Giroux, H. (1983). *Theory and resistance in education: A pedagogy for the opposition*. New York, NY: Bergin and Garvey

Hull, G. (1993). "Critical literacy and beyond: Lessons from students and workers in a vocational program and on the job." *Anthropology and Education Quarterly*, 24 (1), 373–96.

Karabel, J. (1972) "Community colleges and social stratification." *Harvard Educational Review*. 42 (4), 521–59.

Kincheloe, J. (1995). *Toil and trouble: Good work, smart workers and the integration of academic and vocational education*. New York, NY: Peter Lang.

MacLeod, J. (1987). *Ain't no makin' it: Leveled aspirations in a low-income neighborhood*. Boulder, CO: Westview Press.

Ogbu, J. (1978). *Minority education and caste: The American system in cross-cultural perspective*. New York, NY: Academic Press.

Rhoads, R., & Valadez, J. (1996). *Democracy, multiculturalism and the community college: A critical perspective*. New York: Garland Press.

Schultz, K. (1995). "Between school and work: The literacies of urban adolescent females." Paper presented at the annual meeting of the American Educational Research Association, San Francisco.

Pincus, F. (1980). "The false promises of community colleges: Class conflict and vocational education." *Harvard Educational Review*. 50 (3), 332–61.

Valli, L. (1986). *Becoming clerical workers*. Boston: Routledge and Kegan Paul.

Weis, L. (1990). *Working class without work: High school students in a de-industrializing society*. New York, NY: Routledge.

Willis, P. (1977). *Learning to labour: How working class kids get working class jobs*. New York: Columbia University Press.

Wolcott, H. (1990). "On seeking and rejecting validity in qualitative research," (pp.121–52). In E. Eisner, & Peshkin, A. (Eds.).*Qualitative inquiry in education: The continuing debate*. New York: Teachers College Press.

Yin, R. K. (1995). *Case study research*, 2nd Edition. Newbury Park, CA.: Sage.

CHAPTER 6

The Politics of Culture and Identity: Contrasting Images of Multiculturalism and Monoculturalism

ROBERT A. RHOADS

Introduction

A faculty member at a community college questions the commitment of low-income Latino and Latina students at his institution because to him "they are more interested in the up-keep of their cars." Another faculty member sees little reason to discuss theoretical concepts because "the poor and minority students who come here are just not capable of that kind of understanding." A third sees no reason for academically-oriented programs because "low-income students want the immediate returns of technical training." The latter thought is reflected by a group of administrators at one community college who think that their state board of education sets unreasonable expectations for student transfer. As one administrator reasoned, "Minority and low-income kids don't come here to transfer. They come here to learn how to be an electronics technician or a medical assistant. It's unreasonable to put higher expectations on them."

The preceding thoughts about the abilities and interests of community-college students reflect underlying assumptions about the lives of the people these faculty and staff are employed to serve. In the way their comments are phrased, these individuals offer representations not only of students at their institutions, but they also imply a social commentary about various cultural groups with which the students identify. In effect, faculty and staff contribute to the construction of student identities through the interactions they have with students and those they have with other faculty about their students. For example, when an instructor at a community college justifies authoritarian forms of pedagogy because "low-income students need more structure," a representation of low-income students clearly is suggested. Here, two ideas are implied. First, in embracing an authoritarian view of the teacher-student relationship, the teacher is positioned as the keeper of knowledge and students as unknowing neophytes. The second idea implied by this instructor is that middle- and upper-class students do not need knowledge handed to them, but instead are capable of actively engaging in their own knowledge production. Representations such as these call attention to what many critical educational and social theorists describe as "the politics of culture and identity."

As noted in the Introduction to this volume, this chapter follows a more critical qualitative approach to organizational analysis. Accordingly, a critical analysis highlights the fact that culture and identity revolve around issues of power and control and that knowledge gets legitimized through a political process. The politics of culture and identity offer insights into deconstructing social interactions in which power is utilized to situate the self and the other. For example, in the opening comments in which a community college professor claims that low-income Latino and Latina students are more interested in their cars than learning, the students' lives and interests are situated as subordinate to those of the faculty member. The faculty member holds the power to define students' interests and what they ought to be. His construction of social reality has validity, whereas theirs does not. A critical qualitative analysis challenges the researcher to examine the positions from which faculty, staff, and students speak.

Accordingly, the intent of this chapter is to examine the politics of culture and identity as revealed through the kinds of discourses and pedagogical strategies enacted at Western Community College. Western has a high Latina and Latino student enrollment and has struggled to enact effective educational programs and pedagogies for these students.

In what follows, I clarify ideas associated with the politics of culture and identity. I then delineate the methodology used in conducting this study. I go on to provide background information about Western Community College and present findings organized around two contrasting views of culture and identity: monoculturalism versus multiculturalism. I conclude the chapter by discussing the theoretical and practical implications of the findings.

The Politics of Culture and Identity

Over the years, issues of culture and identity have become increasingly central to educational theory and research. Educational institutions play a pivotal role in student identity formation, and schools may be seen as both reflecting and shaping the cultures within which they operate (Giroux, 1992,

1993). For example, Penelope Eckert (1989), Jay MacLeod (1987), Peter McLaren (1986, 1989), and Paul Willis (1977) reveal how social class contributes to students' sense of self and the resistance they offer to the schooling process. Michelle Fine (1991) demonstrates how issues of race, class, and gender relate to persistence among urban high school students. And Angela McRobbie (1978) describes how notions of femininity get reproduced among working-class girls in school settings.

Research on postsecondary settings also reveals the interconnections between culture, identity, and schooling. For example, William Tierney (1992) explores how Native American students oftentimes are forced to leave behind their own cultural heritage in order to be successful in mainstream colleges and universities. Dorothy Holland and Margaret Eisenhart (1990) uncover a "culture of romance" that contributes to a leveling of career aspirations among college women. In my own work (1994, 1995), I examine the struggles gay students face as they "come out" in a university setting in which an oppositional culture hinders their development of a positive sense of gay identity. And finally, Howard London (1978) and Lois Weis (1985) add to this body of literature through studies of working-class and African American students in urban community college contexts. They highlight the obstacles students face when their cultural backgrounds differ significantly from the organizational culture of the community college they attend.

Throughout the aforementioned works—many of which rely on ethnographic and qualitative methods—the experience of students within the educational context is discussed in terms of issues of culture and identity. Emerging from this body of research and corresponding to notions generated largely by critical theory, postmodernism, and feminism is a heightened awareness of how diverse students are situated within educational institutions and subsequently depicted within written texts (Rhoads, 1997b; Tierney & Rhoads, 1993). Depictions of research subjects or "participants" are often discussed in terms of issues of "representation" or "representational practice." Just as critical theory, feminism, and postmodernism have challenged what gets defined as knowledge, and as truth, they also have taken issue with how cultural identities get situated within social hierarchies that elevate some to superior and others to inferior status (Foucault, 1978, 1980; Lyotard, 1984; Minh-ha, 1991; Nicholson, 1990; Ramazanoglu, 1993).

To understand the politics of identity in relation to educational processes, one must make sense of culture. Culture is an often-used expression that conveys the values, beliefs, norms, and attitudes understood by a group of people. It is a concept that can be applied to a wide array of human groups, as large as whole societies, as small as dyads. Culture provides a framework for interaction within social groups and at the same time is continuously revised through those same interactions (Geertz, 1973). And here is why culture and identity may be thought of in terms of politics. Because culture and social interaction have a reciprocal relationship, it is possible through contestation and struggle to engage culture with the hope of transformation.

Culture not only establishes the parameters for social interaction, it also provides a framework for how we define ourselves in relation to others. Definitions of the self and the other contribute to how identities are represented and understood. The politics of identity involve raising questions about how people are represented through culture, and, of course, through language. Such questions in the end serve as challenges to the very means our society has used to define knowledge and truth. As Trinh Minh-ha (1991) maintains, "To raise the question of representing the Other is . . . to reopen endlessly the fundamental issue of science and art; documentary and fiction; masculine and feminine; outsider and insider" (p. 65).

However, the politics of culture and identity move beyond merely understanding how forms of cultural production have positioned various individuals and groups; it also questions the intentions behind representations and seeks to create newer self-representations (Hall, 1990). For people who exist on the margins of society, the struggle to create one's own representations is necessarily a struggle to seize control of the centers of language and discourse. Cornell West (1993) addresses this issue in his explanation of the "new cultural politics of difference," primarily in reference to African American struggle: "The intellectual challenge . . . is how to think about representational practices in terms of history, culture and society. How does one understand, analyze and enact such practices today?" (p. 5). This question cannot be answered for West unless one first comes to terms with previous struggles to create more honest and empowering self-representations. Understanding the role culture, history, and social structure have played in shaping people's lives and identities is critical to offering newer forms of representation.

But history, culture, and social structure are not static concepts; they are theoretical constructs that serve as guides to engage oneself and others in constructing, deconstructing, and reconstructing understandings of knowledge and of truth. As West (1993) explains in his discussion of black struggle, the goal involves more than expanding access and contesting stereotypes: "Black cultural workers must constitute and sustain discursive and institutional networks that deconstruct earlier modern black strategies for identity-formation, demystify power relations that incorporate class, patriarchal and homophobic biases, and construct more multivalent and multidimensional responses that articulate the complexity and diversity of black practices in the modern and postmodern world" (p. 20).

Agency is central to West's call to arms and is crucial to successful engagement in the politics of culture and identity. Agency may be thought of as social action grounded in emancipatory theory and self-reflection. Agency relates to hope in that the goal is to create a more just and equitable society in which those currently positioned on society's borders have a voice in a truly democratic process. As bell hooks (1992) highlights in her work, the emancipatory vision calls for social transformation involving much more than merely criticizing the status quo: "It is also about transforming the image, creating alternatives, asking ourselves questions about what types of images subvert, pose critical alternatives, and transform our world views and move us away from dualistic thinking about good and bad" (p. 4).

Perhaps it may be helpful to move this discussion closer to the educational context. Educational institutions such as community colleges are composed of people who make representations of others to themselves, to students, to colleagues, and to the public. Because a variety of sensibilities guided by specific social norms have taught us to conceal and in effect enact a symbolic form of discrimination—symbolic not because it is not real, but because it is hidden in actions that have underlying meanings—the representations educators adopt regarding students must be deconstructed. Despite a proficiency for hiding prejudice and disdain of the other, representations oftentimes emerge from educational programs and pedagogical practices. To put it another way, the assumptions we have of the other (and necessarily ourselves) are revealed through the educational interactions and endeavors we adopt in relation to our students. For example, when we provide inner-city Latina and Latino students opportunities to acquire vocational skills, but close the door to other possibilities, the racial representations educators adopt about those students is apparent. When we create educational structures that prepare students from lower socioeconomic backgrounds for nonprofessional careers without stressing their potential to assume leadership positions in a variety of social institutions, a representation of class is made. When we steer women away from science and mathematics careers because the demands are too great, a representation of gender gets produced. By the same token, when we offer upper- and middle-class white males the education and training enabling them to assume positions of corporate, political, and economic power, representations of those students are offered as well.

The politics of culture and identity highlight how educational practices and processes may be understood in terms of their support of or opposition to culturally diverse peoples and perspectives. To be more clear, educational practices may be seen as "multicultural" when they seek to include a wide range of culturally diverse peoples and perspectives. "Monocultural" views tend to envision cultural diversity as a threat to dominant conceptions of education and social life. I will elaborate on these concepts later in the chapter as I situate them within a specific community college context.

To understand the kinds of representational practices enacted at a specific institution, one must have a wealth of knowledge about the organizational context. The depth of knowledge I refer to here is typically achieved only through qualitative case studies that draw on ethnographic techniques. In what follows, I discuss the methodology used to explore issues of culture and identity at Western Community College.

Methodology

The data for this chapter derive from a longitudinal organizational case study conducted as part of the "Organizational Structures" research component of the National Center for Postsecondary Teaching, Learning and Assessment (funded by the Office of Educational Research and Information). The first site visit took place during the academic year 1993–94 and the second occurred during the academic year 1994–95. The college was purposely selected as part of a larger project to examine organizational structures designed to improve the educational experiences of underrepresented minority students attending community colleges (Rhoads & Valadez, 1996).

Case study methodology is "an empirical inquiry that: investigates a contemporary phenomenon within its real-life context; when the boundaries between phenomenon and context are not clearly evident; and in which multiple sources of evidence are used" (Yin, 1989, p. 23). In the case of this study, not only are the boundaries of specific institutional structures blurred, as in confused departmental roles, ambiguous faculty assignments, and overlapping administrative responsibilities; but the college, the local community, and the higher education context in general are all interwoven into a complex interdependent system. As Yin notes, researching such fluid social phenomena requires the use of multiple methods. Relatedly, I relied upon the following data collection tools: formal and informal interviews, participant observation, and document analysis. Over 40 students, faculty, and staff participated in formal structured interviews typically lasting about one hour. Interviews either were tape recorded and transcribed verbatim or shorthand notes were kept and transcribed at a later date. Informal interviews also were conducted. Participant observation was a primary data collection tool as well and provided an opportunity to confirm behaviors reported by individuals during the formal and informal interviews. The use of multiple data collection methods amounts to what Norman Denzin (1989) describes as "triangulation" and provides for greater corroboration of evidence.

Site visits were repeated as a means to increase reliability and control for findings that might be time-specific. Case study reports were produced and read by several organizational participants involved in the study. Comments were solicited which in turn led to ongoing dialogues between myself and several organizational members. The practice of involving members of a study more actively in the research process derives from what Yvonna Lincoln and Egon Guba (1986) describe as "member checks"—the idea that research participants have the right to participate in the production of findings.

Member checks contribute to a study's "authenticity," a term akin to the traditional social science notion of "rigor."

Data analysis amounted to what some describe as "cultural analysis." For Clifford Geertz (1973), cultural analysis is a systematic process that involves "guessing at meanings, assessing the guesses, and drawing explanatory conclusions from the better guesses" (p. 103). The process is self-reflective in that a great deal of interpretation and reinterpretation is involved. Such a strategy involves revising questions as well as theories as one progresses toward the conclusion of a study.

In conducting the analyses, I searched for themes that might help make sense of the data gathered. Themes formed in two ways. Some themes reflect the theoretical positioning I brought to the study and were responses to specific questions asked of the research participants. Other themes came to mind after reading and re-reading the data. This latter type of analysis relates to Michael Patton's (1980) notion that the grouping of data is an inductively-derived process whereby salient patterns emerge from the data.

A weakness of case study methodology is that generalizations based on findings are sometimes tentative. This is where theory plays a vital role. Theoretical constructs help to link particular qualitative findings that may be site-specific to the larger organizational context. In this case, findings at Western Community College may have limited significance for other community colleges unless logical theoretical connections can be drawn between the localized findings and the larger community-college context. As noted earlier in this chapter, critical social science provided a general theoretical lens for collecting and analyzing the data. In terms of data analysis, critical notions of culture and identity were most insightful in analyzing the organizational context of Western and the various views faculty held about knowledge and pedagogical practice and the relationship between the two. In what follows, I provide some background information about Western before presenting the findings.

Organizational Context

Western Community College is situated in a suburb of a major urban center. The college serves about 20 surrounding communities known for their cultural diversity as well as their racial and ethnic conflict. Demographically, the area is fairly evenly divided among Latin American, white, African American, and Asian populations. A high percentage of the Asian and Latin American populations are immigrants.

Western enrolls approximately 15,000 students, three-quarters of whom identify as Latina or Latino. The remainder of the student body is composed of Asian, African American, and Anglo students. The large percentage of minority students (roughly 85 percent) is a source of pride for many students, faculty, and staff at Western. A staff member commented, "We are proud of our racial diversity. You see it when you walk around the quad and see all the different students." And a student explained, "Diversity is something many of us here believe in." Indeed, with most of the student body coming from Mexican American backgrounds, "underrepresented" takes on an entirely different meaning at Western.

The college was founded shortly after the end of World War II as part of the city's revised educational mission and in conjunction with statewide efforts to build the community college system. Originally situated at a local high school, Western later moved to its current location near the eastern perimeter of the city. The formal mission of Western includes providing "comprehensive education." For Western, this includes occupational, transfer, transitional, community, and continuing education. The mission statement also emphasizes the responsibility the college has to provide citizenship education and cultural understanding.

During a recent semester, 35 percent of the student body were enrolled in at least 12 hours (fulltime); another 35 percent were enrolled for 6 to 11.5 hours (for some students this unit load is considered parttime, and for others, such as international students, it is fulltime); and the remaining 30 percent were enrolled for less than 6 units (parttime). Eighteen percent of the students are under 20 years of age, 37 percent are between 20 and 24, 28 percent are between 25 and 34, and 17 percent are over 35.

In terms of faculty and staff, the college is composed predominantly of Whites, who occupy roughly half of the professional positions. Nearly 30 percent of faculty and staff are Latin (some of whom identify as Chicana or Chicano) and the remainder derive from Asian or African American backgrounds. Overall, Western employs close to 1,000 full- and parttime faculty and staff with approximately a 60/40 ratio of men to women. Nearly all of the faculty interviewed live outside of the geographic community in which Western is situated.

Monoculturalism and Multiculturalism at Western Community College

I discuss findings related to culture and identity issues in terms of two contrasting perspectives reflected in the educational practices and discourses enacted at Western: (1) monoculturalism and (2) multiculturalism. These categories derive from the theoretical perspective brought to the study contending that all educational settings may be examined by contrasting organizational practices and processes along a spectrum reflecting a singular view of culture (monoculturalism) or a more multifarious view (multiculturalism). Clearly, some institutions will favor one perspective over the other, while others may be more firmly planted in the opposite perspective. To complicate matters, intra-institutional variability may be evident as well with some departments or divisions committed to one perspective and another department more oriented toward the other end of the spectrum. Additionally, there are contextual considerations in that various issues may lend themselves to the application of a multicultural orientation, while at other times monocultural perspectives may be used. The point is that it is overly simplistic to characterize an entire institution or department as simply "multicultural" or "monocultural." A deeper and more contextualized understanding of academic organizations reveals that this is the case (Rhoads & Valadez, 1996). Thus, in conducting my analysis of the general cultural orientations of the faculty and staff at Western, I attempted to employ a complex view of organizational culture.

Based on these theoretically-grounded categories (multiculturalism and monoculturalism), an inductive analysis was then undertaken. Hence, subcategories such as faculty and staff visions of education, pedagogical differences relating to teaching styles, and views faculty and staff have about students emerged from the inductive analysis. The subcategories organize the discussion that follows.

Monoculturalism

Monoculturalism is the idea that a singular culture prevails or ought to prevail within a given society or organization. Schooling based on monoculturalism reinforces an authoritarian view of education. As diverse students enter the institution, they are forced through educational tactics such as grading and other reward or punishment structures to leave behind their cultural ways and replace them with the mainstream values exhibited by the school. Such a process is authoritarian because teachers make the key decisions and provide little to no opportunity for students to alter the cultural norms of the school. Consequently, they offer little hope for students to see themselves as agents in the transformation of the broader society. Socialization and education is a one-directional process: teachers convey the proper norms, values, beliefs, and attitudes to students who must respond appropriately. Thus, from a monocultural perspective, educational institutions serve the purpose of socializing diverse students to the dominant culture of a society. Such a process necessarily involves devaluing the cultural understandings diverse students bring to the educational context.

The majority of the faculty and staff involved in the case study of Western Community College tend to reflect a monocultural and authoritarian view of society and of education. For example, faculty talk about their work with culturally diverse students in terms of helping them to understand how social life is structured in this country and in the mainstream world of work. "Students who come here don't have a clue about the kinds of jobs and limited opportunities available to them. Some seem to think that all they have to do is take a few classes and pretty soon they'll be running some company or programming a computer. Part of our job is helping them to understand the limitations they face in this society. It's not some pie-in-the-sky dream world." A second faculty member adds, "Our students don't really have a clear understanding of how things get done in the U.S. Many are immigrants or children of immigrants and they still hold on to many of the old ways. The kids have a hard time getting away from their families." The last comment could perhaps be restated to read as follows: "The kids have a hard time getting away from their culture."

Vision of Education. The educational goal of many of the faculty and staff at Western is to have students adopt mainstream cultural values. Assimilationist strategies are most pervasive within programs designed specifically for immigrant students whose second language is English. From the perspective of the faculty, these students need to leave behind their cultural baggage and fully embrace not only the English language but American culture as well. One of the problems with this philosophy is that American culture seems to be defined completely by individual faculty and instructors. For example, Western enacted an immigrant education program designed primarily to help legal immigrants "become effective citizens." A faculty member spoke of the program in this way:

> Our goal here is to move the immigrant students into the work force by giving them a technical education. To do that, we must get them to let go of the past and help them realize that they are in a new country, a new culture. They have to learn English and become fairly proficient. They need to learn new ways of thinking and acting. What worked for them in the past will not wash here. There are certain values that employers look for and it's our job to make sure that our students get those values. I try to instill in them the values of hard work by having high expectations. Like getting assignments in on time, coming to class on time, and paying attention in class. Some of the immigrant students are my best.

For faculty and staff at Western, "effective citizens" are defined as those who speak fluent English and obtain vocational training in order to enter the labor force. Faculty feel that classes in the immigrant education program should be structured in an authoritarian manner because "the immigrant students know so little about U.S. culture that they really have a hard time carrying on a conversation." The culture these students bring with them to the pedagogical encounter is treated as irrelevant, which serves to further damage their already fragile view of their place in a new country.

One faculty member talks about advancing cultural understanding as one of the goals of the program. However, the program's vision seems to be grounded in the idea that culture is somewhere *out there* to be discovered and understood. Faculty fail to recognize or even consider the idea that culture is dynamic and that immigrants have culture as well. The consistent message is that immigrants, predominantly Mexican American students, must acquire certain forms of knowledge to more clearly fit into mainstream U.S. culture, and thus embrace the proper ways of their new homeland. Furthermore, there is no place in mainstream culture for the experiences brought by immigrant students.

The view of culture at Western stands in sharp contrast to the idea of culture as continually constituted and reconstituted by people engaged in interaction (Geertz, 1973). Paulo Freire (1970) discusses differing conceptions of culture and of reality in terms of the banking concept versus a problemsolving view of education: "In problemsolving education, people develop their power to perceive critically *the way they exist* in the world *with which* and *in which* they find themselves; they come to see the world not as a static reality, but as a reality in process, in transformation" (p. 70–71). The goal then of education should not only be to prepare people for jobs, but, just as importantly, students ought to be encouraged to develop the critical thinking skills necessary to participate in shaping reality and transforming society. They need to understand their potential as democratic citizens to contribute to the social and political concerns of society.

Pedagogical Style. Related to monoculturalism is the tendency for faculty and staff at Western to enact authoritarian views of the teaching and learning process and of their relationship to students. Inherent throughout much of their interactions is the notion that teachers (and administrators) *absolutely* know what is best for students. Teachers are seen to be the experts and keepers of knowledge and students are seen to be newcomers lacking relevant knowledge or experience and whose success is contingent upon their ability to grasp as many facts and as much information as possible. This perception of the teaching and learning process has been soundly criticized by Freire (1970) and other educational theorists associated with critical and feminist pedagogies (Giroux, 1983, 1988, 1992; Gore, 1993; hooks, 1994; McLaren, 1986, 1989, 1995; Shor, 1987).

Faculty continually stress the role they play in helping students acquire the necessary skills to enter the labor force. Careerism is a pervasive quality of the organizational ethos at Western, and faculty rarely question the preeminence of vocational concerns. "That's what our students come here for," explains one faculty member. "They are here to get jobs." Critical thinking does not seem to be a quality that many faculty and administrators held in high regard. As one administrator states, "Community college education must be practical. Students come here to get important skills. That's what we're here to provide." And another faculty member offers the following comments:

We're not here to produce any Einsteins. These kids come here to get jobs not to be fed a line about how much academic potential they have and that they can be whatever they want if they just work hard enough. There aren't any Horatio Algers here and with the language barriers our students face there's no way they can take on much more than a basic technical education. I have a good idea of the ability of my students and I give them the type of information they need to get entry-level jobs.

The pervasiveness of authoritarian views of learning is quite evident. Faculty pass out facts and information deemed to be appropriate and help students to develop certain skills. Students, on the other hand, receive facts and information and develop the prescribed skills. Clearly, this is not an interactive process.

View of Students. Faculty who tend to view education from an authoritarian perspective see certain qualities in students as positive. For example, they talk about how easy some students are to work with because they rarely complain or create problems. One faculty member explains enthusiastically, "The kids here are so polite. Everything is 'Thank you. God bless you.' It's very rewarding as a staff person." Another happily adds, "Our students are not demanding at all." A third states, "Students here are very compliant. Easy to work with. They do what you ask of them." And a fourth explains, "The students here are hungry to get jobs and are willing to do what we ask of them."

Inherent in much of the discourse among faculty and staff is a belief that docility goes hand-in-hand with being a good student. One administrator voices his observations about Latin American and Asian students, whom he feels are not willing for the most part to speak up for their rights:

> The unique thing about our campus first is the high percentage of Hispanics and Asians, and many of those folks are immigrants from Taiwan and Hong Kong. So we have very few if any Anglos and Blacks, and within this group you have a different attitude toward seeking assistance or help. They tend to be very humble and not seek out things they have a right to. Their culture does not encourage reaching out or being assertive about what they have coming to them. The nature of both these groups, and I'm generalizing, is that they are not aggressive.

Obviously, generalizations about cultural differences run the risk of essentializing racial and ethnic identities. Although the preceding staff member suggests some essential cultural differences, such as "humility," perhaps a better interpretation is that some students may not have the cultural understanding, or "cultural capital" (Bourdieu, 1986), to know how to act assertively at Western Community College. With the general hostility toward immigrants—which often gets enacted against any non-English-speaking, non-

European, as evidenced by the fallout from Proposition 187 in California—
it is certainly no stretch of the imagination to understand why Mexican
Americans and Asian Americans may not want to seem "too assertive."
Becoming actively engaged in educational decision making and in constructing their own educational histories may be seen by some students as a threat
to their very existence in the U.S.—especially for immigrants. And, of course,
the dilemma is that a certain degree of assertiveness is needed to master all
the bureaucratic nuances of both college and public life.

Multiculturalism

Although the dominant view of culture and the teaching and learning
process or Western reflects monocultural and authoritarian perspectives, a
small yet vibrant group of faculty believe strongly in the ideals of multiculturalism and more democratic pedagogical strategies. This group of faculty is generally younger and more actively involved with students on an
everyday basis.

Multiculturalism highlights the notion that multiple cultural identities
exist within a society and therefore colleges ought to reflect the different
ways of knowing and cultural forms diverse peoples bring to educational
institutions. Such a perspective suggests a democratic form of education in
which diverse voices are to be represented not only within the curriculum but
within the organizing structures of the institutions. Thus, multiculturalism in
its most powerful sense implies more than simply transforming the curriculum, it also involves an organizational transformation. Patrick Hill (1991)
discusses this broad vision of multiculturalism: "We would not have changed
much if all we achieve is a sprinkling of multicultural courses in the departments. . . . Marginalization will be perpetuated . . . if new voices and perspectives are added while the priorities and core of the organization remain
unchanged" (pp. 44–45). And Estela Bensimon (1994) reminds us that
multiculturalism is fundamentally connected to issues of cultural and identity
struggle: "We must recognize that the perspective of multiculturalism, the
struggle to create a more democratic, pluralistic education system in this
country, is part of the struggle to empower people. . . . Such an education
seeks not to inform but to transform" (p. 7).

A faculty member at Western committed to multicultural education discusses one of the biggest problems at the college: "We have one of the
highest Hispanic student populations of any college in the country and yet
most of our faculty are White. Many administrators here do not even see this
as a problem." Several students at Western also comment on faculty diversity
as well. One notes that it is hard for him to go to Anglo instructors when he
has personal problems. Another feels that her language problems are not
nearly as evident when she interacted with Latin American teachers. "They

seem to understand the problems I have explaining things. They are able to translate some of my mistakes and help me learn how to speak better English." And a third student discusses some of the problems he has had with instructors who only speak English: "I can't even understand what they are trying to say to me sometimes. I know my English is not that great but why don't they make some effort to better understand Spanish? Why can't they meet me half of the way?"

Vision of Education. Faculty committed to multiculturalism tend to see education in a broad sense. For them, a community college education is more than preparation for a job. These faculty feel that one of their roles is to get students to think of themselves in terms of multiple roles: as family members, as residents of a community, as citizens of a country. Several faculty talk about how education can be used to bring out these multiple roles and how the classroom can be a vehicle for interaction and learning among students. To engage students, faculty try to create open and accepting learning environments. "If you want students to share with one another and talk about important issues that relate to their lives, you can't set them up for failure by pointing out how something they said was stupid or wrong. If you want students to participate you have to set the stage by being open to different points of view."

One program enacted by Western builds upon the ideals of multiculturalism. This program is part of a statewide initiative and is designed to increase the retention and transfer rates of Mexican–American and Latin American community college students. The program focuses on the development of reading and writing abilities by bringing English teachers and Mexican American counselors together as part of a collaborative effort. Part of the program's success is the integration of culturally-based academic counseling. The Mexican American counselors share the cultural background of many of their students and thus are able to bridge some of the communication difficulties compounded by cultural and language differences.

Students at Western give the program glowing reviews. One student states that the instructors involved in the program helped him with his self-confidence. Another feels that the program has been crucial to her academic success. "[That program] has helped me to see the possibilities in education for me. I never imagined myself as college material. Coming to school here just seemed like the best alternative for me. But now, I can see myself getting my bachelor's degree and maybe even a masters someday." Several other students involved in the program also plan to transfer at the completion of the associate's degree program to pursue the baccalaureate. Additionally, statistics kept at the state level indicate that the program has made positive contributions to increasing student transfer: the rate of transfer to state universities for students in the program is 13.5 percent compared with 9 percent for the overall student population.

Pedagogical Style. Faculty committed to multicultural education tend to see the pedagogical process in a different manner than faculty who reflect a monocultural perspective. For example, while monoculturalists speak of passing knowledge and skills on to students so that they could get jobs, multiculturalists tend to see the process as more interactive. "I see teaching students as more of a process. They learn from me and I learn from them. It's like a two-way street. It goes both ways." Another adds, "If I can't get my students to talk about their experiences and what they bring of value to the classroom, then I think I have failed." A third states, "I do everything I can to avoid lecturing to my students. It's easy for them to just sit there and listen to me talk but they have to learn some where along the way that they can have ideas too. Good ideas."

The words of the preceding professors highlight an essential ingredient of multicultural pedagogy: an emphasis on democratic classrooms in which all students have opportunities to discuss their own experiences, and, in a very real sense, write their own educational histories. Other faculty feel that more open classrooms were especially important at Western since "most of the students here are minorities and they're used to being silenced. We have to somehow break through that barrier." A student offers some insight into the diverse pedagogical styles at Western and what suited his needs: "One thing I've learned is that teachers teach differently. One teacher doesn't give you a chance. He doesn't really let students interact and make class exciting. I find the classes that are the most fun, the most interactive, are also the most helpful." And a second student explains, "I've had some good teachers and I've had some bad teachers. I think the thing that good teachers have in common is that they are good listeners. To be a good listener you have to care about what someone else has to say. So I guess they have that in common too—that they care about what you have to say."

View of Students. Faculty supporting multicultural education tend to discuss students at Western in different terms when compared to monoculturally-inclined faculty. While monoculturalists feel it is their obligation to teach students the ways of society and of the world of work, multiculturalists see students both as learners and as teachers. "Students need to learn from one another, not just from me. That means they have to play the role of teacher sometimes," comments one faculty member. A second adds, "I learn from my students all the time. They continually surprise me with the knowledge they have." And a third instructor explains his perspective on students:

You have to help students see themselves in a new light. And I don't think you can do that by standing in front of them lecturing at them. You have to try to develop their confidence. In every class I try to do something different each time to get the students to relax and feel good about themselves. I use a lot of group stuff where they can help each other to succeed. They see that there are others who also struggle with certain ideas and that there are also students to whom they can turn for help. Some are more comfortable getting help from a peer than from a teacher like myself.

Consistent throughout the discourse of multicultural teachers is a view of students as "equals" or as "partners" in the learning process. Although this group of faculty recognize that they have expertise and knowledge that students might not have, they also believe that students bring a great deal to the college in terms of their own understandings. As one teacher explains, "The challenge is to share the knowledge I have and at the same time create opportunities for students to share with one another."

Discussion

My intent is not to vilify faculty at Western Community College who emphasize monocultural views of culture. They have good intentions (such as helping students get jobs) for enacting authoritarian pedagogical strategies. For students from low-income backgrounds, it is hard to underestimate the importance and relevance of finding a decent paying job. Clearly, many of the faculty at Western recognize this need. The problem at Western, however, is in the manner in which education for work gets enacted. As one teacher explains, "These students need to be taught how to look and act out there." By "out there" this faculty member alludes to the world of work. Although it is certainly important for community college students to acquire skills that will help them gain employment, there is something missing from an educational experience solely rooted in preparation for employment. The question I pose here is whether or not it is possible to envision community college students as something more than prospective employees.

I am not suggesting that helping students prepare for careers is not important. Indeed, students from low-income backgrounds need to develop the skills necessary to gain meaningful employment if the idea of social mobility is to become something more than myth. My criticism of the faculty ethos reflected among monoculturalists relates more to what is lacking—a critical discourse about education and its role in the development of citizens who have lives beyond the world of work. Western, like many other two- and four-year colleges and universities, suffers from a lack of vision of underrepresented students as full participants in social and political processes. Careerism frames nearly all the decision making at Western, and any notion of preparing thoughtful and critical citizens seems a distant echo. Steven Brint and Jerome Karabel speak to this very issue:

> The task is not simply to help them [community college students] acquire a marketable skill, though that is desirable; it is also to assist them in developing the capacities that will prepare them for life as citizens in a democratic society, where the gap between leaders and the general population may be growing ever more profound. According to the precepts of classical democratic theory, the citizenry of a democratic society must be able not only to participate in the governance of its own affairs, but to do so in a thoughtful and informed fashion. (1989, p. 231)

A goal of multiculturalism is to create educational institutions that affirm diverse cultural identities and embrace a wide range of cultural knowledge. At the same time, however, such institutions must build opportunities for diverse students to develop the knowledge and skills necessary to succeed in mainstream society. To focus only on developing students' skills and understandings for the sake of improving their economic opportunities reflects little understanding of the importance of culture and identity. Just as problematic is a focus on cultural issues at the expense of career-enhancing experiences, be they vocational or transfer education. To be effective institutions of higher learning, community colleges must meet both of these challenges.

From a multicultural perspective, community college faculty and administrators must ask themselves what they might learn from the lives and perspectives of the students they serve. The stories and experiences students bring to the educational process have the same transformative potential as the experiences teachers and administrators bring with them. To construct one-directional educational strategies is to devalue the understandings and ways of knowing that culturally diverse students have.

Latina/o students attending Western Community College bring their own knowledge of the world to the classes they attend and the campus settings in which they interact. As Hugh Mehan, Lea Hubbard, and Irene Villanueva (1994) point out, "Latinos have a different folk model of schooling that encourages different patterns of behavior. . . . [Latinos and Latinas] tend to equate schooling with assimilation into the dominant group, a course of action that they actively resist" (p. 95). Despite what is known about the experiences of Latin American students, the majority of faculty and staff at Western follow assimilationist educational practices and ignore the significant cultural differences associated with Latin American identity.

In *Hunger of Memory*, Richard Rodriguez (1982) provides an autobiographical account of his socialization into mainstream American culture, his growing reliance on the English language, and the increasing sense of distance separating himself from his parents and from his native tongue: "After English became my primary language, I no longer knew what words to use in addressing my parents. The old Spanish words (those tender accents of sound) I had used earlier—*mamá* and *papá*—I couldn't use anymore. They would have been too painful reminders of how much had changed in my life" (pp. 23–24). For Rodriguez, the cost of education in U.S. schools was his Mexican heritage and cultural identity. His assimilation into U.S. society meant leaving behind the ways of his parents that left him with feelings that his parents were "no longer my parents, in a cultural sense" (p. 4).

For some, it may seem ironic that I call upon the life of Richard Rodriguez. After all, this is the same Richard Rodriguez who made a name for himself as an opponent of affirmative action and bilingual education. Success in U.S public life, for him, has meant adopting the language and the ways of life of mainstream U.S. society. "Americanization" is the term he uses in describing his education and subsequent career success. Only when he was able to think of himself as an "American," and not as an "alien" in a white society, was he confidently able to pursue the rights and opportunities associated with social and vocational achievement.

Yet the life of Richard Rodriguez highlights some of the negative effects of a one-directional form of socialization carried out by traditional schools. This kind of socialization involves a remaking of individuals so that they conform to an image organizational members have about what is "desirable and proper" (Van Maanen, 1983, p. 211). Socialization grounded in assimilationism force diverse individuals to leave behind their own cultural heritage in order to succeed in their new surroundings. What assimilationists fail to take into account is that culture is not a static phenomena. As Geertz (1973) points out in his work, people are not only shaped by culture, but they also continually reshape culture through their lives and their social interactions. Because culture is continually reshaped, the culture that diverse students are confronted with should also be reshaped to reflect their unique experiences and understandings. Again, the fact that culture is transformable is the reason many speak of the "politics" of culture and identity. This means that institutions, in general, and schools, in particular, must do more than help diverse students to learn about mainstream culture; these same organizations must be willing and able to change as well.

Conclusion

Obviously, we live in quite a heterogeneous society. Multicultural education is about celebrating heterogeneity. Such a process necessarily involves coming together to learn from one another, to care about one another. In drawing on the work of Carol Gilligan (1982), Steven Mittelstet (1994) suggests that community colleges ought to be structured more in terms of caring relationships (webs of connection) rather than the more common authoritarian patterns. "Seeing relationship as web [webs of connection] rather than hierarchy provides an image of community that is more affiliative, cooperative, and creative" (p. 558). An ethic of care, as discussed by Mittelstet, is consistent with feminist interpretations of education and organizational life, and is a central concern of an educational process grounded in an inclusive vision of diversity (Ferguson, 1984; Iannello, 1992; Larrabee, 1993; Noddings, 1984; Rhoads, 1997a). Caring necessarily implies embracing the cultural differences of others as more celebratory forms of socialization prevail over assimilationist strategies (Rhoads & Solorzano, 1995).

The challenge facing community colleges such as Western Community College is helping faculty, staff, and students to recognize the interconnections between educational processes and student identities. Central to this challenge is coming to terms with the interconnectedness of culture, knowledge, and power. We need to recognize that teaching and learning is a contextualized process in which certain cultural forms become legitimized through their inclusion or delegitimized through their absence. This legitimization process has serious consequences for a student's sense of self and sense of cultural identity. Nowhere perhaps are these issues more relevant than in the context of the community college where more and more diverse students are seeking educational opportunities and social mobility.

References

Bensimon, E. M. (Ed.). (1994). *Multicultural teaching and learning.* University Park, PA: National Center on Postsecondary Teaching, Learning & Assessment.

Bourdieu, P. (1986). "The forms of capital." In J. G. Richardson (Ed.), *Handbook of theory and research in the sociology of education* (pp. 241–28). New York: Greenwood Press.

Brint, S., & Karabel, J. (1989). *The diverted dream: Community colleges and the promise of educational opportunity in America, 1900–1985.* New York: Oxford University Press.

Denzin, N. (1989). *The research act* (3rd ed.). New York: Prentice-Hall.

Eckert, P. (1989). *Jocks & burnouts: Social categories and identity in the high school.* New York: Teachers College Press.

Ferguson, K. E. (1984). *The feminist case against bureaucracy.* Philadelphia: Temple University Press.

Fine, M. (1991). *Framing dropouts: Notes on the politics of an urban high school.* Albany: State University of New York Press.

Foucault, M. (1978). *The history of sexuality, volume I: An introduction* (R. Hurley, Trans.). New York: Vintage.

――――. (1980). *Power/Knowledge* (C. Gordan, *et al.,* Trans.). New York: Vintage.

Freire, P. (1970). *Pedagogy of the oppressed.* New York: Continuum.

Geertz, C. (1973). *The interpretation of cultures.* New York: Basic Books.

Gilligan, C. (1982). *In a different voice.* Boston: Harvard University Press.

Giroux, H. A. (1983). *Theory & resistance in education: A pedagogy for the opposition.* South Hadley, MA: Bergin & Garvey.

――――. (1988). *Teachers as intellectuals: Toward a critical pedagogy of learning.* Granby, MA: Bergin & Garvey.

――――. (1992). *Border crossings: Cultural workers and the politics of education.* New York: Routledge.

――――. (1993). *Living dangerously: Multiculturalism and the politics of difference.* New York: Peter Lang.

Gore, J. (1993). *The struggle for pedagogies: Critical and feminist discourses as regimes of truth.* New York: Routledge.

Hall, S. (1990). Cultural identity and diaspora. In J. Rutherford (Ed.), *Identity: Community, culture, difference* (pp. 222–237). London: Lawrence & Wishart.

Hill, P. J. (1991). Multiculturalism: The crucial philosophical and organizational issues. *Change, 23*(4), 38–47.

Holland, D. C., & Eisenhart, M. A. (1990). *Educated in romance: Women, achievement, and college.* Chicago: University of Chicago Press.

hooks, b. (1992). *Black looks: Race and representation.* Boston: South End Press.

――――. (1994). *Teaching to transgress: Education as the practice of freedom.* New York: Routledge.

Iannello, K. P. (1992). *Decisions without hierarchy: Feminist interventions in organization theory and practice.* New York: Routledge.

Larrabee, M. J. (Ed.). (1993). *An ethic of care: Feminist and interdisciplinary perspectives.* New York: Routledge.

Lincoln, Y., S., & Guba, E. G. (1986). "But is it rigorous? Trustworthiness and authenticity in naturalistic evaluation." In D. D. Williams (Ed.), *Naturalistic evaluation* (pp. 73–84). *New Directions for Program Evaluation,* No. 30. San Francisco: Jossey-Bass.

London, H. B. (1978). *The culture of a community college.* New York: Praeger.

Lyotard, J.-F. (1984). *The postmodern condition.* Minneapolis: University of Minnesota Press.

MacLeod, J. (1987). *Ain't no makin' it.* Boulder, CO: Westview.

McLaren, P. (1986). *Schooling as a ritual performance.* London: Routledge.

――――. (1989). *Life in schools.* New York: Longman.

――――. (1995). *Critical pedagogy and predatory culture.* New York: Routledge.

McRobbie, A. (1978). "Working class girls and the culture of femininity." In Centre for Contemporary Cultural Studies (Ed.), *Women take issue* (pp. 96–108). London: Routledge & Kegan Paul.

Mehan, H.; Hubbard, L.; & Villanueva, I. (1994). "Forming academic identities: accommodation without assimilation among involuntary minorities." *Anthropology & Education Quarterly*, 25(2), 91–117.

Minh-ha, T. T. (1991). *When the moon waxes red: Representation, gender and cultural politics*. New York: Routledge.

Mittelstet, S. K. (1994). "A synthesis of the literature on understanding the new vision from community college culture: The concept of community building." In G. A. Baker III (Ed.), *A handbook on the community college in America* (pp. 549–64). Westport, CT: Greenwood Press.

Nicholson, L. J. (Ed.). (1990). *Feminism/postmodernism*. New York: Routledge.

Noddings, N. (1984). *Caring: A feminine approach to ethics and moral education*. Berkeley: University of California Press.

Patton, M. Q. (1980). *Qualitative evaluation methods*. Beverly Hills, CA: Sage.

Ramazanoglu, C. (Ed.). (1993). *Up against Foucault: Explorations of some tensions between Foucault and feminism*. London: Routledge.

Rhoads, R. A. (1994). *Coming out in college: The struggle for a queer identity*. Westport, CT: Bergin & Garvey.

———. (1995). "The cultural politics of coming out in college: Experiences of gay male college students." *The Review of Higher Education*, 19(1), 1– 22.

———. (1997a). *Community service and higher learning: Explorations of the caring self*. Albany: SUNY Press.

———. (1997b) "Crossing sexual orientation borders: Collaborative strategies for dealing with issues of positionality and representation." *Qualitative Studies in Education*, 10(1), 7–23.

Rhoads, R. A., & Solorzano, S. M. (1995). "Multiculturalism and the community college: A case study of an immigrant education program." *Community College Review*, 23(2), 3–16.

Rhoads, R. A., & Valadez, J. R. (1996). *Democracy, multiculturalism, and the community college: A critical perspective*. New York: Garland.

Rodriguez, R. (1982). *Hunger of memory*. Boston: David R. Godine.

Shor, I. (1987). *Critical teaching and everyday life*. Chicago: University of Chicago Press.

Tierney, W. G. (1992). *Official encouragement, institutional discouragement: Minorities in academe—The Native American experience*. Norwood, NJ: Ablex.

Tierney, W. G., & Rhoads, R. A. (1993). "Postmodernism and critical theory in higher education: Implications for research and practice." In J. C. Smart (Ed.), *Higher education: Handbook of theory and research* (pp. 308–43). New York: Agathon.

Van Maanen, J. (1983). Doing new things in old ways: The chains of socialization. In J. L. Bess (Ed.), *College and university organization: Insights from the behavioral sciences* (pp. 211–47). New York: New York University Press.

Weis, L. (1985). *Between two worlds*. Boston: Routledge.

West, C. (1993). *Keeping faith: Philosophy and race in America*. New York: Routledge.

Willis, P. E. (1977). *Learning to labor*. Aldershot: Gower.

Yin, R. K. (1989). *Case study research: Design and methods* (rev. ed.). Newbury Park, CA: Sage.

CHAPTER 7

"Be a Name, Not a Number": The Role of Cultural and Social Capital in the Transfer Process

ARMANDO TRUJILLO and EUSEBIO DIAZ

Introduction

Community colleges play an important role in facilitating access to higher education, especially among the poor, the working-class and racial or ethnic minorities. A high percentage of students who begin their collegiate careers at community colleges do so with the intent of transferring to four-year colleges in order to complete their studies. However, research shows that students who start their academic careers in community colleges are significantly less likely to earn a baccalaureate degree than students who begin their collegiate careers at a four-year university (Grubb, 1991; Austin, 1985; Dougherty, 1987; Richardson & Bender, 1987). Even though data on transfer rates vary significantly by college, overall transfer rates to four-year institutions remain low. Cohen's research on this topic (1991) reveals that on average only 23.5 percent transfer successfully, and when the focus is on urban community colleges the rate drops to about 11 percent.

Research that has sought to decipher behavior and attitudes related to transfer presents contrasting profiles. Community college students that display a higher propensity towards successful transfer are characterized by variables such as high levels of initial commitment to the institution and their educational goals; high levels of academic and social integration; parents with higher level of educational attainment; positive attitudes towards transferring to a senior institution; and engagement in some form of transfer behavior at the two-year institution (Nora & Rendon, 1990). On the other hand, factors associated with low transfer and non–completion of associate degrees are both student- and institution-related. One study conducted in urban community colleges and universities with high minority-student enrollment identified factors that constrain student success and transfer options. College faculty and administrators pointed to low levels of academic preparation; unfamiliarity with the higher education system; conflict between shortrange occupational objectives and long range baccalaureate aspirations; poor concepts of time; and financial pressures due to job and family responsibilities (Richardson & Bender, 1987). Institutional factors affecting student success and transfer encompass both high schools and community colleges. For example, Rendon, Justiz, and Resta (1988) report that college staff complain that minority students receive poor academic preparation in high school and lack access to college-preparatory courses. In addition, they identify a number of problems inherent within community college and senior institutions which served as barriers to transfer.

These studies shed light on the numerous pitfalls and obstacles that community-college students face. However, they capture only part of the picture of what the college student experience entails. They do not capture the richness and complexity of the educational experience for many working-class and minority students as they confront and overcome obstacles on their navigational course through the community college. As the first in their family to attend college, many community college students undergo transformations in identity and outlook as a result of their interactions with faculty, staff and other students. An exploration of these experiences will shed light on why students may not succeed despite having the characteristics of successful students, or why students with poor preparation and support networks are able to overcome obstacles and become success stories.

Despite the persistently low transfer rates of most community colleges, some have attained relatively high transfer rates. An equally important part of the picture, therefore, is the role that the community college as an institution can play in helping students build the confidence and academic skills needed for further achievement. Recently, a large ethnographic research project has focused on urban community colleges that have attained relatively high levels of transfer of students to a four-year institution. This research, carried out in multiple urban community colleges that enroll high numbers of working-class and minority students, has sought to understand what, in the culture of these institutions, contributes to their relative success in transfer (Shaw & London, 1995). This paper draws on the data collected at Palo Alto College in San Antonio, Texas (PAC), which was one of eight urban community colleges studied in the larger project.[1]

In this chapter, we analyze student culture at an urban community college and the extent to which the institution accommodates student diversity as a way of promoting success and transfer. Our aim is to describe the complexity of interactions between students, faculty and staff that take place within various institutional contexts, and to explore their contributions to academic success and eventual transfer. In undertaking this analysis, we argue that faculty and staff at PAC recognize and value the cultural capital of the student and community culture. Further, we argue that this recognition is manifested in both the formal and informal curriculum. It is our contention that this recognition develops the social capital necessary for students to succeed and pursue transfer to a university.

The Role of Social and Cultural Capital

Student success in community colleges is often determined by the fit of the institution's culture with the culture that the student brings into the college setting (London, 1978; Weis, 1985; Valadez, 1995). However, because student populations are becoming increasingly diverse (cf. Almanac, 1995), there is less likelihood of a good fit between the institutional culture and student cultures. This is especially true of institutions that have a history of rigorous admission standards prior to the arrival of "open admissions" (cf. Traub, 1994).

The two primary concepts that we use to explain the nature of the fit between institutional culture and student culture are cultural capital and social capital. These concepts have distinct theoretical grounding but are complimentary in that they bridge the constructs of culture and social structure through a focus on human agency. Drawing on the concept of capital, both refer to resources that have "exchange value" in different institutional settings of the broader political economy such as the community college. Below, we elaborate on the nature of their differences and their interrelation.

Cultural Capital and Social Structure

Cultural capital refers to different sets of linguistic and cultural competencies that individuals inherit by virtue of their family's class position (Bourdieu, 1977). Dominant classes give certain social value and status to language forms, sets of meanings, qualities of style, modes of thinking, and types of dispositions (Giroux, 1981). As a result, the cultural capital that gets the most social value and status in educational institutions is that of the dominant classes. The culture of schools, including community colleges, reflects the dominant social relations of a class-based society. As such, schools play a vital role in legitimating and reproducing the cultural capital of the dominant classes. Bourdieu (1977) argues that the educational system reproduces the structure of the distribution of cultural capital among social classes because the culture, practices, and belief systems it transmits is closer to the dominant culture.

Research in community colleges with high enrollments of minority, working-class, and poor students suggests that the community college is subject to the same class dynamics as other types of schools. That is, community colleges tend to reproduce the structured inequality present in society through the mechanisms of the institutional culture (Weis, 1985; Wilson, 1986; Valadez, 1993). Academic success in community colleges, then, is often determined by possession of the cultural capital with the most "exchange value," which we term academic cultural capital. Working- class students, minorities, and other marginalized groups do not possess the academic cultural capital necessary for success given that the culture and knowledge of the dominant classes forms the basis for education and for administering the community college (Rhoads & Valadez, 1996). Consequently, minority and working-class students often find that their cultural capital (cultural knowledge) and academic preparation does not facilitate movement through the educational pipeline.

Yet some community colleges with high minority and low-income student enrollment have actively sought to address the incongruity of fit between the institutional culture and student culture through strategies that promote a multicultural environment conducive to learning for all students. One such strategy involves the recognition and incorporation of the cultural capital of a diverse student body in both the formal and informal curriculum. Palo Alto College (PAC) is such a place. In pursuing this strategy, PAC has developed what Rhoads and Valadez (1996) call a "critical multicultural pedagogy" that stresses inclusiveness. The strategies that contribute to critical multicultural education facilitate active participation and learning on the part of students, faculty and staff. As such, PAC recognizes cultural differences and actively seeks to incorporate the cultural capital of students and the surrounding community in its formal pedagogical and informal curricular practices. The process by which faculty and staff acknowledge the cultural diversity and educational needs of students, we believe, contributes to the formation of social capital.

Developing Social Capital

The concept of social capital refers to "features of social organization such as networks, norms, and social trust that facilitate coordination and cooperation for mutual benefits" (Putnam 1995, p. 67). The presence of these features in a community enriches life for its members in various ways. Putnam (1995) stresses that, through their networks of civic engagement, people generate norms of reciprocity and the emergence of social trust. One of the principal features of networks of civic engagement is that they facilitate coordination and communication—practices which lead to collective benefits. We argue that the relationships developed by students, faculty and staff are an important form of civic engagement in the educational process. The activities that these groups engage in promote the norms and social trust for learning and subsequently for eventual transfer. Successful community colleges are those that help students overcome barriers to educational success and in so doing, provide an important transformational function (Shaw & London, 1995). An important aspect in uncovering this transformational process, we believe, is to describe the dense networks of interaction students engage in and how this process may lead to a broadened sense of self.

A person's sense of self does not develop in a vacuum. It develops as an interconnected network of relationships, starting within the family and community and expanding outward to other institutions in society as the person progresses through the life cycle. In the process, a person's sense of self develops in the context of others and should be understood within this context. As such, in order to understand a person's broader sense of self, it is necessary to examine the group context. In other words, the process of self-identity is, in actuality, the development of the "I" into the "we" (Putnam, 1995). A person's sense of self gains clarity and explanatory strength when it also reflects a sense of "we" or collective identity.

Institutions of higher learning cultivate a collective sense of self through a range of formal curricular and informal extracurricular activities. In this context, a student's sense of self may reflect the institutions' collective identity. PAC students, for example, when asked about their sense of self in the community college often respond by saying: "At Palo Alto, you are a name, not a number." Most students expressing this sentiment recognize that PAC faculty and staff treat students genuinely. They often contrast the treatment received at PAC with the more impersonal experiences some have had at the other community colleges in the city or the local state university. Students at PAC say they receive personable, friendly, and concerned treatment which, in turn, makes them feel accepted, nurtured, and part of the collective effort of success.

How did PAC develop this type of supportive, nurturing culture? We would argue that the history of how PAC came to be is a crucial contributor to its current culture. Hence, we begin our examination of the college at its beginning. Before discussing the accommodation of students' cultural capital within the formal pedagogical and informal curricular practices and how these contribute to the development of social capital, we first discuss the historical setting—the college, community, and student makeup.

Palo Alto College: A Recognition of Mexican American Cultural Capital

Palo Alto College, established in 1985, is one of four community colleges that comprise the Alamo Community College District (ACCD). Like its sister institutions, PAC is an urban community college. However, based on density of buildings and population per square mile, its immediate surroundings are not highly urbanized. The college is found in the southern sector of San Antonio, virtually at the fringes of the city limits, with industrial and residential areas to the North and West and rural areas to the East and South. Located at the intersection of a highway system that connects the inner-city to the outlying areas, and an interstate loop that surrounds the city and intersects with two other interstate highways that run north-south and east-west, it is easily accessible. Students who drive to school like the ease of getting to and from the campus and never complain about a lack of parking. Those that don't drive use the metro bus service which runs on a daily schedule but takes considerably more time, often requiring several bus transfers before getting to the campus.

PAC originated as a result of community grassroots political mobilization, a fact which sets it apart in significant ways from most community colleges, and reverberates through its current culture. As pointed out in Dougherty's study of community colleges in four states (1994), most (86 percent) locally-developed community colleges were founded with little or no participation by minority groups. PAC, in contrast, emerged via the sustained and energetic work of Communities Organized for Public Service (COPS), a Hispanic, community-based organization. COPS led a twelve-year struggle with politicians, educational leaders, and the Board of Trustees of the ACCD to establish an institution of higher learning in the predominantly working-class, minority and low-income southern sector of San Antonio and Bexar County. Initial enrollment, after the college opened in 1985, was 250 students. Lacking a permanent campus at the time, classes were held in various locations throughout the city, including local high schools and military bases. The permanent campus opened on a 118-acre site in January 1987. COP's membership, made up primarily of blue-collar Mexican Americans, played an active role in a door-to-door campaign informing households of PAC's existence, and along with the founding faculty and staff, actively engaged in recruitment of students. Twelve years later, enrollment has increased to more than 7,000.

The college serves students who come from throughout the city and county; however, most are drawn from the southern sector of San Antonio, with a small but significant number from the rural areas south and east of Bexar County, as well as three nearby military bases. The vast majority of students are from working-class backgrounds and among the first in their families to attend college. Student demographics reveal that 60 percent of the student body are from Mexican American or Hispanic backgrounds. The other major ethnic groups represented are white or Anglo (33 percent) and African American (5 percent). The gender composition of the student body is also of interest: 60 percent are female.

PAC is a primary example of the power that grassroots community organizing can exert in developing necessary community resources. In its short history, the college has provided educational access to students hoping to complete their baccalaureate degree at a senior institution. Approximately 90 percent of its students enroll in transfer-oriented programs, with nearly 55 percent transferring to four-year institutions (Shaw & London, 1995). Why does PAC experience such success? We believe that part of the answer lies in the history of the political struggle that established the college in the south side, creating an explicit political statement committed to making postsecondary education accessible to the community. In the early 1970s, when the city's only public state university was built, it was placed in the far northwest side of the county. Community leaders argued that its location, not to mention tuition costs and admission standards, made it inaccessible to the majority of poor, working-class, and minority students who are heavily concentrated in the south, east and near-west side of San Antonio. Public transportation to and from the university was almost nonexistent and created an additional hardship on these students.

The push to build PAC in the south side was in part a reaction to the placement of the state university in the northwest sector of the county. Mexican American leaders who sought to build a community college in the south side were, therefore, guided by a philosophy of equal access to higher education. This philosophy has become an integral component of PAC's institutional culture and serves as a guiding beacon for faculty and staff. Important components of the equal access philosophy include location, open admissions, and most importantly, emphasis on liberal arts over vocational education. The reaction against vocational education is a significant one in the Mexican American community, whose members have traditionally been tracked away from college and toward blue-collar occupations. The experiences of Roger, a 30-year-old Mexican American PAC student, are typical. He recalls being discouraged by his high school counselor when he inquired about college: "In high school . . . I went in one day and told the counselor, 'I'm thinking of going to college.' She pulled out my record and said, 'You're not really college material, you ought to think about getting a vocational job.'" Because such experiences have been so common, Mexican American community leaders and PAC faculty made a conscious political decision to push for a strong liberal-arts education in order to counteract a history of vocational-education tracking.

The implicit message and clear political statement in establishing a college in the south side of San Antonio is a recognition of the Mexican American community's own cultural capital and the community college's ability to help students develop the academic cultural capital they will need to succeed in a four-year institution. PAC education leaders emphasize the need for liberal-arts preparation and transfer and resist the encroachment of vocational-education programs. As the college has grown, a few Applied Science programs have been developed, but they are not as numerous as in PAC's sister institutions. While new state education policy affecting community colleges has placed pressure on PAC to diversify its vocational programs, faculty and staff remain loyal to a strong liberal arts program that facilitates transfer.

In what follows we clarify how PAC faculty and staff, in their daily interactions with students, recognize and legitimate the nonmainstream cultural capital that students bring with them to college and, in turn, help them obtain the necessary academic cultural capital that they will need to succeed in senior institutions. In the process, students develop sufficient social capital to insure their success while at PAC and facilitate their eventual transfer.

We discuss our findings through the prism of student diversity at PAC and how the institution accommodates student's cultural capital in both the formal and informal curriculum. We organize our findings into three sections. In the first section, we discuss the nature of the student population at PAC and the range of obstacles that confront students as they pursue further education. In the second section, we look at what students say about accommodation in the formal curriculum, and how this facilitates acquisition of academic cultural capital and development of social capital. We conclude in the third section by analyzing aspects of the informal curriculum that acknowledge and legitimate students' cultural capital as part of the campus culture and builds social capital.

Student Diversity and Cultural Capital

PAC, like most urban community colleges, has a diverse student body spanning the spectrum of academic preparation and social class background. At one end of the spectrum are students with solid academic preparation who have acquired the cultural capital in high school necessary for them to make the transition to college without much difficulty. They are usually labeled "traditional students," in that they are 18 to 22 years of age and have achieved a high degree of social and academic integration in their schooling. Students with high levels of social and academic integration tend to have a higher predisposition to transfer (Nora & Rendon, 1990). Although it is difficult to identify the percentage of students who fall under this category, they are a significant part of the student population. The age range of student population at PAC is 16 to 82, with the most frequent age being 19, and median age 23. More that half of the student body is under age 25, indicating that a high percentage of students at the college enroll soon after high school. Based on age distribution, the student population is relatively young.

At the other end of the spectrum are the "nontraditional students" who were average to poor performers in high school and did not immediately pursue a postsecondary education. Many of them found a job, married, had a family, and have returned to college relatively late in life. Many students classified in the nontraditional category includes minorities, immigrants, working-class students, and students over age 25. Transition to college life for these students is often very difficult; many have poor academic and study skills and external pressures of family and work responsibilities. To facilitate their transition to the regular college curriculum, PAC offers developmental studies classes in math, reading, and language. Taken as a whole, these students, much like traditional students, hope to obtain the skills and knowledge necessary to enter the workforce in a sector of the economy with stable employment. Some of them are definite about their program of study. Others have not yet identified a career field and are pursuing a general program of study while they identify a promising vocation. PAC has an abundance of this type of nontraditional student.

Whether traditional or nontraditional, students at PAC look to the community college as an avenue to further academic, social, and economic advancement. The vast majority are transfer oriented and hope to attain a baccalaureate degree. Of the two broad groups, the traditional student is more likely to possess the traits and cultural capital which positively affect his or her success toward this end. Conversely, the nontraditional student often possesses only part, in some cases very little, of this cultural capital. Consequently, the latter group turns to PAC for further development in their pursuit of advancement. To gain a better understanding of the differences between the traditional student and the nontraditional student, while also gaining a better understanding of the differences in the cultural capital possessed by the members of these groups, we present a few portraits of PAC students. While the students described in these cases are meant to be representations of these groups, and consequently, to illustrate the differences between them, we make the caveat that theirs is not the story of all students. However, these portraits provide a more detailed understanding of the type of cultural capital each type of student possesses, and the challenges that PAC faces in accommodating the diversity of its students.

How PAC Is Experienced by "Traditional" Students

PAC sees itself as a link between local high schools and universities. To cultivate its links to the secondary schools, it has established an early admission program for high school junior and senior students who qualify for dual high school and college credit. At minimum, these students must have good grades, sufficient high school credits completed, and have successfully passed the Texas Assessment of Academic Skills (TAAS) test to qualify.[2] These qualifications assure that students have sufficient academic cultural capital to be successful in college courses. Through these types of programs, PAC makes it a point to attract students with a strong cultural capital foundation. One such student, Gil, a 19-year-old Mexican American student who qualified for early admission, initially found out about the program through a friend that was already participating. He recalls,

> A friend of mine was telling me she was going to college. She said she wanted to go into a dual credit program . . . . I asked her how she found out about this. She said she went to the counselor, and they told her about it. So I went to the counselor, and my grades were good enough, and I had enough credits, so I was able to qualify for it.

Seeking the support and guidance of his high school counselors has helped him prepare for college life.

According to Gil, he was always a good student who maneuvered easily within the high school setting and sought to pick up sufficient academic cultural capital to facilitate his transition to college course work. While in high school, he consciously selected courses that would enhance his preparation even though they were not required for graduation. He adds,

> I figured I might as well take the hardest courses now, that way I'll have a feel of things. I always wanted to take the hardest courses. People though I was crazy. My friends would say . . . take PE . . . I'd be taking pre-calculus for my electives . . . economics . . . geometry . . . the courses nobody else wants to take. People would think I was weird. Why are you taking that? You don't have to take that . . . Take something fun, like art . . . take sewing or something like that . . . I wanted to sometimes, but no . . . I was taking some really weird classes for my electives . . . physics . . . I didn't need more science. I just took it because I thought it would look good on my transcript. A lot of my friends thought I was crazy.

He acknowledges that college requires a great deal of time and effort but believes he will eventually be rewarded. His mother, herself a college graduate, has been supportive and has encouraged him to succeed academically. Moreover, she has been a role model for Gil, struggling through nursing school while raising him as a child. As Gil figures it, "If she can do it, why can't I do it?"

Gil demonstrates several essential attributes that are central to many students who successfully transfer. For example, he received support from his parents, took challenging courses in high school, and sought and received advisement from counselors. However, although Gil displays some "traditional" tendencies, he also displays some nontraditional tendencies. He works nearly fulltime, an average of 36 hours per week. Moreover, he is a significant contributor to the household budget, still lives with his mother, pays for some household expenses and also helps with household chores. In many respects though, Gil exhibits the characteristics of students with high propensity for success and eventual transfer, possessing enough cultural capital to keep on this success track despite the obstacles of work and home responsibilities. Even though he is undecided on a major, Gil is certain that he will transfer to a four-year university.

Being a good student in high school and getting admitted to a senior college does not necessarily indicate that the transition will be a smooth one, however. A few students with high social and academic integration in high school find that their academic and social skills do not bring them immediate success in college course work. We talked to a few students at PAC who had transferred from a four-year university to the community college after encountering academic, social, or financial difficulties. While these students initially exhibited the characteristics of traditional students in that they were academically successful in high school, once they enrolled in the university they discovered they did not possess the cultural capital necessary for a successful transition.

An example of such a student is Betty. She received a scholarship after high school and attended a local state university. She reported getting A's and B's in high school, but felt she was not really prepared for the university: "The classes were really hard, and I wasn't prepared for college. I didn't know what to expect. At ——— University they don't care if you do or don't do the homework. . . . I lost all my scholarships because I started to do bad in school."

A similar situation was described by Monica, a 22-year-old Mexican American student. She was a straight-A student in high school and enrolled in ——— University after graduating. Her experience there was not positive and she did not do as well academically as she had hoped. She says,

> I didn't like the system there. It was very discouraging. I felt that their main goal was to weed out people. They're not there to help. There is only one in a few that help you. You're just a number, you're not a name. Here at Palo Alto it's a one-on-one basis. I really enjoy that. I enjoy the way the instructors and the counselors and everybody helps you. Over at ——— I didn't find that.

Minority, working-class and low-income students who do relatively well in high school but lack sufficient academic cultural capital to feel comfortable or be successful at a four-year institution see advantages to attending a community college. It allows these students to gain first-hand familiarity with the college environment and avoid getting lost at a big university. Gil comments on this:

> I think it's smart to come to a community college and then jump to a university. . . . We're not used to being a number in a big crowd. I think it's better to go to a community college. It's more cost efficient too. It gives you more of an incentive to want to go. You go to a university and you're lost. It gives you an image that college is hard . . . . You come here and it gets you ready to go

to a university, for what you're going to have to go through. It will be harder and more difficult, but you're ready now because you've been here.

Gil's statement is a powerful critique of the ways in which big universities do not accommodate students' culture. Much of the heterogeneous student population at PAC would agree with such an assessment. Even students like Betty and Monica, who successfully acquired academic skills in their primary and secondary schooling, are nevertheless still at a disadvantage because they lack the social capital needed to successfully navigate the new environment of the university. The importance of social capital is highlighted in their situation. At the four-year university, they did not find networks of civic engagement that generated sufficient social trust for them to feel comfortable and experience success. In contrast, PAC, by cultivating norms of reciprocity and social trust, provides an environment where students are accepted and given an opportunity to succeed in college course work.

Nontraditional Students

According to some scholars, community colleges have evolved with the goal of providing the masses with access to higher education (Cohen & Brawer, 1989). They have become the main avenue to higher education for minority, working-class, and immigrant students (Richardson & Bender, 1987). In San Antonio, PAC serves this role well. Based exclusively on the criteria of ethnicity, working-class background, immigrant status, and age over 25, the majority of students attending PAC are classified as nontraditional. Furthermore, most are also first generation college students, since few of their parents have attended college. However, there are additional factors that contribute to their nontraditional status. Nontraditional students at PAC also tend to be married, work full-time (PAC's proximity to three Air Force bases attracts students who are military personnel), are generally older, did not enroll in college immediately after high school, and lack familiarity with the college environment as a whole.

Other nontraditional students have taken different pathways to PAC. For example, students who for some reason were not able to navigate through the high school environment as a necessary first step towards postsecondary education have followed alternate routes, most often dropping out and obtaining a GED. Consequently, upon entering PAC's academic environment, they lack the essential academic cultural capital that traditional students have gained through schooling.

To illustrate this situation, we present the case of Josephine, a 20-year-old Mexican American. She dropped out of high school at age 16 because she had lost interest. She reflects on her high school experience and says,

I just started goofing off.... I wouldn't pay attention... I mean, school was back seat to my friends.... It was just something where me and friends would just go in to see each other. I would always go to parties and that's all we would talk about. What are we going to do this weekend?... Stuff like that. Every time we would go to class we would get out. We would just talk and talk and talk. That's basically what high school was about.

Josephine had been in high school three years but had not advanced past her freshman year. She decided it was better to drop out and get her GED instead of staying in high school four more years until graduating. She reasoned, "I can stay a freshman for another year and go to school for four more years, or I can drop out and go get my GED and start college." She told her parents about her decision and her plan and they supported her. She adds, "I needed to better myself... I didn't want to be home all day or working at McDonald's or things like that. Now I want to come to school and be able to earn money and go out and get what I want."

Josephine's lack of academic and social integration in high school prevented her from gaining any kind of support and guidance from counselors. As a result, she was limited to her network of family and friends for guidance. Since neither of Josephine's parents finished high school, consequently they could not offer her much help with college. She credits her cousin with helping her sign up for GED classes and later enroll in college. She states, "She was the one who pushed and pushed me. She was just the one who brought me and helped me to get my paperwork done." Josephine obtained her certificate within three months of enrolling. The GED program at PAC allowed her to get exposure and familiarity with the community college. She is currently a sophomore and plans to transfer to a local university to study social work.

Although Josephine's situation is not necessarily representative of all nontraditional students, it demonstrates the lack of cultural and social capital possessed by students in this category. The cultural knowledge provided by their class, ethnic, or immigrant background does not have the same exchange value in institutions of higher learning as middle-class cultural knowledge. As a result, nontraditional students are often restricted to the one institution that accepts them, the community college.

The examples above give a selective representation of traditional and nontraditional students attending PAC. Our aim has been to give insight to the heterogeneity of students' backgrounds and experiences as well as to the reasoning and strategies utilized by them in making the transition to the community college. In the next section, we describe the ways in which both formal and informal aspects of PAC's institutional culture address the varying needs of its students.

Formal Curriculum and Cultural Accommodation

The formal curriculum is an important part of the institutional culture of a community college, and the principal mechanism whereby students acquire the necessary cultural and social capital that will enable them to be successful in a senior institution. At PAC the formal curriculum is comprised of both liberal arts and vocational-technical programs of study. The liberal arts track, however, remains the predominant and most visible component of the institutional culture. Close to 90 percent of the students enroll in transfer-oriented programs. The historical basis for the high percentage of students enrolled in transfer programs has been discussed above. In this section, we explore what happens within the transfer curriculum—that is, what faculty do to accommodate students and help them acquire the cultural and social capital necessary to succeed.

Faculty have been instrumental in establishing an institutional culture that recognizes and values students' culture as a way of promoting learning. When PAC was established, the founding faculty was comprised of eleven members. The new administration gave them the responsibility to implement the philosophy of equal access as it took form through the community struggle for higher education. One of the founding faculty members elaborates on this:

> We didn't want PAC to be another vocational school. We want to give these kids a chance to make a decision for themselves. If you lock it into vocational, that's it, you've made a decision for them. If they want to go vocational, they have every right, and they should have access to those kinds of programs, but don't create something like that and say this is where you belong.

This faculty member views a liberal-arts education at the community college level as a necessary step leading to further study at a senior institution. This is a lofty goal for PAC students, given that on average less than 12 percent of students enrolled in urban community colleges transfer successfully (Cohen, 1991).

Nonetheless, this transfer mission remains a key aspect of the teaching ideology shared by faculty at PAC. Given the high percentage of students that do transfer to a four-year institution, the strategies employed by faculty are central in helping students to acquire the cultural and social capital necessary to transfer. We asked students to describe their experience on campus, especially in the classroom with faculty and other students, and we observed the classroom setting as well. The data we collected provides insightful accounts of pedagogical strategies used by faculty to facilitate student learning. They also provide evidence of a negotiation between students and faculty leading to more culturally relevant teaching. We discuss three strategies that illustrate this process below.

Faculty-Initiated Pedagogy

In the early years, the eleven founding faculty at PAC collaborated in developing a curriculum that stressed writing and critical thinking skills. Since they were so few in number, they worked closely together and reached consensus. A member of the faculty recalls:

> I know when it was smaller . . . there was eleven of us and . . . there was more opportunity to bring about some kind of consensus. . . . I think all of us agreed that we needed to make something different at Palo Alto. . . . So we worked pretty good together at the beginning, and we established that notion of writing across the curriculum. . . . We decided that writing was one of the most important things that we had to get across. If a student developed some good writing skills, they could succeed almost anywhere.

This process established networks of civic engagement among faculty, which in turn promulgated a supportive intellectual environment in the classroom for students. That is, faculty accommodated students and at the same time challenged them. The faculty member above adds, "I want to make them feel important, and the way you make people feel important, which is a process of empowerment, is that you don't baby them, on the one hand, but on the other hand, you don't throw them out in the cold and let them freeze. . . . You address them like a human being."

Students recognize this dynamic in the classroom and find it appealing. For example, Maricela, a 21-year-old Mexican American student, had attended a private four-year university for a year, but found that she could not afford the tuition. She reasoned that she could take the same courses at PAC for significantly less money. She finds the courses fairly comparable and adds that while the instructors at PAC are easy to understand because they take time to explain, they are also challenging. She states: "I like Dr. ———. A lot of people think he's a difficult teacher . . . a hard instructor. But I don't think so. He challenges you and that's what I like, instructors to challenge you, not to just hand you the homework, the questions, the right answers. . . . I mean, you've got to work for your grade to earn it."

The supportive intellectual environment at PAC also encourages networks of civic engagement that extend from students to faculty. These networks facilitate communication and social trust leading to collective benefits. In other words, there is evidence that students engage in negotiation with instructors to make class material more accessible. An example of this process is provided by Ester, an older student pursing studies towards a nursing program. She comments that she and other students were having problems with a first-year instructor at PAC, and they spoke up: "The frustration gets so bad at times that you have to communicate with the instructor to let him/her know that something's not right, or I'm having problems with this class."

She adds that while there are some instructors that can relate the materials to the student's level, some can not. She recalls that she had trouble with the quizzes and tests in her Human Anatomy class and had to approach the instructor:

> The questions and the wording were difficult, so we told her. . . . She is a very strict tester. She has changed her wording and the test I took today, I found it a lot easier. I think even the other instructors let her know that, "hey, the students that have been making As before are making Cs, what's going on?"

This example illustrates how social capital takes form through civic engagement for mutual benefits. Students help new instructors accommodate through communicating needs, and instructors, in turn, are willing to listen and change their instruction.

The networks of civic engagement that have evolved at PAC emphasize a commitment to students and community. As such, faculty continue to cultivate collaborative pedagogical efforts that address student needs. During our year of data collection at PAC, we found that these efforts took different forms. Perhaps the best example is provided by an officially sanctioned faculty forum that met every Friday during the spring semester in which faculty gave presentations on their own successful pedagogical approaches. The forums were open to all faculty members on campus and were well represented across disciplines. Presentations generally generated an expanded discussion on how to accommodate students academically and socially. The feedback faculty received in an open forum setting helped cultivate support networks focused on students and effective teaching. Such activities suggest that faculty are attentive to student cultural diversity in the classroom and actively seek out a variety of methods and materials that motivate students to learn.

Making Class Material Relevant

The majority of students we interviewed were positive about their classes and about transferring. We sough to decipher why students were so enthusiastic about continuing their studies. They reported that the majority of faculty use a student-centered teaching style that is nonthreatening and motivates them to learn. Central to this style is the technique of making class material relevant to students and illustrates how faculty accommodate student needs. For example, Rudy, a 21-year-old computer graphics student, makes reference to his English instructor, one of PAC's founding faculty.

> He makes his English and literature classes real interesting because he gets all the students involved. . . . Like right now, we're studying Shakespeare and . . . the way he teaches class makes it more fun for the students. He tries to put it to

where we can see from our point of view and not only his point of view. He tries to put it in our generation, in our terms. . . . So that way you get a better understanding of what they're talking about.

Other students also identify the ability of faculty to present classroom material in an interesting and relevant manner. Donny, a 20-year-old Mexican American student, notes that the teaching style of a certain instructor makes it easy for students to learn the material: "He applies algebra to real life. I've never seen another teacher who could do that, who actually applies algebra to real life. You know, that's great. I think that's really good. It helps people understand, like the people in class who can't get it. It's a pretty nice teaching method."

Nontraditional students returning to school after a long absence report that faculty have facilitated their re-entry. Roger, who originally was discouraged from pursuing post secondary education by his high school counselor, enrolled after working ten years at a warehouse and getting passed over for promotion. His first semester was a difficult one. He felt out of place because of his age (30 years old), and because he did not know any other students. Additionally, he thought college was going to "be like high school" where teachers were the authority. He was surprised that PAC was not like that; his teachers treated him with respect and motivated him to learn. When talking about his instructors he says,

> They get me motivated. Most of them get me motivated by teaching the subject . . . in an interesting way that keeps you interested, and makes you want to learn more. For example, I don't like math, but my college algebra teacher . . . got me interested in it by explaining it to me. . . . The teacher was able to do that because if I had a question, I'd ask during class or after class, or I'd go to the office. They were very willing to sit down and talk with me and explain it.

Roger, a radio, television and film major, is close to getting his Associates degree and plans to transfer to an area university to complete his bachelor's. He feels that he has been able to make the transition to college and experience success primarily because his instructors have helped him.

Another example is provided by Dulce, a nontraditional student and product of home schooling. She elaborates on how faculty are flexible and always willing to help:

> Teachers who realize that I have to have an unusual schedule . . . they're willing to bend over backwards to make sure that everything is perfect for their students. It's never the pass or die kind of thing. It's always . . . how can I help you? If you have to work, let's rearrange the class schedule. Let's give you another day so you can make up the work instead of just saying tough. . . . They're very kind.

The type of feedback that faculty provide, she believes, encourages students and builds self esteem: "One of my teachers, Mr. ———, gives a two-page analysis that he types up on his own time for every paper that he receives, telling you how the paper was good and how it needs to be improved. When you read and see that the teacher goes out of his way to do that, you feel great."

Epi, a student taking classes at both PAC and a local university, provides a further example of civic engagement generating norms of reciprocity and social trust. She embellishes on the importance of faculty-student interaction and quality of instruction:

> One of the differences I've noticed is that all of the professors at Palo Alto that I've had have always done more for the students. They have given them that attention. It didn't matter how big the class was or how stupid the question was. I didn't feel intimidated by them . . . that I couldn't go up to them and speak to them and ask them to explain things, no. . . . The professors that I've had have always made me feel comfortable. That's why I keep coming back.

Faculty responsiveness to student needs cultivates networks of civic engagement that facilitate coordination and communication leading to collective benefits, i.e., the formation of social and cultural capital.

Collaborative Learning Activities and Faculty Feedback

Another feature of networks of civic engagement that contributes to acceptance, self esteem and social trust are interactive activities organized in the classroom. This type of pedagogical technique was common at PAC. Roger notes that in English class small groups were formed where "we read each others' papers and give feedback on them . . . like, I like this part about it, or I didn't understand that. . . . You would get all this feedback, and you take it, and you would rewrite your paper." He adds that he was surprised with this type of interaction: "I thought the competition [in college] would be very intense, but for the most part people here try to help me out, and I try to help them out."

Small group activities in the classroom bring together students of diverse backgrounds; yet in this setting, diversity is not a deterrent in promoting norms of reciprocity and social trust. Rick, when describing the small group activities in his economics class, says, "I think it's a good idea to have study groups. You all come to a decision and you all give your different viewpoints. . . . We found out own answers, and we compared them. We discussed how we found them. We came to one general agreement . . . You're putting more heads together, and you come up with more logical answers." He adds that the group ranges in age from 17 to late 30s, a fact that has never been a problem, nor has ethnicity.

Another example of the value of collaborative learning is provided by Juan, a 22-year-old son of immigrant parents. He credits his success to the quality of instruction, as well as to the diversity of students in the classroom.

> I've had night classes . . . with students that are older than me, late 40s, even 50s. It seems like you kind of fit in because they help too. You're not just learning from a teacher, but you're learning from classmates that are wise and have done a lot of things before. It kind of makes you be more self-centered in the sense that you're trying to get to where they're at, even though they're not finished with school. . . . They talk to you; they don't act superior or anything like that.

In general, younger students regard older students as more serious because they know what they want and have more life experience. Esmeralda, a student in her early 40s, says, "What's nice about Palo Alto is that the younger generation looks towards the older generation and the older encourage them. I tell them, look at me. Get your education now, don't wait too long, until you're my age to come back." She states that younger students do not feel that they are being lectured: "We're probably telling them the same thing that their parents are telling them. But it seems that they don't feel pressured by hearing it. They take it as an encouraging word instead of being told what to do."

The curricular practices of faculty, then, reflect a self-conscious effort to convey a commitment to serving students and community. In Bourdieu's terminology, it is the "habitus"—the social practices and subjective dispositions of faculty, staff, and students—which promotes a conducive environment for success at PAC. In other words, in the classroom the interaction between certain fulltime faculty and students instills in students the message that faculty members are there to help students learn. This interaction, in turn, helps students develop the confidence that they can do college-level work. Students feel comfortable asking questions in class or during office hours. Some faculty give extensive feedback on student's papers that both praises and constructively critiques their work. Others organize small study groups in class that encourage students to collaborate on assignments. As a result, students not only learn from instructors but from each other as well. This practice promotes networks of civic engagement that validate student's personal experiences and culture. As one student remarks, "we put our heads together to arrive at a more logical answer." Furthermore, some faculty are able to apply academic knowledge such as math to real life situations which facilitates learning and bridges the gap between practical knowledge and academic knowledge. In short, the empathy and feedback provided by faculty helps students acquire cultural and social capital, and reinforces their self esteem and positive outlook towards education. Taken as a whole, the pedagogical strategies employed by faculty and the corresponding response from students illustrate networks of civic engagement supporting students and community. Through these networks, the cultural capital of students is recognized and social capital development is promoted.

Informal Curriculum and Cultural Accommodation

By informal curriculum, we mean those affairs and activities that constitute a large part of community college life outside of the classroom but which nonetheless solicit and involve the participation of students, faculty, and staff. This concept is closely aligned to the concept of the hidden curriculum, which is said to transmit norms, values, and dispositions to students through the process of daily living and coping with the institutional expectations and routines of schools (Apple, 1979). As such, it is part of both the formal and informal curriculum.

At PAC many informal curricular activities are sponsored by the Student Activities Office (SAO) throughout the academic year in conjunction with special recognition dates such as Hispanic-heritage month, PAChanga, women's-history week, black-awareness week, PAC Fest, job fairs, and student-services fairs. Student support service program offices—the Transfer Center, the Returning Adult Center, and the Student Health Center—sponsor numerous other activities: brown-bag lectures, picnics, educational-excursion trips, and TB, depression and blood screenings. These events and activities help create an active campus life involving students, staff, and faculty and in so doing disseminate integral knowledge (cultural capital) as well as norms, values, and dispositions (social capital). The college does not approach the transmission of norms and values unilaterally. Rather, this process is intricately linked into the norms and values of the broader community. The various events and activities sponsored by the college cultivates linkages with the community and validates working-class cultural capital, thereby providing a bridge to middle-class academic culture. We explore the nature of these linkages and their connection to social and cultural capital through a two-pronged focus. First, we look at the college activities that help integrate students to the college environment. Second, we explore linkages between the college and community.

Student Activities and Support Services

To promote the acquisition of social and cultural capital, PAC extends to its students several programs and facilities that help integrate them into the college environment. These are housed in the Student Center (SC), an accessible and highly trafficked location. The Student Activities Office, Transfer Center, Returning Adult Center, Student Health Office, bookstore, and the dining area are found here. The dining area contains a cafeteria, a large well-lit area with a TV and stage at one end, various vending machines along one wall, and numerous tables and chairs where students gather in groups to interact, dine, or do their work. Much of the socializing that occurs on campus as well as cultural and other educational events take place in the SC dining area. Students passing through to get to a class frequently stop for a few minutes if there is an activity such as a musical performance in connection with a special recognition day. They are also drawn to the SC by sponsored fairs that expose students to university recruiters, career or job opportunities, and health information services.

The SC, therefore, serves as the central location for student socializing and campus activities. As such, it serves to bridge the institutional culture and student culture and facilitates interaction between students, faculty, and staff. PAC is unique in that there are no separate dining facilities for students and faculty. Both groups purchase their food, dine and socialize in close proximity. There are few other eating establishments near the campus, a fact which further helps to draw both groups to the SC. Often students and their instructors can be seen dining and interacting at the tables of the SC. This interaction outside the classroom reduces barriers and adds to students' perceptions that faculty are approachable. Perhaps most importantly, it contributes to the development of social capital by providing consistent, extensive opportunity to interact with faculty in meaningful ways.

As is illustrated above, one of the primary goals of the college is to help students achieve academic success and prepare for transfer to a senior institution. To this end, PAC has established a Transfer Center (TC) that serves to demystify the transfer process and four-year colleges and universities. Initiated in 1992 through a joint venture with the Hispanic Association of Colleges and Universities and funded through a grant from the Ford Foundation, the TC provides students with information that facilitates the transfer process, such as two-plus-two agreements, transfer requirements, course substitutions, deadlines, applications and advisement from many four-year state and out-of-state institutions. The two-plus-two program is an integral component of the transfer process and involves curriculum coordination between PAC and specific four-year institutions.

Center personnel also schedule recruiter visits to campus and field trips to area universities. At least one transfer fair per semester is scheduled, in which recruiters from four-year institutions have contact with students, distribute literature, and answer questions. Educational excursion trips in which students register to visit area universities are held throughout the year. One excursion went as far as Texas A & M University-Kingsville, a trip that took well over two hours one way and required an overnight stay.

Of all the programs and services available through the TC, the educational excursion trips are the most unique. They help students transcend the boundaries between the community college and the four-year university as well as build social capital. An example of this process is provided by Margaret, a second-semester 19-year-old Mexican American, following the two-plus-two program at a local private university where she plans to transfer and major in education. When the educational excursion signup sheet was posted at the TC, she was interested in going but very reluctant because she did not know any of the students who had signed up. "I saw the signup list and I didn't know anybody, so I told [my friend] to signup with me so I wouldn't be all by myself. . . . I would have said no, I'm not going to go if it's just going to be me by myself." Margaret's friend accompanied her on the trip and provided the support she needed even though he is not planning to transfer to this particular university. She was nervous about the trip because she did not know what to expect. Afterwards she said: "I liked it. I liked the fact that they had people there that you could talk to about financial aid and what to expect. I would have liked to have seen the college a little bit more. . . . We ran out of time and only saw half of it." The trip helped Margaret transcend the boundary separating her from a bachelors degree and demystify the first steps in enrolling at the four-year university. While she knew the university had a reputable education department and was familiar with its location, she had never been on the campus.

I had never actually been inside. I had just always seen it from the outside. I knew where it was located, and that's about all I knew . . . other than it had a good elementary education major. When I went inside it was just huge, and I thought it was so pretty too with the chapels and everything. . . . Now that I know what it is like and what it looks like, I have an idea of what I need to do when I transfer and where to go.

The services of the Transfer Center function to provide the social and cultural capital that students need to make the transition to the four-year institution smoothly. Just as important as receiving information about a particular four-year institution is the fact that students can also make an experiential connection with a senior institution. First, students are familiarized with the transfer process. Second, they are able to meet and talk with representatives from an institution. Third, through educational excursion trips, students can visit and in some cases attend a four-year institution through joint admissions while still enrolled at PAC. Consequently, students can actually visualize themselves at a senior campus and establish a sense of familiarity, thereby demystifying the process.

PAC's Returning Adult Center (RAC) plays a crucial role in helping non-traditional students adjust to the community college by providing them support and access to the social and cultural capital operative in institutions of higher learning. For example, many single parents enrolled at PAC have been out of school for some time, or have not finished their high school education. The RAC assists these students with personal development, life coping skills, career exploration, and college-resource information. It also sponsors various brown bag lectures that motivate students and exposes them to topics and issues of concern to the academic community. In short, the RAC helps nontraditional students build up their confidence, academic skills, and the cultural and social capital they need to succeed in the college environment.

Imelda describes RAC's positive effects by commenting on the encouragement and skills learned:

> I took an orientation class with Ms. ———, the career resource coordinator. I learned a lot from that class. Good study habits, how not to get discouraged or . . . distracted. . . . They taught you how to juggle." The counselors talk to you a lot when you come in . . . . They give you a lot of encouragement. They tell you that you can make it. They tell you that it is not impossible.

College–Community Linkages

The gap between college life and the working-class community served by PAC is a significant one. If students are to be successful at bridging this gap, PAC must find ways to reach out and bring in the community. To this end, the SAO and other program offices sponsor activities that extend into and incorporate the students' community—particularly the Hispanic community. These activities acknowledge and incorporate aspects of the student and community culture and in so doing, help students feel that their culture is valued and accepted by the institution. PAC in turn helps them acquire the necessary cultural and social capital to facilitate their transfer to a four-year university.

This dynamic is best exemplified by PAChanga, a community-based festival that is organized each fall. This festival is intended to reach students and their families as well as the community at-large. *Pachanga* is the Spanish word for fiesta or celebration. PAC has incorporated the word into "PAChanga: Celebrating Community." PAC began this celebration in 1993 as a way of fostering greater social interaction between the college and its surrounding community. The all-day event features food, crafts, information booths, performances by college departments, children's games and activities, music, dancing, and demonstrations. One of the local Spanish language radio stations does live broadcasting from the festival grounds. A variety of musical entertainment is provided including a PAC student and her band. The group plays the Tejano music that is very popular in San Antonio and South Texas.

The various events and activities that make up the festival serve to validate students' Hispanic and working-class cultural capital. By hosting the festival on campus, PAC introduces the community, family members and friends of PAC students to the college environment. Mr. Zapata, a member of the festival organizing committee, stresses that the festival is conducted for the purpose of highlighting the various things that are happening on campus and opening up the college to the surrounding community. In particular, he wants students and their extended families to feel comfortable on campus: "I want them to feel comfortable with bringing their abuelita (grandmother) to school even though she may not speak any English. Or for some students who say, 'my dad *trabaja levantando basura*' (works as a garbage man). Well that's OK, that doesn't matter. I want them to feel comfortable with their family background and culture and not feel ashamed."

Just as importantly, these activities and events further serve to accommodate students into the college community. By establishing such an association, PAC extends into the greater community and simultaneously allows the community to feel it is part of the campus. By cultivating community linkages, PAC helps validate working-class cultural capital and provide a bridge to middle class academic culture. These linkages augment students' feelings of belonging and collective identity. Moreover, they establish networks of civic engagement that enrich the lives of students, faculty, staff and community members.

Palo Alto College: The Heart of the Community

The predominant ethos at PAC is student and community centered. It has its historical foundation in the grassroots community struggle to establish an institution of higher learning in the underserved southern sector of San Antonio. The successful founding of PAC has made postsecondary education available to the predominately Hispanic, working-class, and low-income residents in southern Bexar County. The philosophy of educational access has been the guiding beacon as the college has evolved and remains a key characteristic of the institutional culture. Founding faculty and staff have responded by accommodating and even embracing student culture in both the formal and informal curriculum. As the college has grown and new faculty and staff are hired, there is care to employ people that have the knowledge, experience and disposition to serve the diverse student population attending PAC.

Approximately 25 percent of the faculty and staff are from Mexican American or Hispanic background and a good portion of them are from the surrounding community. As a program office staff member put it:

People aren't here just for a job. You can tell that these people really care. I think a lot of times it's because a lot of the people that work here come from the same area of town. If you look who's around here, the counselors . . . the Vice President, these are people who grew up in this area. I come from the west side, [the nurse] comes from the west side. We have an affiliation to this area. When we talk to a student, hey, that's my neighbor, that's my sister, that's somebody I grew up with. I think that we see them that way, and I think students can see that we are just like them, and I think that we take an interest in them.

This statement captures the sense of commitment that faculty and staff have to serving students and the institution. This outlook has filtered out to the community, and students have responded accordingly. Students are attracted to PAC by its proximity, friendly family atmosphere, small class size, supportive program services, and attentive faculty and staff. These factors contribute to making students feel comfortable and confident in crossing the boundary to postsecondary education.

Informal curricular activities and events involving staff, students and faculty also promote practices and subjective dispositions that instill in students the message that college is a warm, friendly place to learn and establish positive social relationships that will help them throughout their life. One college administrator noted that when PAC opened there was a shortage of support personnel necessary for the college to function effectively. Consequently, many students were hired as staff through the work study program to assist different program offices and became an "intimate part of the development of the college." Students continue to serve in this capacity. The Student Activities Office Director comments that their continued involvement has given them a sense of "part ownership in what's going on." These networks demonstrate the importance of social bonds within each group, and contribute to the formation of social capital.

PAC's commitment to students and the community is captured in its slogan—"The Heart of the Community." The slogan was selected from 189 entries during a campus-wide contest in 1994. Contributed by a student from the south side community, it captures the essence of the college. As a metaphor, the slogan reflects PAC's sense of collective identity, an institution that bridges the high school and university for students. It also extends out to the community at large through various community outreach activities such as off campus courses, blood drives and depression screenings, income tax preparation, and festivals like PAChanga. In short, through its formal and informal curricula, PAC recognizes and values the culture of its students and community. Through this process, the college helps students develop necessary cultural and social capital to succeed and eventually transfer to a four-year institution.

Notes

1. The data reported here was collected during the 1994-95 academic year as part of Cultures of Success: A Study of Community Colleges With High Transfer Rates (see London & Shaw, 1994)

2. Successful completion of the TAAS test is required before students graduate from high school

References

Apple, M. (1979). *Ideology and curriculum.* London: Routledge & Kegan Paul.

Astin, A. W. (1985). *Achieving educational excellence.* San Francisco: Jossey-Bass.

Almanac: Facts about higher education in the U. S., each of the 50 states and D. C. (1995, September 1). *Chronicle of Higher Education,* XLII (1).

Bourdieu, P. (1977). "Cultural reproduction and social reproduction." In J. Karabel & A. H. Helsey (Eds.), *Power and ideology of education* (pp. 487–511). New York: Oxford University Press.

Cohen, A. M., & Brawer, F. B. (1989). *The American community college* (2nd ed.). San Francisco: Jossey-Bass.

Dougherty, K. (1987). "The effects of community colleges: Aid or hindrance to socioeconomic attainment?" *Sociology of Education,* 60, 86–103.

Giroux, H. A. (1981). "Hegemony, resistance, and the paradox of educational reform." *Interchange,* 12(2–3), 3–26.

London, H. B., & Shaw, K. M. (1994). "Cultures of success: A study of community colleges with high transfer rates." Research proposal overview. Ford Foundation. Unpublished.

London, H. B. (1978). *The culture of a community college.* New York: Praeger Publishers.

Nora, A., & Rendon, L. I. (1990). "Determinants of predisposition to transfer among community college students: A structural model." *Research in Higher Education,* 31(3), 235–55.

Putnam, R. D. (1995) "Bowling alone: America's declining social capital." *Journal of Democracy,* 6 (1), 65–78.

Rhoads, R. A., & Valadez, J. A. (1996) *Democracy, multiculturalism, and the community college: A critical perspective.* New York: Garland.

Rendon, L.; Justiz, M.; & Resta, P. (1988). *Transfer education in southwest community colleges.* Columbia: University of South Carolina Press.

Richardson, R. C., & Bender, L. W. (1987). *Fostering minority access and achievement in higher education.* San Francisco: Jossey-Bass.

Shaw, K. M., & London, H. B. (1995). "Negotiating class and cultural boundaries: Toward an expanded definition of the transfer process." Paper presented at the Association for the Study of Higher Education. Orlando, FL.

Traub, J. (1994). *City on a hill: Testing the American dream at city college.* Reading, MA: Addison-Wesley.

Weis, L. (1985). *Between two worlds: Black students in an urban community college.* Boston: Routledge and Kegan Paul.

Wilson, R. (1986). "Minority students and the community college." *New Directions for Community Colleges,* 54, 61–70.

Valadez, J. R. (1995). "Culture and class relations in a rural community college: Influences on student academic achievement." Paper presented at the American Educational Research Association Meeting. San Francisco, CA.

Valadez, J. R. (1993). "Cultural capital and its impact on the aspirations of nontraditional community college students." *Community College Review,* 21, 30–43.

CHAPTER 8

Defining the Self:
Constructions of Identity in Community
College Students

KATHLEEN M. SHAW

Introduction

The lives of community college students are, in many ways, defined by complexity. In contrast to more "traditional" college students, community college students are more likely to be employed either part- or full-time; to have spouses, children, or both; and to encounter financial or logistical difficulties that make attending college a difficult endeavor. In fact, for many students, community college attendance often represents a real attempt to improve their social status—a process that can be fraught with confusion regarding one's definition of self (London, 1991).

In addition to the struggles inherent in adding the role of student to the already full roster of responsibilities held by these students, they are also defined, and define themselves, as members of particular social categories, such as race, culture, and gender. Indeed, since community colleges enroll disproportionate numbers of women and ethnic or racial minorities, identification with such categories is particularly relevant within the context of these institutions. This interplay of assumed roles and social categories interact to produce an experience of identity that is multifaceted, situation-specific, and fragmented. In short, community college students are engaged in a juggling act of sorts with an array of identities. If these students are to successfully manage their various roles—that is, if they are to maintain their identity as students while they also function as parents, workers, and members of a particular racial or ethnic category—

community colleges must recognize, embrace, and accommodate the complexity of these students' lives.

Critical theorists of all stripes point to the importance of recognizing differences in power that emerge from membership in particular social or cultural categories. Non-whites, women, the poor, the disabled, and sexual minorities occupy the lower rungs of the power structure in American society. As such, they are excluded from the economic and social benefits that members of the dominant culture enjoy. Since community colleges are increasingly the path through which such marginalized groups attempt to overcome structural inequities, it is particularly important that these institutions recognize and embrace the cultures and lived experiences of students who are not members of the white, middle-class, Western culture upon which educational institutions are based in the United States. However, as tempting as it is to reduce community college students to the sum of their membership in one or more of these marginalized categories, their sense of identity is, by their own description, much more complex and multifaceted. Indeed, as I have found in examining data from interviews with hundreds of such students across the United States, students define themselves in terms of voluntarily assumed roles (e.g., spouse, caretaker) as frequently as they do in terms of their race, class, or gender. Repeatedly, individual agency interacts with both social characteristics and social structure to produce fluid, multiple identities.

While most community colleges adopt strategies designed to emphasize and reinforce the actions and behavior associated with the role of "student," some have adopted pedagogical and organizational strategies designed to help students adjust to the fluidity and inherent contradictions of their multiple roles and identities. In this chapter, I employ critical qualitative methodology to use the words and experiences of community college students to explore and expand upon recent theories of identity, particularly those that have emerged from postmodernism, critical theory, and cultural studies. While this data does not negate the relevance of social categories of identity (e.g., race, class and gender) that have gained ground in recent years under the moniker of "identity politics," it builds upon them by establishing other sources of identity, and suggests a somewhat different process of identity formation and adaptation. Secondly, I examine the ways in which community colleges define students, and identify a typology of institutional responses ranging from those in which students are defined primarily by their roles as community college students, to institutions that recognize and embrace student identity based on social categories, to those that approach students in a more holistic manner, and attempt to address their multifaceted identities in a number of ways.

Identity Theory in the Context of the Community College

Despite the fact that community colleges are largely ignored by educational researchers and the general public, they are far from being "marginal" to the educational structure in this country. In fact, community colleges enroll 36 percent of all college students (The Chronicle of Higher Education Almanac, 1995). Yet the demographics of community college students reveal a student population that is striking in its diversity, and in its diversion from what is generally considered to be the "traditional" college student. For example, 57 percent of community college students are female, 22 percent are classified as minority, 10 percent have family incomes beneath $15,000, and 25 percent carry a high school grade-point average of a C-plus or lower. In contrast, 53 percent of four-year college students are female, 18 percent are minority, only 6 percent have incomes of $15,000 or lower, and 14 percent have C-plus or lower high school grade-point averages (Dougherty, 1994, p. 4). In short, community colleges serve a disproportionate number of poor, working-class, ethnic or racial minority, and female students.

As has been pointed out by numerous social critics, structurally, these groups occupy a social strata which at best can be described as "disadvantaged," and at worst, as "oppressed" (West, 1990; Gates, 1986; Lorde, 1984). Not only are women, people of color and the poor and working class systematically shut out of many of the economic, educational, and social opportunities that present themselves to those occupying a higher place in the social structure; they also experience the world differently. As a result, they must function in a world in which unequal power differentials maintain and reinforce their disenfranchised positions.

This emphasis on power differentials is the nexus of a strand of identity theory that has been appropriated by those interested in challenging the primacy of traditional modes of discourse and education. It departs from more traditional theories of identity in several ways. According to more standard notions of identity, such as those based on Erikson's psychosocial theory of developmental stages (1956, 1959), identity is defined as a "solid sense of self" (Chickering, 1969, p. 80), resulting in a "fixed" or "given" fully constituted whole (Rothstein, 1991, p. 78). Underlying these theories is the assumption that developing an "integrated", stable, and autonomous sense of self is the mark of a "mature" individual (Heath, 1978, p. 193–94). While identity may change over time, one fully formed identity is substituted for another. Thus, identity is defined by a set of intrinsic personality characteristics; while individuals may weigh "competing" identities, they ultimately commit to one (Marcia, 1966; Marcia and Friedman, 1970).

In contrast, identity theories based on power differentials and difference borrow from both symbolic interactionism and postmodern theories of the self as a social construction (Goffman, 1963; Berger and Luckmann, 1966; Denzin, 1992). In doing so, these theorists portray identity as the unstable, situation-specific effect of difference—specifically, the effect of differential power relations. As Lawrence Grossberg asserts, "like notions of knowledge and truth, cultural identities also are framed by discourses contingent to a large degree on power relations" (1994, p. 12). Moreover, since identity is defined only in reaction to what one is *not*, it becomes not an essence, but a positioning. Hence, "there is always a politics of identity, a politics of position, which has no absolute guarantee in an unproblematic, transcendental 'law of origin.'" (Hall, 1990, p. 226). Thus, multiple identities are possible, because identity is mutable and subject to change on the basis of finding oneself in a specific situation. Furthermore, it is constructed and reconstructed through the prism of membership in one or more gender, race, or class categories.

In part because this definition of identity points to inequities based on differences of class, gender and race, it has become politicized in the form of identity politics. In fact, those who have used identity politics to challenge the assumptions and practices of the academy have given rise to new, and sometimes radical, pedagogies and curricula designed to uncover existing inequities and create the intellectual and emotional "space" to explore the experiences and perceptions of those inhabiting one or more marginalized social categories (e.g., Giroux's notion of "representational pedagogy", 1992).

Yet as theorists have begun to grapple with the somewhat deterministic relationship which these theories draw between specific social categories and identity, some have begun to express discontent, arguing that "race, class, and gender are not . . . the bottom line explanation to which all life may be reduced" (Denning, 1992, p. 38). Indeed, there has emerged the sense that there are different kinds of difference, and that, along with both social categories and social structure, *individual agency*—that is, the ability to make conscious choices—has a role in identity formations. "We need," says Peter McLaren, "to envision identity as a subjective formation which avoids assuming narrative forms based on race and gender essentialism—an essentialism which 'forcibly' fragments experience in the name of a commonality" (1995, p. 101).

This third theory of identity (also referred to as a theory of human agency) does not negate the power of race, gender, or class in determining the ways in which we define ourselves and are defined by others; it simply adds a category of "difference" that is determined by individual agency, or choice. For example, the identity experience of a black female will undoubtedly be influenced by both her gender and her race, since both categories mark her as "other" and thus situate her within a disadvantaged social position. But her identity may also at times be affected by her choice to become a community college student, or a spouse, or to care for a sick relative or friend. The degree to which she self-identifies with one or more of these positions at any given moment will depend upon the relative importance placed on each. Thus, as Grossberg points out, "the relations of ethnicity or agency are determined, not merely by ideological practices of representation, but also in *affective practices of investment*" (italics added) (1994, p. 15).

The three major strands of identity theory discussed above suggest major differences in both the source and process of identity formation. Conventional theories of identity posit that identity is an intrinsic characteristic that is comprised of stable elements of personality. While an individual may encounter identity "crises" in which she is unsure of her identity, ultimately such crises are resolved, and a definitive identity is adopted. In contrast, postmodern and critical identity theorists see identity as situational, and the result of differences in status and power. Since status differences are most often the result of membership in a particular social category such as gender, race or class, these characteristics are seen as the primary framers of identity. The third strand of identity theory builds on postmodern theories in its assumption of situational identity formation. Yet in addition to allowing for identity based on membership in a particular social category, this agency-based identity theory also allows for voluntarily assumed identities, such as the decision to become a student.

But how do community college students describe themselves? How do they experience identity formation and re-formation, and how do organizational contexts define and respond to them? While the theories of identity discussed above have much intuitive appeal, there have been few empirical investigations of their relevance to date within the sphere of community colleges. Yet As Peter McLaren points out, the challenge of all scholarship, but particularly that which focuses on the disenfranchised, is to "speak to the lived experiences of oppressed people—people who possess a natural suspicion of academics writing from the high-altitude vistas of Mount Olympus" (1995, p. 110). Community college students, with their exceedingly complex and multifaceted lives, provide a particularly rich testing ground on which to explore the experience of identity formation. In the spirit of McLaren's exhortation, this chapter presents representations of identity as described by community college students themselves, and uses these descriptions to enhance our understanding of identity formation and re-formation. In this way, I employ a critical qualitative methodology as a way to illustrate, via data, differences in the theoretical constructs of identity. The chapter then explores the ways in which community colleges define and respond to students, and identifies policies and practices that reflect three major ideologies regarding identity.

Methodology

The data used in this chapter are drawn from a larger research project entitled *Cultures of Success: A Study of Community Colleges with High Transfer Rates,* which is funded by the Ford and Spencer foundations. The project is a four-year ethnographic examination of eight urban community colleges, each of which enrolls high numbers of working-class and minority students and boasts a transfer rate that is significantly above the national norm for urban institutions. The larger purpose of the research project is to identify aspects of the organizational culture that contribute to their relative success in transfer. These colleges vary along a number of other dimensions as well, including size, ethnic and racial mix, percentage of minority faculty members, age and history, structure of the state higher education system, and curriculum.

Ethnographers familiar with the research topic were recruited locally at each site. These ethnographers conducted field work on a half-time basis during the academic years 1994–95, and 1995–96. They followed general guidelines established by the Project Directors, including a series of interview protocols, but were also free to follow leads peculiar to their own institutions. The research protocol followed a grounded theory format (Glaser and Strauss, 1967), in that research questions evolved and were adjusted according to close and continuous analysis of the data. The Project Directors developed the research protocol, monitored and coordinated the field work of the ethnographers, conducted intensive site visits, and analyzed the data.

The ethnographers collected data from many sources and used a variety of techniques, including formal and informal interviews of students, faculty, staff and administrators; observations of students in both formal (classroom) and informal (e.g., cafeteria, library) settings; observations of faculty in both formal (classroom) and informal (social) settings; and observations of staff and administrators in formal settings (staff meetings). They also attended an array of institution-wide events, such as first-year orientation, cultural festivals, and college recruitment events, and collected a wide variety of historical and archival documents, including student newspapers, course catalogs, mission statements, syllabi, and accreditation reports.

Over 1,000 data elements (interviews, observations, and documents) have been gathered from the community colleges and are being analyzed using *HyperResearch* (1991), a content analysis program for qualitative researchers. After developing a coding scheme based on what was learned in the field and gleaned from the literature, the Project Directors began individual and cross-institutional analyses.

Experiencing Identity: Three Students Describe Themselves

Community college students can be quite eloquent when asked to define themselves, often embarking on rich and detailed descriptions of change, conflict, and confusion as they attempt to juggle their myriad roles. Yet far from defining themselves in terms of only one type of identity, these students will most often describe the ways in which two or even three of these identity elements intersect with one another. In what follows, I present three students' experience of identity to highlight the commonalities and differences in the ways in which community college students describe themselves. While not wholly representative of all community colleges in the eight institutions studied, they provide prototypes of three general ways in which these students define their lives within the context of attending community college.

Michael: Multiple Identities Adding Up to a Coherent Whole

A student enrolled at Harold Washington College in Chicago provides a good example of the manner in which several types of differences and experiences contribute to students' experience of identity. Formerly a blue-collar employee of a paper mill and a Vietnam veteran, Michael is an African-American man in his 40s who came to Harold Washington College as a victim of the "new economy"—he was laid off. Cognizant of the constraints imposed on him by his status as a working-class man, Michael said "I worked for a paper mill . . . There was a sense of security. Now I realize there's no more job security. There wasn't any then. It's just that my mind thought there was."

Yet Michael does not define himself merely in relation to his class membership; he also sees himself as a budding intellectual, and describes significant changes that have occurred as a result of deciding to become a student:

I decided to stop and took a look at myself. I said what have I really learned . . . I can read the book, answer the questions, get As on the test, but what have I really learned? I have to apply what I'm learning. If I apply what I'm learning then I truly know what it is I've learned . . . That changed me right there.

In fact, Michael draws a connection between his class status (what he refers to as his "past circumstances") and his student identity, crediting both with the way in which he has come to see and define himself. He commented, "It's revelation and past experience. A lot of things combined to get me where I'm at, to get me here right now. . . . My ideas are changing. I'm thinking about teaching. When I came here my major was business." In this way, Michael's class consciousness and individual agency in the form of assuming the role of student combine to re-define Michael's sense of himself. Often, shifts in what students see as intrinsic components of their identities are attributed to attending college, since education can be a revelatory experience, especially for students like Michael who neither planned nor expected to go to college. Indeed, Michael speaks eloquently about the ways in which his student identity re-formulated his sense of self, describing a "transformational experience" seen in other studies of community college students by Rendon (1994) and Shaw and London (1996).

Despite the different facets of Michael's life, he describes them as pieces that are integral to the whole of his identity. In other words, he sees his class standing and student status converging to create a "new" Michael, and does not appear to experience a sense of fragmentation or conflict.

Julia: Losing Oneself Amidst Multiple Identities

While the sense of a "converging" identity described by Michael is not unheard of in our data, neither is it common. Much more common are students who simultaneously map out situated identities that do *not* converge to form a coherent "whole." Indeed, some students describe a sense of losing themselves amidst their fragmented identities.

Julia provides a good example of this type of experience of identity. Currently a master's student at a local university, Julia first enrolled in a community college when she became convinced that her husband was preparing to leave her. Frightened by the prospect, she decided to develop some marketable skills. In the process, she was introduced to feminist theory and became politicized, eventually becoming president of the student government association. Julia describes her growing awareness of herself as a feminist in this way:

> They asked me to be president and I said OK. I did that and I loved it. I grew. I just kept growing and changing and becoming more political. It's what education does to you. Ever since then I became a feminist.

Julia's recognition of the role that gender plays in her life grew out of her decision to become a student. Yet she also discovered that the role of student did not replace any of her other identities; indeed, this choice added to the complexity of her life immensely:

> I had to go to school; I had to do the homework. But when you're a woman and you're a Chicana, and you're a mother, a wife, you lose yourself in all of that and there is no time for you.

In her multilayered description of herself, Julia self-identifies as both a woman and a Chicana, pointing out her membership and allegiance to both a gender and ethnically-based identity. However, she also sees herself as much more, and describes a series of identities that are the result not of membership in particular social categories, but of life choices that she has made and embraced. Julia also identifies herself as a student, a mother, and a wife. Moreover, she points out as well the difficulty inherent in simultaneously inhabiting all of these roles; in fact, she suggests that in assuming such a large set of multiple identities, one can paradoxically "lose yourself in all of that." Yet she does not rescind on any of them, and instead continues to self-identify on multiple dimensions.

Isabel: The Conflict Inherent in Multiple Identities

"Losing yourself" occurs in another way for students. While Julia only hinted at the conflict inherent in self-identifying in multiple ways, other students can be quite explicit about their discomfort when faced with pressures from a variety of sources. In the following conversation, Isabel, a Columbian-born liberal arts student, gradually uncovers the ways in which her identity as wife and as worker conflicts with her identity as student.

Interviewer: What does your husband think about you coming to school?

Isabel: He loves it (pause); he likes it. Sometimes it's hard to give time for him also with school and work. Sometimes we get a little unhappy there.

Interviewer: So does it cause any tensions?

Isabel: Yes it does because I guess it's human nature. Men always want to get some attention. It's my husband. I want to give attention too. Sometimes you're too busy to give attention . . . I try to juggle both things at the same time.

Interviewer: Do you feel like your relationship with him is changing as a result?

Isabel: I guess it has changed a little bit, but for the better. When you realize that you have to not be so self-centered; think of the other person. At the beginning it hurts and you don't want to accept it. You go against it, but after a while, OK, this is the way it goes.

Initially, Isabel struggles against choosing between her identities as student and wife. Believing her husband's initial encouragement, she enthusiastically takes on the additional role of student. Yet when she begins experiencing conflict between the two roles, she realizes that there is an emotional cost ("it hurts and you don't want to accept it"). While she does not rescind her student identity, she does accept responsibility for her husband's dissatisfaction, and devotes more attention to him. In fact, she embraces her role of wife, stating "It's my husband; I want to give attention too." In doing so, Isabel highlights the role of individual agency in the formation of identity— the "affective practices of investment" that Hall (1990) speaks of.

However, Isabel does not abandon the role of either worker or student. Instead she finds a way to simultaneously be all three. The type of conflict inherent in this choice is especially frequent when the role of student extends

outside of the community college—e.g., when a student attempts to do school-
related work at home. Students often pay a high price for adding the role of
student to their constellation of identities. Another student's description of
what happens is not atypical: "As soon as I open my books, my son needs
my attention. I'm waking up at 4:00 in the morning to try to do work for
school."

The complex, layered identity descriptions seen in the words of the three
students profiled above were common in discussions with community college
students, and are the antithesis of the "essentialism" rejected by McLaren.
Few, if any students describe the fully-constituted, fixed sense of identity
seen in the more traditional identity theories of Erikson and Heath. While
some will talk about portions of their identities as though they are "intrinsic"
(that is, not defined in relation to difference or "otherness"), these same
students also describe their identities in terms of both socially ascribed and
choice-based characteristics such as their roles as fathers, students, black
men, etc.

Identity based primarily on membership in a gender, class, or race category is also uncommon. For example, all three of the students profiled above
are members of ethnic or racial minorities; two are women; and one is
foreign-born. Yet in their descriptions of themselves, they mention these aspects
as only one portion of their identities. Moreover, their refusal to define themselves simply in terms of these social characteristics is not due to ignorance
regarding the ways in which these characteristics situate them within the
power structures they encounter; Michael is extremely active in student government and the politics of the college, and Julia is a committed, active
feminist. The "politics of difference" spoken of by multiculturalists such as
Iris Marion Young (1995) are quite real to these students, and all three acknowledge the ways in which this aspect of their identities affect their lives.
However, gender, race, or class are described as only one contributor to a
myriad of identities, many of which are not constructed in terms of differences in power relations.

Of the three, only Michael does not experience a sense of fragmentation.
Although he describes a changing identity, he perceives each aspect of his
identity as part of a coherent whole. Julia and Isabel, on the other hand,
describe identities that are very much fractured along a complex pattern of
fault lines. Not only do these identities not converge into a coherent whole;
when they intersect, they create conflict. The process described by these two
students is akin to Paul Patton's discussion of narratives as a metaphor for
describing multiple identities: "Narratives are not unitary: they are better
understood as assemblages created within the different kinds of segmentarity
which divide up modern social life" (1986, p. 143).

Institutional Definitions of Student Identity

As individuals who juggle a myriad of roles in addition to that of a student, community college students' sense of identity is complex and multifaceted. It incorporates elements that they consider intrinsic to their personalities, but also includes membership in particular race, gender, and/or class categories, and the assumption of identities resulting from individual agency and choice as well, such as that of student. Community colleges, as the institutions in which these students are situated, also attempt to define them, sending messages through both formal policies and informal interactions which convey both an overall theory of identity and the degree to which different facets of identity are recognized and responded to. These messages are important, because identity occupies contested terrain, and the culture of institutions such as community colleges provides the context in which identities are interpreted and understood. As Rhoads and Valadez (1996) have pointed out, "Culture not only provides the parameters for our social interactions; it provides a framework for how we define ourselves in relation to others" (p. 23).

Below, I use the discourse of individual faculty and administrators, along with examples of institutional policy, to explore the ways in which students are defined within these colleges, and the implications for their experiences within the community college setting. In fact, a typology of institutional ideologies regarding identity has emerged which mirrors in many ways the three strands of identity theory outlined in an earlier section of this chapter, ranging from rather narrow and unidimensional definitions of students, to those that recognize the multiplicity of students' identities. In the following pages, three elements of this typology are described and analyzed.

Essentializing Identity

Given the extreme diversity of students found in urban community colleges, few faculty and administrators, when queried directly, fail to acknowledge the complexity of their students' lives. However, many tend to define students in terms of intrinsic personality characteristics—specifically as played out in their performance as students. Traits such as motivation, the ability to set and maintain goals, and level of intelligence are mentioned repeatedly when faculty and administrators are asked to characterize students. This type of essentialism is no more clear than when faculty and administrators are queried about why students succeed, or fail, in their institution. The following quotation by a faculty member is typical:

> It's my philosophy of human life that we are given by God a free will. That is what made western civilization what it is today, and I emphasize that to my

students . . . I just believe that in normal human nature, not all people can be Einsteins . . . I believe in individual responsibility. Some people may have the flame in them, but it's dead; they don't want to fan the ember. Those are the people that don't make it. They don't want to.

This faculty member attributes success to the presence or absence of an innate characteristic—"the flame," which refers to motivation, intelligence, or a combination of both. Both this characteristic and the "free will" he speaks of are seen as innate characteristics, "given by God." In defining students in this way, this faculty member reveals an underlying ideology of identity that assumes that personality traits are intrinsic, static, and basically immutable. He does not consider, for example, other explanations for student failure, such as structural barriers or an inferior educational system, nor does he consider the effects that students' other roles and responsibilities may have on their ability or desire to persist in college. Those who don't make it have only themselves to blame, fatally flawed by an intrinsic lack of desire or intelligence.

In another form of essentialism, personality traits such as those mentioned above are linked to membership in particular social categories, such as ethnic groups, age, or gender. Yet rather than seeing group membership as an *additional* component of identity, it is viewed instead as the *cause* of innate characteristics that distinguish one group from another. An administrator displayed his proclivity for this type of identity definition when queried about why transfer rates from the community college to four-year institutions varied.

I think it's the same reason you have Asians come here and they band together and they're going to open those businesses and go on to be successful in this country. I think part of it's cultural. They understand that higher education is important and they're going to work that way. When you're in this country, and it's not just if you're black or Hispanic, that push to get your bachelor's degree isn't as apparent . . . We have to explain to them how important it is. They need that extra nudge.

In this description, the administrator recognizes that students are members of particular ethnic and racial groups, and that they can be defined in terms of immigrant status as well. But he uses such categories to essentialize students' identities; in doing so, the attitudes and other personality characteristics attributed to these students are portrayed as a natural outgrowth of their cultural upbringing. Again, identity is seen as an organic whole; the fragmentation and conflict inherent in students' descriptions of their identities is not recognized.

This unidimensional definition of identity can be reflected in the context of formal college policies as well. For example, in some of the colleges we studied, the lion's share of student services personnel and program costs are directed at students' academic performance only. Both faculty and support staff alike express discomfort in dealing with students' "personal problems," and do not view such issues as central to students' experience in the college. The strict, inflexible set of academic standards seen in several of these colleges are, in part, an outgrowth of this ideology. When students are defined simply in terms of their status as students, critical aspects of their lives go largely unaddressed.

Essentialism based on ethnic or racial identity can also be seen in institutional approaches to issues of diversity or multiculturalism. All of the colleges in our sample address the diversity of their student bodies in some way, but the approach to diversity varies dramatically. When diversity is compartmentalized into "Women's History Month" or "Martin Luther King Day," the college is simultaneously reducing such students to the sum of their social or cultural characteristics, and sending the message that this aspect of students' lives is not an integral part of their identity. Instead, it is something that should be recognized once a year, and then politely ignored.

Embracing Students' Racial, Gender, and Class Identities

I have also discerned an expanded definition of identity among some portions of the faculty and administrations covered in our study, one that recognizes and encompasses what Lemert calls "the varying combinations of several fracturing, yet integrating, political and cultural identities" (1993, p. 498) that emerge from identification with a specific set of racial, gender, and class categories. In this type of identity construction, membership in these categories is seen as resulting in a sense of "other" and "difference" and as the primary components of identity, since they situate individuals within a complex "matrix of domination" (Collins, 1990, p. 617). Acknowledging structural power differentials and the ways in which they are played out in terms of identity is considered a critical aspect of the educational process from this perspective. One administrator, in describing how he views his responsibilities to students, implicitly recognizes the relationship between power and (in this case) ethnicity.

> Through my office I feel that I am trying to guide students so that you have to find your own self identity. Part of that identity can be the correct pronunciation of a [Spanish] name . . . You have to know who you are and feel comfortable with that before you can truly move on . . . giving them an awareness of their culture gives a better understanding of who they are and how they are related to the bigger picture and how they could use this knowledge to help them succeed.

This commitment to acknowledging the importance of cultural, class, racial, and gender sources of identity can also be seen in the curriculum of some of the colleges studied. Courses that are built on feminist, post-Marxist, and/or critical theories of social interaction are common at several of the schools in our sample, and lecture series regarding the intersection of oppression and membership in various social groups permeate the culture of one of the colleges. Although quite rare, another community college has developed an entire women's studies program; still another sees as its primary mission the empowerment of a specific cultural group, e.g., low-income Mexican Americans. By connecting students' disadvantaged situation within power structures with their membership in one or more racial, class, or gender categories, some individuals and institutional policies can help students understand the ways in which this aspect of their identities contributes to their own lived experiences.

These types of organizational policies and pedagogical practices are the exception to the rule in our sample of colleges. However, they certainly speak to the identity experiences of students to a greater degree than those reflecting the identity-as-essentialism ideology discussed previously. Yet as affirming as such practices are, they can sometimes downplay or ignore other situational or choice-based aspects of students' identities. Certainly, issues of oppression and domination are critical to community college students, and in some ways may be the most important aspects of identity to address. However, by focusing exclusively on identities as defined primarily in terms of race, gender, or class, institutions can become blinded to other critical aspects of students' identities.

Recognizing the Multiplicity of Student Identities

This third category of identity construction most closely reflects the ways in which students in our study self-identify. Not only are student identities seen to comprise intrinsic qualities and racial, gender, or class identities; situational or choice-based aspects of identity, such as the role of student, mother, or caregiver are also acknowledged. Most times, recognition of the complexity of student identities carries with it a recognition of the difficulties inherent in such complexity. In a description of her students, a philosophy professor points to the fragmentation inherent in their lives.

> The tremendous juggling of work and family and school—these kids do not have the time to study—they don't have time to go to school. Very few of my students really have the time necessary to gain a command of the material. So I tell them all the time . . . you've got to give your brain a chance. Your brain is fine . . . but it's like expecting somebody to be ready for a football game when they haven't been able to go to practice but fifteen minutes the week before. There's lots of absenteeism, but people miss class for totally correct reasons. The priorities in their lives are ones that I would agree with.

This faculty member not only recognizes the multiple identities of her students; she also points to the ways in which various identities take precedence for students at different times in their lives. By stating that she agrees with choices that sometime reduce the primacy of student identity, this faculty member recognizes the conflict inherent in the multiplicity of students' identities. In her conception of identity, there is no coherent whole; only multiple pieces that compete and conflict in a situational manner. Moreover, the conflict inherent in occupying multiple identities is born of the conflict between different sources of identity—that is, between cultural identity (member of ethnic family and community), class identity (worker), and an identity born of personal agency (student).

Institutions can also acknowledge and respond to the multiplicity of student identities. The creation of a day care center, for example, addresses some students' struggle to combine parenthood with student-hood, as does the willingness of faculty members to allow students to bring their children to class if child care is not available. Both types of policies are seen in more than one of the colleges in our sample. Most times, individuals and institutions that display a sensitivity toward choice-based identities are also sensitive to identities formed through membership in social categories as well. For example, support groups for returning adult students, courses reflecting Afrocentric and feminist ideologies, a deaf studies program and a day care center can all be found at one institution.

A sensitivity to the intersection between institutional policy and students' struggles with their own identities can also be seen in the hiring practices of one institution. Here, adoption of a multiculturalist ideology is seen as at least as important as actual racial or ethnic diversity itself in the hiring practices of the college. Experience and degree of comfort with diversity defined in the broadest sense is an explicit criteria for hiring at the college. Because diversity in all of its manifestations—socially-defined, choice-based, and intrinsic—is valued, the social hierarchy which can result from Euro-centrism has been displaced to some degree. As one administrator says, "There is no dominant group, no sense of whose culture has primacy. Stability comes from this distribution of power. In some ways, [the college] demythologizes the importance of ethnic identity." In recognizing the primary importance of difference, this college paradoxically reduces the importance of specific kinds of difference in favor of a philosophy which sees difference as intrinsically valuable.

The Intersection Between Individual and Institutional Definitions of Identity

Community college students see themselves as multifaceted. Faced with a myriad of roles, both assumed and imposed, their identities derive from several different sources—their relation to particular power structures (class, race, or gender); what they see as intrinsic aspects of their personalities (self-esteem; motivation); and as the result of individual agency (student; caregiver). As can be seen in students' descriptions of themselves, identifying oneself in multiple ways can lead to confusion and sometimes pain, since the primacy of specific identities is situational and can lead to conflict. Whether multiple identities converge into a unified whole as is the case with Michael, or remain fragmented and in disarray, as we see with Julia and Isabel, it is clear that individuals can and do choose which identities will take precedence at particular points in time. Hall's (1990) notion of the role of "affective practices of investment" in identity formation is born out in these students' descriptions of themselves.

Yet it is important to note that these narratives are in and of themselves an act of "presentation of self" (Goffman, 1963), since discourse is an interactive event in which one "recalls and recasts experience into meaningful signposts and supports" (Conquergood, 1993). One's underlying ideology regarding such questions as the essence of human experience is revealed in both words and deed. And just as the presentation of self is not based on some essence of objective "truth," neither are actions. As McLaren points out, "theories are not just about seeing the world in different ways, some truer than others, *but about living in particular ways*" (1995, p. 93) (italics added).

Thus, in the same way that students' ways of self-identifying reveal certain ideologies, so too do the words and actions of institutions and those employed by them. The community colleges in our study reveal an array of ideologies regarding identity. Some reflect a more traditional, essentialist notion of identity based on an a-contextual, psychological notion of intrinsic characteristics—usually those related to success as a student. In this type of identity construct, students' needs and experiences are not placed or understood within the context of power structures or other assumed roles, except insofar as characteristics such as race contribute to these personality traits. Moreover, student services are designed to help those outside of the mainstream "adapt" to the dominant academic culture. Differences of any sort are a liability to be dealt with, rather than embraced as a source of strength.

Notions of identity as derived primarily in terms of differential power relations take us closer to students' lived experiences of identity, since many (though not all) of the students interviewed as part of our larger study identify themselves with one or more marginalized category of race, gender, or class. Institutional efforts to help students recognize the role of these social characteristics on their life trajectories—"how they are related to the bigger picture"—reveal an identity ideology that places "difference" as a defining factor in one's identity formation. Moreover, they link knowledge of the relationship between racial, class, or gender identities and structural inequalities to action and empowerment.

We have also seen policies and practices—reflected in both the actions and words of both individual faculty members and the institution writ large—

that most closely reflect and address students' experience of identity as a multilayered, multidimensional phenomenon. In these rare instances, the multiple identities that result from categories of both difference *and* individual agency are acknowledged, and students are given both the tools and the space to address their changing, shifting needs. In instances in which this third strand of identity theory is enacted, sensitivity to the ways in which students juggle multiple identities is seen, and an appreciation of a contextualized identity is most pronounced.

Toward More Inclusive Institutional Cultures

Although community college students consistently describe their identities as multifaceted, multisourced, and multilayered, the colleges that they attend are more likely than not to define students in much narrower terms. When they do so, they ignore or negate the lived experiences of students, and increase the chances that these students will maintain neither the desire nor the ability to persist. Given that community colleges serve the most marginalized of college student populations, this type of exclusionary college culture threatens to alienate that portion of the population for whom education is most critical. Institutions which acknowledge and address the full compliment of student identities—regardless of whether they originate from intrinsic characteristics, social or cultural characteristics, or human agency—have the best chance for helping students to integrate identity and the educational process.

By focusing on the words and narratives of students themselves, this chapter adds empirical evidence to the validity of emerging theories of identity that incorporate individual agency and personal investment. In addition to identity based on "difference" or in relation to existing power structures, a new strand of identity theory recognizes identities that are voluntarily assumed as well. I have identified examples in which the multiplicity of identities is recognized by community colleges. The challenge for the sector as a whole is to work toward embracing not just identity born of social or cultural differences, although such a goal alone will be reached only in the distant future; but to recognize and adapt as well to other categories of identities exhibited by their students.

References

Berger, P. L., & Luckmann, T. (1966). *The social construction of reality: A treatise in the sociology of knowledge.* New York: Doubleday.
Chickering, A. (1969). *Education and identity.* San Francisco: Jossey-Bass.

Collins, P. H. (1990). *Black feminist thought: Knowledge, consciousness, and the politics of empowerment.* Boston: Unwin Hyman

Denning, M. (1992). "The academic left and the rise of cultural studies." *Radical History Review* 54:21–48

Denzin, N. K. (1992). *Symbolic interaction and cultural studies: The politics of interpretation.* Oxford: Blackwell.

Dougherty, K. J. (1994). *The contradictory college: The conflicting origins, impacts, and futures of the community college.* Albany: SUNY Press.

Erikson, E. (1956). "The problem of ego identity." *Journal of the American Psychoanalytic Assocation* 4:56–121.

———. (1959). "Identity and the life cycle." *Psychological Issues Monograph*, 1(1), 1–171. New York: International Universities Press.

Gates, H. L. Jr. (1986). "Race as the trope of the world." In H. L. Gates, Jr., (ed)., *"Race," writing, and difference.* Chicago: University of Chicago Press, p. 4–13.

Giroux, H. A. (1992). *Border crossings: Cultural workers and the politics of education.* New York: Routledge.

Glaser, B. G., and A. Strauss (1967). *The discovery of grounded theory: Strategies for qualitative research.* Chicago: Aldine.

Goffman, E. (1963). *Stigma: Notes on the management of spoiled identity.* Englewood Cliffs, NJ: Prentice-Hall.

Grossberg, L. (1994). "Introduction." In H. Giroux & P. McLaren. *Between borders: Pedagogy and the politics of cultural studies.* New York: Routledge.

Hall, S. (1990). "The emergence of cultural studies and the crisis of the humanities." *October* 53:11–23.

Heath, D. (1978). "A model of becoming a liberally educated and mature student." In C. Parker (ed.), *Encouraging development in college students.* Minneapolis: University of Minnesota Press.

Lemert, C. (ed.) *Social theory: The multicultural and classic readings.* Boulder, CO: Westview Press.

Lorde, A. (1995). "Age, race, class, and sex: Women redefining difference." In A. Lorde (ed.), *Sister outsider.* Trumansburg, NY: The Crossing Press.

Marcia, J. (1966). "Development and validation of ego-identity status." *Journal of Personality and Social Psychology* 3:551–58.

Marcia, J., & Friedman, M. (1970). "Ego identity status in college women." *Journal of Personality* 38:249–63.

McLaren, P. (1995). *Critical pedagogy and predatory culture.* New York: Bergin & Garvey.

Patton, P. (1986). "Ethics and postmodernity." In E.A. Grosz; T. Threadgold; A. Cholodenko; & E. Colless (eds.), *Future fall: Excursions into postmodernity.* Sydney: Power Institute of Fine Arts, University of Sydney.

Rendon, L. I. (1994). "Clearing the pathways: Improving opportunities for minority students to transfer." In M. J. Justiz; R. Wilson; and L. G. Bjork. *Minorities in higher education.* Phoenix, AZ: Oryx Press.

Rhoads, R. A., & Valadez, J. (1996). *Democracy, multiculturalism and the community college: A Critical Perspective.* New York: Garland Press.

Rothstein, G. (1991). *Identity and ideology: Sociocultural theories of schooling.* New York: Greenwood Press.

Shaw, K., and London, H. (1995). "Negotiating boundaries and borders: Institutional and student cultures in high transfer urban community colleges." Paper presented at the Assocation for the Study of Higher Education Annual Meeting. Orlando, Florida.

U.S. National Center for Educational Statistics, 1991. *Digest of education statistics, 1991.* NCES 91–697. Washington, D.C.: Government Printing Office.

West, C. (1990). "The new cultural politics of difference." In Ferguson, R.; Gever, M.; Minh-ha, T. T.; and West, C. (eds). *Out there: Marginalization and contemporary cultures.* Cambridge, MA: MIT Press, 19–32.

Young, I. M. (1995). "Social movements and the politics of difference." In Arthur, John and Shapiro, Amy (eds.), *Campus wars: Multiculturalism and the politics of difference.* Boulder, CO: Westview Press.

CHAPTER 9

Celebratory Socialization of Culturally Diverse Students Through Academic Programs and Support Services

Introduction

Culture exists in every context and plays a role in the way people function. It is a social sharing of cognitive codes and maps, norms of appropriate behavior, and assumptions about values and beliefs which profoundly influence our thoughts and actions (Delgado-Gaitan and Trueba, 1991). Observing, understanding and interpreting the cultural behavior and needs of ethnically and linguistically diverse students is critically important, yet remains problematic in community colleges. Students once labeled "nontraditional"— namely, those from low socioeconomic backgrounds, who are first-generation college-going, 25 years and older, from diverse racial or ethnic and cultural backgrounds, with limited English and linguistically diverse, recent immigrants, academically underprepared, fulltime workers and parttime enrollees, reentry women, and learning- and physically-challenged—have become the majority students in most community colleges in the 1990s (Cohen & Brawer, 1996).

Going to college is an eventful point in all students' lives, one that both prompts and hastens movement into a culture that differs from the one they have known all their lives. When this transition occurs, powerful social and personal dramas are played out, for cultural membership helps define who we are in the eyes of others as well as ourselves (London, 1992). What happens, however, is that all too often, students of diverse backgrounds are forced to

173

live between two worlds (Weis, 1985). These students must either maintain separate identities, behavioral patterns, and peer associations, or they are forced to leave one cultural world behind and uneasily accept the dominant culture. Frequently, they become uncomfortable in both cultures, resulting in a profound sense of isolation or loss.

Crossing these cultural borders is an integral part of the community college experience for many students. Hence, the question of how community colleges can help students to make a successful transition into the academic world while retaining their own sense of cultural identity is a critical one. Those who possess border knowledge—knowledge that resides outside the canon, outside of the cultural mainstream (Rhoads and Valadez, 1996, p.7)— must be incorporated into a learning community that recognizes distinct groups, builds on their socialization experiences, and provides culturally appropriate academic and student support programs. While ambitious, these goals can no longer be ignored by educators today if a learned, informed democratic citizenry is to be realized that can also function competently and competitively in the economic and technological spheres of the twenty-first century. How then do community colleges provide for such diverse groups and meet their multicultural, multilingual, and complex needs without violating their cultural identities?

Van Maanen's (1984) concept of celebratory socialization refers to creating an institutional culture in which students not only celebrate their own cultural knowledge, values, skills, and histories, but also take an active role in their learning process, transforming the organization's culture through their participation and contributions (Giroux, 1992; Tierney, 1992; Van Maanen, 1984). By accepting the cultural knowledge that diverse students bring to the institution and building an educational experience on its foundation, community colleges can help to break down the difficulties inherent in border crossings.

This chapter utilizes the notion of celebratory socialization to assess how the critical cultural knowledge and values which ethnically diverse students bring with them to the community college can become positive influences on their motivation and academic achievement. More specifically, I illustrate the ways in which a community college can help students learn the new organizational culture of the community college while it simultaneously embraces students' diverse experiences and multiple ways of knowing. In doing so, I utilize Rhoads and Valadez's (1996) notion of organizational socialization, in which the organization specifically seeks to create conditions of celebration and affirmation that embrace students' border knowledge. Acknowledging border knowledge allows diverse students to take an active role in participating in their own education along with classroom teachers and other college personnel (Giroux, 1992; Rhoads and Valadez, 1996).

As an example of the way in which community colleges can utilize celebratory socialization to empower culturally diverse students, I examine academic and support programs in two community colleges. These programs are specifically designed to motivate and encourage Hispanics and others to excel academically. The first is a suburban community college with a low but rising enrollment of these students; and the second is an urban community college with a majority population of ethnically diverse students. In both institutions, students are provided with opportunities to become powerful learners while the schooling process is transformed at the same time (Hull, 1993).

Creating a Web of Empowerment

How students who are distinct from the mainstream, dominant, college-going group experience college continues to be the subject of much research attention (Astin, 1988; Attinasi, 1989; Pascarella and Terenzini, 1991; Tinto, 1975, 1987, 1988; Olivas, 1979; Rendon, 1982; Rendon, Justiz, and Resta, 1988; Nora, 1987). Some researchers (Nora, Attinasi, and Matonak, 1990; Pavel, 1991; Tierney, 1992; Cabrera and Nora, 1994) have sought to understand how the constructs of academic and social integration leading to persistence or departure as conceptualized by Tinto (1975; 1989, 1993) are applicable to different institutional types and student populations. Tinto's (1987, 1988) process model of separation, transition, and incorporation leading to integration and embedded in the concept of rites of passage (Van Gennep, 1960) dominates the literature. However, several researchers (Tierney, 1992; Attinasi, 1994; Nora and Cabrera, 1994), have explored its applicability for students of racial or ethnic backgrounds, and found it to be culturally inappropriate.

Tierney (1992), for example, argues that the underlying assumptions of acculturation embedded in Tinto's model ignore cultural differences of ethnic groups. Moreover, he suggests that Tinto's use of the term integration is perhaps a veiled synonym for assimilation. Attinasi (1994) posits that Van Gennep's (1960) theory of rites of passage is actually a series of "nested passages" (p.5) leading to passage-within-passages stages that occur over a longer period of time than just during the freshman year, as Tinto asserts. Nora and Cabrera (1994) found that individuals from various cultures and segments of society can and do undergo successful passages of initiation into the college community. However, they found that encouragement and support for ethnic students from significant others was critical for these students to adjust to their academic and social environments.

As noted above, culture exists in every social context and plays a role in the way that people can function and make sense of their world. Individuals within a cultural group share a common language, norms and patterns of appropriate behavior, beliefs, values, world views, and similar lifestyles (Delgado-Gaitan and Trueba, 1991). Within the context of community colleges, students' cultural differences can be an advantage if conditions are provided which enable the students to empower themselves by understanding their place in the world, and changing the relationships that constrain and silence them (Tierney, 1992). In particular, the curriculum, part of which remains largely hidden to those on the borders outside of the dominant group, can be explored and examined for its multiple meanings and interpretations by ethnically diverse students.

Tierney (1992) suggests that educational organizations can examine how "to transform power relations so that all the participants within are encouraged to reconstruct and transform the organization's culture" (p. 41). Seeking a metaphor to explain this process, Tierney and others reject the image of students floating—somewhat powerlessly—through an educational pipeline. Instead, the metaphor of the web (Geertz, 1973) is seen as the symbol of greater equalization and empowerment for all participants, in that each individual is both inside the web as a participant in all the activities and outside the web as a constructor of new layers. That is, each is "at the center of the web," (Helgesen, 1990b, F 13, cited in DiCroce, 1995) while also acting as a spinner producing the web itself. Moreover, if one thinks of the rites of passage as distinct intersections where distinct processes come together, all that passes through becomes a part of the web that is interwoven and crossed with a multiplicity of voices (Tierney, 1992, p. 53–4). These rites of passage, in turn, can be transformed to empower students to find their own voices and manage their own lives, and thus become powerful, independent learners in their own right. Using this concept of student empowerment, it is important to understand how the community college can transform itself into a webbed organizational structure which will empower ethnic students in the process.

Methodology

This chapter is drawn from a larger study which focused on first-year students of color enrolled in community college with the goal of transferring to four-year institutions (Laden, 1994). Two community colleges in northern California offer examples of how two-year institutions can promote culturally-sensitive and culturally-specific programs in academic and student services to increase ethnic student motivation and commitment to college while also changing the institution as a result of the commitment to the students. The outcomes resulted in improved student persistence and academic achievement, a sense of belonging within the institution, and the transforming of these students into powerful learners. The programs examined here were selected because of their efforts to improve academic and support services and increase the transfer rates for students of color who had enrolled with the goal of transferring to a four-year institution.

This study utilizes an ecological model which considers the cultural context of students' lives. Students are connected to families and communities and function within cultural, economic and geographical boundaries. An ethnographic case study methodology was adopted for this study. The two cases provide rich, descriptive analysis of events, interactions, and experiences of students involved in culturally specific academic and support services programs as seen through the lenses of the organization, that is, individuals involved with the transfer function in various ways, and as observed by this writer over the period of an academic year.

The Colleges

Suburban College has an enrollment of 14,016 students with a majority population of white students, reflective of its affluent, predominantly white suburban area. Suburban College is well regarded in its community and as evidence has historically offered a comprehensive day and evening curriculum, with most students attending fulltime. Moreover it enjoys high transfer rates to a variety of public and private four-year institutions for its majority students. However, in 1989 the college began to experience a shift in student demographics, drawing an increasing number of students from diverse racial, ethnic, and socioeconomic backgrounds in the greater metropolitan community. In 1988 Suburban College enrolled 89 percent white students; by 1991 this percentage had dropped to 73 percent.

In contrast, Urban College has an enrollment of 11,341 students, with 59 percent of its student population coming from very diverse racial and ethnic backgrounds, many of whom are first-generation college-going, nearly 30 percent enrolled in English as a Second Language, attending on a parttime basis, mainly in the evening, and often selecting vocational programs as the most expedient for providing faster career mobility. A much younger college still trying to build more needed physical facilities on its campus, Urban College is located in a rapidly developing urban area of electronic and computer technology firms, with more high-tech firms moving in each year and surrounding the campus. Moreover, Urban College is shifting its curricular emphasis from being primarily a vocationally-oriented institution to increasing its academic and transfer programs, especially during the day. This shift has attracted younger, fulltime students, and raised the transfer rates of its students of color in particular. Table 9.1 provides more detailed demographic information on each college.

Thirty-eight administrators, faculty, and support staff involved with transfer were interviewed to get an organizational perspective on how the two colleges were developing programmatic efforts to increase the transfer rates for students of color. Table 9.2 lists the respondents who were interviewed. In-depth interviews using semistructured questions with probes for expanding on

TABLE 9.1
Demographic Information by Community College

	Suburban College	Urban College
Enrollment	14,016	11,341
Race/Ethnicity:		
African American	2.0	5.0
Asian American	11.0	28.0
Filipino	1.0	10.0
Hispanic	10.0	13.0
Middle Eastern	2.0	2.0
Native American	1.0	1.0
White	73.0	41.0
Gender:		
Women	60.0	48.0
Men	40.0	52.0

individuals' responses, yielded context-specific data, insights, and anecdotes. Interviews were audio taped and verbatim transcripts obtained. Observation and a collection of archival data (e.g., college catalogs, governing board agendas and minutes, reports, and other varied campus literature for students) provided additional descriptive data. Observations occurred at different times of both day and evening throughout the academic year and in a variety of settings (e.g., classrooms, transfer center, cafeteria, student center, library) on each campus.

Pattern matching prototypes and relational matrices of merging and repeated themes (Yin, 1984; Miles and Huberman, 1984) were used to code and analyze the data. The data were separated out by academic and student services programs and activities. The emergent themes provide the framework for the analysis. Themes were triangulated in order to enhance validity of findings and alternative explanations were sought and compared to initial findings in an attempt to disconfirm the hypotheses (Lincoln and Guba, 1985).

TABLE 9.2
Community College Respondents Interviewed

N=31	Suburban College	Urban College
Administrators	4	6
Faculty	9	7
Support Staff	3	2
Total Interviewed	16	15

Models of Culturally-Responsive Institutions

The efforts undertaken by Suburban College and Urban College to meet the needs of its ethnically diverse students offer models for how an organization can develop a process for responding to and empowering racially and ethnically different groups through culturally-specific offerings. While different in many ways, these community colleges have in common several aspects of presidential leadership, resource allocation, and faculty commitment which facilitates changes in the curriculum, programs, and student services. The influence of leadership and commitment are discussed first, followed by descriptions of some of the programmatic offerings specific to each college.

Leadership, Commitment, and Resources

An organizational commitment to any goal must be publicly articulated and embraced by the institution's leadership so that all participants are aware of and understand it. Leadership and commitment come from both the president and the faculty in Suburban College. The president's commitment to addressing issues of diversity is fundamental in this college. As a new president and a Latino himself, early in his tenure he publicly embraced and articulated a vision for the college which included increasing the transfer offerings and transfer rates of students traditionally underrepresented in the institution, namely, Hispanics, African Americans, Asian Americans, and Native Americans. He remarked, "We have put the emphasis on transfer for Hispanic and other ethnic students. There is no reason why we cannot put our resources to work to help these students succeed. It is up to us to make that happen." He added, "While transfer has always been a priority at this college, now the focus is on special groups. It's put center-stage."

With the support of the governing board, the president has also allocated financial resources to address the needs of these groups. Use of these funds include hiring new faculty from more ethnically diverse backgrounds, creating a center which combined all career and transfer information and activities, having more active on-campus and outreach and recruitment efforts in high schools in the greater community, and supporting the development of innovative curriculum and programs. From the very beginning, these changes were expected to have a positive and direct effect on ethnic students and in transforming the college. One of the counselors remarked on the president's and the faculty's commitment to focusing human and capital resources on minority students by stating, "It's always been in place, the philosophy of "Let's get everyone transferred," but never really distinctly to given [special] populations until now. That's a big difference."

The hiring of faculty from different racial or ethnic backgrounds in particular has had a galvanizing effect on changing the composition of the faculty.

For example, in a period of growth between 1989 and 1991, 14 new faculty were hired which included three Hispanics, one African American, and three Asian Americans. Faculty comment on the hirings as an affirmative action commitment to diversity and the beginning of a "critical mass" of students and staff representative of the society at large. As an academic dean notes:

> It is well documented that if students connect with the institution, they are more likely to stay, and they are more likely to connect with people who look like them, or talk like them, or dress like them. When students come on campus and find no reflection of themselves or their culture, then the alienation is just multiplied and the likelihood of their remaining is less.

The president noted that the new faculty of color had an immediate effect on the college in terms of curriculum and programs. He gave credit to "the new hires who are promoting and increasing equal educational opportunities for students not traditionally attracted to higher education in significant numbers." Faculty and administrators commented on the contributions of the new faculty in creating new programs, supporting innovative changes, and display a willingness to assume responsibilities even when not explicitly stated as part of their responsibilities. A new Hispanic counselor stated, for example, "No one put me in charge of being the transfer counselor for students [of color]. I put myself in charge."

The faculty's commitment to improving the environment for students of color was expressed initially in two documents: the college master plan and a minority task force report. In the college master plan, armed with empirical data and national reports, the faculty acknowledged the changing demographics of the state, the community, and the college, and cited the need to reach out into the community and expand outreach efforts to the new majority students. This report was approved overwhelming by the faculty as its master plan for leading Suburban College into the next century.

The minority task force report was based on an assessment of the college regarding (1) how to respond to the changing ethnic patterns of the communities the college now serves; (2) how to focus campus attention on the "new majority" students emerging in California; and (3) how to focus on minority students' transition into four–year institutions and into the job market. The task force made recommendations to the governing board, the administration, and to the faculty accordingly. These recommendations included one stating that Suburban College make efforts to develop an improved image and campus climate to meet the needs of the increasing number of students of color matriculating at Suburban College, undertake appropriate curriculum changes that addressed the needs of this new population, and offer more culturally-oriented and culturally-sensitive student services.

At Urban College, leadership comes primarily from the academic and student-services vice-presidents and faculty with the backing of the president. The president commented that he thought the "process ought to be more proactive in trying to get students of color interested who have never thought of going to a four-year college. We need to work more closely with the faculty in the various disciplines and programs to incorporate changes that attract and keep these students in college."

Faculty at Urban College, however, credit the two vice-presidents directly for finally giving prominence to the transfer function by making a commitment to develop new transfer courses and upgrade existing ones, raising aspirations of current students and recruiting new minority students interested in transfer, and creating a transfer center. With the support of the president, the vice presidents allocated fiscal and human resources to develop a strong transfer program in Urban College—which has hitherto been relatively weak due to the institution's primary emphasis on vocational programs that had historically generated larger enrollments but were now declining sharply in some areas. For example, interested faculty have not only developed and strengthened transfer core courses, but they formed a special core transfer program for young, daytime students who were attending in increasing numbers. The new transfer program focuses on this younger, rapidly growing population at Urban College. A core of general education transfer requirements is offered in convenient time slots so that day transfer students can easily take a full load, yet still have time to study and go work—a necessity for more than 50 percent of these students, who express a need to work at least parttime while in college. Faculty who teach transferable general education courses in the evening have been offered incentives to also teach in the day.

Counselors have also formalized recruitment activities at high schools with large minority populations beyond the local feeder schools, and meet with parents as well as students, faculty, and administrators in their efforts to publicize Urban College as a transfer institution with a diverse student body. As part of the overall effort, college literature was revamped and revised to highlight the new curriculum and transfer offerings. Moreover, the strength of Urban College, which is its highly diverse student population, is prominently profiled in all its new literature and publicity.

Curriculum and Programs

The goal of creating powerful learners can be achieved in a number of ways; however, the most powerful approach is by transforming the curriculum and supporting programs. Both Suburban College and Urban College have undertaken various efforts to promote curricular and programmatic changes which affirm students' border knowledge and cultural heritage.

Curriculum, the fiercely protected prerogative of the faculty, has received attention at Suburban College in response to ethnic students' call for courses reflecting their own heritage. Integrated into the general education offerings are new transfer credit courses which are culturally specific, such as African American Literature, Mexican American History, Culture and the Humanities, and Cross Cultural Counseling. An ethnic studies requirement was added to the associate degree to give salience to the courses. The student services dean acknowledged, "We are very excited about the degree requirement and all of these courses, including the cross counseling course which was developed and is team taught by Hispanic and African American counseling faculty."

In addition, a cross disciplinary honors program has been developed which recruits high-achieving students, according to the program coordinator, "from every socioeconomic and racial or ethnic group because we don't want this to be an elitist group of white privileged students, but a program for everyone who excels academically and wants to be even more intellectually challenged and stimulated. Five of our first ten honors students to transfer are Latinos [or Latinas] and African Americans, for example."

The Urban College faculty, on the other hand, has taken an across-the-curriculum approach that incorporates a multicultural perspective with new and revised courses whenever possible. A faculty member commented, "We want everyone to be exposed to multiple perspectives and students will not get that if we restrict the curriculum to just a few courses not everyone will take." New and revised courses such as Cross-Cultural Communication, Southeast Asian and American Literature, and Math Across Cultures have emerged as a result of the institutional decision. To further encourage transformation of the curriculum, faculty development workshops are offered at the beginning of each semester for new and other interested faculty to orient them to multiculturalism and to demonstrate ways they can incorporate cultural perspectives into their curriculum.

At Suburban College, a powerful and distinctive program specifically for Hispanic students, the Puente Project, has been instituted. The Puente Project integrates students' culture, academic preparation, and college orientation through the curriculum. Fittingly, the Puente Project[1] was initially developed by a local community college in 1981 with the goal of increasing the number of Hispanic students transferring to a four-year institution. It met with immediate success and by 1985 the University of California was a collaborative partner with the California Community Colleges in financing and expanding the Puente Project to interested community colleges. As of summer 1997, at least 38 other community colleges were participating in the Puente Project (Laden, in press).

Of special emphasis in the Puente Project are the threefold goals, which include: (1) two semesters of intensive English instruction focusing on writing and reading about the students' Hispanic cultural experiences and identity; (2) Hispanic counselors who have first-hand knowledge of the challenges the students face; and (3) mentors from the Latino and Latina professional and academic community (McGrath and Galaviz, 1996).

The Puente Project is a practical, cost-effective model for Hispanic students that addresses their unique needs by not only being sensitive to but also affirming their ethnic identity by building on their cultural strengths—much along the lines of the celebratory socialization advocated by some researchers (Van Maanen, 1984; Rhoads and Valadez, 1996; Tierney, 1997; Laden, in press). In effect, the students' border knowledge is validated and incorporated into the curriculum rather than ignored or dismissed. The Puente Project cultural model offers a tri–bridge approach that leads to successful academic outcomes, increased self-esteem, and greater self-confidence for Hispanic students.

The writing component of the project is based on a two-semester sequence of accelerated writing instruction with approximately 30 Hispanic students. In the fall semester, students take a pretransfer developmental English course and read Hispanic literature and write compositions based on their own cultural and community experiences. The rationale is that students are able to write about what they know best, that is, drawing from their own Latin American life experiences, their families and friends, their neighborhoods, and all that is most intimately familiar to them. In the second semester, students enroll in a transfer-level English composition class with the same Puente faculty. Hispanic literature and personal cultural experiences continue to be integrated into the curriculum. Oral and written mentor activities in the classroom are incorporated during this semester. Additionally, guest Hispanic writers and artists share their work and experiences with the Puentistas, stressing the ways they are able to remain true to their own cultural identities while functioning successfully in the mainstream society.

The academic counseling component strives to provide daily close contact between the counselor and the students, thus placing the counselor in a proactive a position to address student needs whenever necessary. The counselor also takes an active role in the courses, offering practical academic advice, teaching study skills, and assisting in the English course work. The counselor offers not only typical academic and career guidance and advice about degree requirements, transfer eligibility, financial aid information and assistance, and the college application process, but provides the necessary day-to-day understanding, encouragement, motivation, and psychological support to persist and succeed in what for many is still an alien environment.

Working closely with parents also is critical to the success of the program by helping them to understand and become involved with their children's pursuit of higher education. Hence, a variety of activities are held in the evenings or weekends that include the parents of the students. Parents are also invited to attend off-campus trips with the class and any Puente Project regional and state events. An added bonus is that some parents have enrolled in college themselves and some have become students in the Puente Project as well.

The program is funded by the respective colleges. Therefore, it is an expensive one for community colleges to undertake, as the Puente Project faculty team of two must attend an intensive two-week summer institute at the University of California, Berkeley, participate in followup conferences and workshops throughout the year, attend a number of evening and weekend events, and dedicate 50 percent of their faculty load exclusively to the program.

Another hallmark of the program is that the two faculty members' commitment to the program and the student transcends the typical expectation of faculty involvement. They must contend with students' academic and personal in-class and out of class concerns. These students are typically the first in their families to attend college, and as Zwerling, London and associates (1992) point out, regardless of race and ethnicity, first-generation college students need special understanding and support to make the cultural and academic socialization experiences positive. They also frequently have financial concerns, often work at least parttime, and usually have other competing interests and demands in their lives. The Puente counselor's remarks about her relationship specific to the Hispanic students can be applied to all students: "You have to go after them. You have to establish personal relationships with them. They want to know you because you have been referred by someone they know and trust, so they then trust you. It is all very culturally specific what we do with them."

Throughout the year-long process, due to the combined efforts of the faculty, the mentors, and the culturally enriched curricular activities, the students gain a sense of empowerment and academic success. An administrator commented, "It is one of the best things we do on this campus. We validate the students, respect who they are as Latinos, and what they bring with them to college. They connect with role models in the community, their mentors, who encourage them and support them, too. Is it any wonder these Latinos succeed and do as well as they do?" The dean of student services added, "The retention and success rates of these students far exceed the normal rates for Hispanic students. One of the best things is that Puente deals with the issue of self-worth and valuing who the students are. It does not try to change them."

In talking about the Puente Project's success on campus, the president of Suburban College echoed the concepts embedded in celebratory socialization. He stated:

> The Puente Project is the most successful program in the state for helping Hispanics succeed. Students get a strong sense of self-esteem and develop good coping skills in an environment that tells them they are okay just the way they

are. But at the same time, it raises their aspirations by showing them that education can offer them a whole lot more without losing a sense of who they are. I think every college, whether it be a community college or a university, should have Puente programs for their students. It is a model we should be emulating in higher education to help all low income and minority students succeed.

Urban College has created a similar program modeled on the Puente Project called *La Mision*,[2] but because of the high cost of training, implementing, and maintaining the program, it does not affiliate directly with the Puente Project or participate in any of the Puente Project state and regional activities. Nonetheless, an English instructor and an Hispanic counselor have formed a teaching partnership to offer a developmental English composition class together using some of the Puente Project's culturally-specific curricular strategies. The two faculty members also work with La Mision students collaboratively in and out of the classroom with a selected cohort of first-year Hispanic students for the full academic year. As a team akin to the Puente Project faculty, drawing from their respective areas of expertise, the faculty provide in-depth instruction in English composition, career and college orientation, culturally-specific readings and guest speakers, and an understanding of the "hidden curriculum" of college.

From the very beginning, the students are encouraged in the English class to use their own voices, thus, they write about what they know intimately—their own personal and family cultural experiences. As in the Puente classes, the students learn the formal mechanics of grammar and syntax through the context of their culturally-specific writings. Integrated into the English course is explicit information regarding how to understand and use the organizational structure to the students' own advantage. The La Mision students receive specific guidance in transfer preparation, and obtain information and role models through guest speakers and off-campus college visits. Unlike the Puente Project, however, La Mision does not incorporate the use of mentors. The counseling faculty member commented:

I knew we could make a difference for Latino students and get more of them to not only do well in English, but get them to start thinking about at least a B.A. degree, and helping them prepare academically for transferring to a university. La Mision is working just as I knew it would. We are attracting more Latinos to [Urban College] and many of them are interested in transferring. They like the personal approach we offer through La Mision. College does not seem so alien to them and they do not feel isolated in their new setting. La Mision is definitely a successful program!

At the beginning of the third year of the program, the dean with program oversight commented, "It is really what we needed for our Hispanic students.

The faculty are committed to making it work and we are having a huge success with it. We have students transferring to some selective universities when they had never even thought of going to college before we recruited them." He added that he thought including a mentoring component would be especially beneficial to La Mision students and was encouraging the La Mision faculty to consider it for the next cohort of students. He concluded by stating:

> Ideally, the most desirable for our college and for our students would be to affiliate with the statewide Puente Project, but with the financial retrenchment that the college is in, we are fortunate to have La Mision at all. Fortunately, the program is a huge success, one I wish we could offer it to every student of color, if not to every student who comes to [Urban College].

Thus, La Mision at Urban College—much like the Puente Project at Suburban College—offers Hispanic students an opportunity to develop their writing and oral proficiency in English in a classroom setting that validates and daily honors their cultural heritage through the curriculum, increases their self-esteem and self-confidence, and raises their commitment to persist in college, while preparing them to transfer to a four-year institution in pursuit of the bachelor's degree.

Also at Suburban College is a summer bridge program called the Summer Leadership Institute for high school graduates with the express goal of giving these incoming freshman students of color a "head-start" preparation for the fall. The six-week summer program offers six one-unit credit courses in English fundamentals, effective reading, career exploration, study skills, and computer literacy. The director of the program and the faculty work closely with the students on a daily basis to ensure the students feel welcomed and connected to Suburban College. Among the many activities are a variety of guest speakers, field trips, cultural events, and meetings with parents about the benefits of college and financial aid availability are part of the six-week experience. For example, the summer bridge students also visit several nearby universities and meet with campus representatives and students of color who spend the day with them showing them the campus and talking about the four-year college experience. These students get priority registration as well an opportunity to meet with some of the faculty they will have in fall classes before they leave the summer program.

Student Services and Activities

How else can students be affirmed in their cultural heritage while still instilling a sense of belonging and achieving? A prospective student's first contact with a college is often with student services staff, frequently during off-campus or on-campus recruitment activities. Student services staff are typically responsible in one way or another for most activities held outside of the classroom. The transformation of the organization frequently begins in this area of the college community because administrators, counselors, and support staff typically deal with a variety of student issues and concerns first. Often they are able to recognize and respond to the need for changes first. Even small changes can have an unexpected impact.

For example, transforming traditional activities such as College Day or Transfer Day can produce surprising results. College Day or Transfer Day is a typical, large scale fall event held in community colleges that brings four-year college recruiters to campus to provide students with information about postsecondary choices and opportunities. In keeping with the concept of celebratory socialization, Suburban College offers an additional fall college information day specifically for Hispanics and other students of color. Started by the Puente Project counselor at Suburban College, the event is called Raza Day.[3] It features ethnic four-year college and university representatives who offer a more personalized presentation of the academic and social aspects of their institutions, including information about special campus programs offered for students of color. They also offer workshops on academic majors, student affairs programs, financial assistance and scholarships, extracurricular and social programs, and a myriad of activities of special interest for racial or ethnic students. In keeping with their own outreach efforts in the community, Suburban College invites ethnic students from surrounding high schools to attend Raza Day. According to the student affairs dean:

> The event has become very popular with our students of color here and in the high schools. They all like the special day just for them. It gives them an opportunity to talk with college representatives they feel comfortable with and who can understand a little bit better who they are and how their needs may be different from our mainstream students. In fact, this event has been so successful that we are thinking of changing the name to Minority Transfer Day to be more inclusive for all races and ethnic groups even though they are all invited.

In keeping with its commitment to provide alternative experiences for its students, Urban College offers a second transfer-day event at night time to address the needs of the evening students, many who are older, working fulltime, often the first in their families to attend college, and from diverse racial and ethnic backgrounds. Known as College Night, the event is held in the late afternoon and early evening to capture working students arriving for evening classes between 4:00 p.m. and 7:00 p.m. The transfer counselor explained:

> We wanted to inform our evening, working students about four-year college opportunities and about the variety of evening and accelerated programs oriented to this special population, especially for our minority students, that can

make it possible for them to get a bachelor's degree in a reasonable amount of time. We keep finding that so many of our first-generation students just are not aware that there are a variety of transfer options open to them after they complete their requirements here. We're one of the few community colleges that actually puts on College Night—and I know this event makes a difference for so many of our evening students.

Recruitment and outreach activities are common in every postsecondary institution. However, both Suburban College and Urban College have increased their recruitment into the larger community where large ethnically and socio-economically diverse populations reside. Both colleges hire buses to bring in junior and senior students from high schools every fall and spring for High School Days, and for Raza Day in the case of Suburban College, and tailor their on-campus events to the groups invited.

At Suburban College, students spend the entire day going to class with peer mentors and attending a variety of academic, culturally-specific, and social activities. Already a favorite series of events are the buffet luncheon followed by a fashion show featuring the elaborate work of students in the state awarding-winning Fashion Design program, and a cultural program featuring considerable student talent. During the spring visit, for example, I observed a group of Aztec dancers with elaborate feather headdresses who swayed to rhythmic chants and drumbeats while faculty, administrators, students, and visiting high school students along with their peer college guides watched, smiling and clapping along with the drummers. "Everyone—faculty, administrators, the president, staff, and of course, students—gets involved in High School Days. It is a major event on our campus and we are all very committed to having it be a success each and every time," remarked one faculty member.

At Urban College, high school students attend a half-day of activities coordinated by the counselors and members of the student body association. The visit culminates with a lunch which features speakers and entertainment by college faculty and students. On the day I visited, the entertainment included a group of Vietnamese students who read poetry, and a band who sang in Vietnamese several recognizable rock songs, and several Latin American students who performed folkloric dances. In speaking about the high school visits, a dean explained, "We have such a highly diverse student population already that when our high school visitors see our mix of students and faculty as people they can identity with racially and ethnically, this image sells our college to them."

Emphasis on Transfer

Access to knowledge pertinent to meeting one's goals and meeting people whom one can identify with have a great deal to do with becoming self-empowered. Both community colleges have developed transfer centers which integrate career and academic information and make its dissemination and utilization accessible. At Suburban College, the new transfer center has gone from "being nearly in a closet" to being located in the counseling building in a high traffic area, and staffed with a counselor, a career specialist, and a counselor aide. All community college information is consolidated with information on four-year institutions so that students go to only one site for all academic information. Four-year college representatives regularly meet with transfer students there and also present motivational, application, and financial aid workshops. Specific ethnic recruiters from different universities are invited often to speak with and meet students of color on the campus. An administrator commented, "When minority students see people who look like them, they are more likely to want to talk with them. It is an important connection we try to provide and one students seem to appreciate."

A unique component to the transfer center at Suburban College is the addition of a counselor aide. The position of counselor aide is still uncommon in most California community college counseling departments. In those few instances where the position does exist, it is used not only as a way to add staff in budget crunch times, but to create greater diversity within the counseling department. In the case of Suburban College, an Asian American was hired while she was enrolled in a counseling master's-degree program to assist the transfer counselor and the career specialist. Her presence was credited in part to attracting students of color to the transfer center. A counselor not directly affiliated with the transfer center commented that he saw students using the transfer center whom he had not seen there before the counselor aide was hired. The counselor added:

> I cannot say for sure that it because of [the counselor aide] that more minority students are using the transfer center, but it certainly looks like that to me. I think students who are not too familiar with college, who may be the first in their family to go to college, tend to feel more comfortable asking for information from someone who is more like them, who may understand something about how they feel being there.

The creation of a transfer center at Urban College was considered long overdue by some faculty. Bringing the transfer center to fruition is attributed to the efforts of several counselors and the vice president of student services. While "a career center of sorts had existed off and on for several years," according to one of the counselors, "we were working out of cardboard boxes that held our catalogs and transfer materials." With the remodeling of the student services area, a transfer center was created next to the counseling center and a full-time coordinator and career specialist were hired. The career specialist noted that being located next door to counseling and across from the bookstore and the cafeteria "gave us an ideal location for students to find us." Credit for attracting students of color to the transfer center in increasing numbers is attributed to the hiring of student workers from diverse racial and ethnic backgrounds "because students know that there is someone here who can speak their language if they need to ask questions and can understand some of their cultural needs or situations more readily."

The transfer counselor noted that student of color are using the transfer center with increasing frequency. She attributed that to "making the students feel welcomed, specially when they see the student workers and meet with our diverse counseling faculty. The transfer counselor added:

> It is terrific having diverse student workers because they attract students who are like them—students who might not come in here otherwise. The student workers can relate to these students in a way we cannot. They also tell us what students are thinking or need and we can try to address their needs. It really makes such a difference to have them, such that I don't know how we could serve our diverse students in the same way without them.

Toward A More Empowering Organizational Culture

Culturally sensitive academic and support programs and activities especially designed to provide a sense of welcome and belonging, to motivate and empower, and to make knowledge meaningful and accessible to ethnically diverse students remain crucial in community colleges that enroll high numbers of these students. As Tierney (1992), Rhoads and Valadez (1996), and others (London, 1992; Rendon, 1993; Rendon and Nora, 1992; Turner, 1988; Laden, 1994, in press) remind us, empowering students involves helping them to understand and make sense of their relationship to the world and to the complex organizations, that is, the community colleges, they inhabit. In the environment of the community college, the process of empowerment is one that individuals take on themselves as they come to an understanding of their place in the world, and are then able to transform themselves in light of their new knowledge in an organizational context that welcomes and affirms their presence.

The task for educators is to create conditions for change. Educators must transform organizational practices and policies in ways that acknowledge the range and diversity of the contextual experiences students bring to higher education institutions. The programmatic efforts described here suggest how two community colleges initiated efforts that addressed some of the cultural and academic needs of diverse students. The interactions occurring among the various elements—academic offerings, cultural identity, motivation, and student support services—have the potential for creating a web effect that leads to student empowerment and success. Such programs and activities, however, cannot occur without the dedicated commitment and leadership of all members of the organization—that is, the president, administrators and faculty—to transform the college community in ways that celebrate and emphasize differences positively.

Moreover, it is the allocation of critical human and financial resources that also enable the structural and psychological changes to occur. Individuals at Suburban College and Urban College take active roles in using the available resources to promote the recruitment, retention, and academic achievement of Hispanics and other racial and ethnic students by creating environments on their campuses which welcome them, give them a sense of belonging, and value them for who they are. The resources allocated are used to create or strengthen programmatic efforts and to develop culturally-specific offerings and services encouraging student acceptance and empowering them toward the goals of personal and academic accomplishment. A comment by the president of Suburban College may best sum up the critical necessity of allocating resources and transforming the institution for populations who are currently under served and under represented in higher education in general. He exclaimed:

> For years, the biggest flaw in the educational system is that we took students from different backgrounds and said, 'if you want to succeed, you have to adopt our values, our mores, our culture, or you die'—die meaning drop out. Well, now that the numbers are changing in our colleges and universities, they have to change or they will shrivel up and die from lack of traditional students. So, the question is what new things do we do to accommodate the new majority, the diverse population? There is something that Hispanics have, that blacks have, that Asians have, that's good and that's unique to being Hispanic, black, or Asian. The challenge for us is to not have those groups become like us, but rather have the institutions become like them. There are a lot of things that need to occur in terms of what we call reverse acculturation. We need to change the institutions now. We need to stop having the institution change us. To me, education is simply as set of options—a *set of keys* which just open up more doors. Whatever we do with our students, we need to give them as many keys on that key ring as possible so that they have options in their own lives.

It is only by first understanding the culture of the students that the process of organizational and individual transformation can yield significant outcomes for these students or the community college as a whole. Students of different cultural groups, no less than those of the dominant group, who "come to college believing that they may be unsuccessful . . . can be transformed into powerful learners" (Rendon and Jalomo, 1993, p. 1), and powerful participants in the institution. This can be accomplished through the institution's efforts to transform the students' experiences into meaningful in- and out-of-class experiences which facilitate their psychological growth, cognitive development, and learning experiences while recognizing and valuing their cultural distinctiveness—and transforming themselves as institutions at the same time.

Notes

1. The term *puente* has several meanings. *Puente* is Spanish for "bridge." A student who participates in the Puente Project also is referred to as a *puentista*. In this form, the word also refers to someone who crosses a bridge or someone who works on a bridge, hence all individuals who are affiliated with the Puente Project can also be referred to as *puentistas*.

2. *La mision* is Spanish for "the mission."

3. *Raza* is Spanish for "race." It is also an inclusive term often used by Latinos and Latinas to refer to themselves as *la Raza,* meaning "our people."

References

Astin, A. W. (1988). *Minorities in American higher education.* San Francisco: Jossey-Bass.

Attinasi, L. C., Jr. (1989). Mexican Americans' perceptions of university attendance and the implications for freshman year persistence. *Journal of Higher Education*, (60) 3.

———. (1994). "Is going to college a rite of passage?" Paper presented at the annual meeting of the American Educational Research Association, New Orleans, April.

Cabrera, A. F. & Nora, A. (1994). "The role of perceptions of prejudice and discrimination on the adjustment of minority students to college." Paper presented at the annual meeting of the Association for the Student of Higher Education, Tucson, November.

Cohen, A. M., & Brawer, F. B. (1996) *The American community college.* (3rd Ed.) San Francisco: Jossey-Bass.

Delgado-Gaitan, C., & Trueba, H. (1991). *Crossing cultural borders: Education for immigrant families in America.* London: Falmer Press.

DiCroce, D. M. (1995). "Women and the community college presidency: Challenges and possibilities," in B. K. Townsend (Ed.), *Gender and power in the community college. New Directions in Community Colleges*, 89. San Francisco: Jossey-Bass.

Geertz, C. (1973). *Local knowledge.* New York: Basic Books.

Giroux, H. A. (1992). *Border crossings.* New York: Routledge, Chapman and Hill.

Helgesen, S. (1990b). The pyramid and the web. *New York Times Forum,* May 27, 1990, p. F13, cited in DiCroce, Deborah M. (1995) "Women and the community college presidency: Challenges and possibilities," in B. K. Townsend (Ed.), *Gender and power in the community college. New Directions in Community Colleges,* 89. San Francisco: Jossey-Bass.

Hull, G. (1993). Critical literacy and beyond: Lessons learned from students and workers in a vocational program on the job. *Anthropology and Education Quarterly,* 24 (3), 373–96.

Laden, B. V. (1994). "The educational pipeline: Organizational and protective factoring influencing the academic progress of Hispanic community college students with potential at risk characteristics." Unpublished Ph.D. dissertation. Stanford University.

———. (In press). "An organizational response to welcoming students of color," in Levin, John S. (Ed.), *Organizational change in the community college: A ripple or a sea of change? New Directions in Community Colleges.* San Francisco: Jossey-Bass.

Lincoln, Y. S., & Guba, E. G. (1985). *Naturalistic inquiry.* Newbury Park: Sage.

London, H. B. (1992). "Transformations: Cultural challenges faced by first–generation students," in S. L. Zwerling & H. B. Howard London (Eds.), *First–generation students: Confronting the cultural issues. New Directions for Community Colleges,* 80. San Francisco: Jossey-Bass.

McGrath, P., & Galaviz, F. (1996). "Message from the co–directors." *Puente News,* (Fall), 1. Oakland: University of California Office of the President.

Miles, M. B., & Huberman, A. M. (1984). *Qualitative data analysis.* Beverly Hills: Sage.

Nora, A.; Attinasi, L. C.; & Matonark, A. (1990). "Testing qualitative indicators of precollege factors in Tinto's attrition model: A community college student population." *The Review of Higher Education,* 23 (4), 351–73.

Olivas, M. A. (1979). *The dilemma of access.* Washington, D. C: Howard University Press.

Pascarella, E. T., & Terenzini, P. T. (1991). *How college affects students.* San Francisco: Jossey-Bass.

Pavel, M. (1991). *Assessing Tinto's model of institutional departure using American Indian and Alaskan Native longitudinal data.* Paper presented at the annual meeting of the Association for the Study of Higher Education, Boston, November.

Rendon, L. I. (1982). "Chicanos in south Texas community colleges: A study of student institutional-related determinants of educational outcomes." Unpublished Ph.D. Dissertation. University of Michigan.

Rendon, L. I.; Justiz, M. J.; & Restas, P. (1988). *Transfer education on southwest border community colleges.* New York: The Ford Foundation.

Rendon, L. I., & Nora, A. (1992). "A synthesis and application of research on Hispanic students on community colleges." *Community College Review*, 17 (1), 17–24.

Rendon, L. I., & Jalomo, R. (1993). *The in- and out-of-class experiences of first-year community college students.* Paper presented at the annual meeting of the Association for the Study of Higher Education, Pittsburgh, November.

Rhoads, R. A., & Valadez, J. R. (1996). *Democracy, multiculturalism, and the community college.* New York: Garland.

Tierney, W. G. (1992). *Official encouragement, institutional discouragement: Minorities in academe—the Native American experience.* Norwood: Ablex.

Tinto, V. (1975). "Dropout from higher education: A theoretical synthesis of recent research." *Review of Educational Research*, 45 (1), 89–125.

———. (1987). *Leaving college.* Chicago: The University of Chicago Press.

———. (1988). "Stages of student departure: Reflections on the longitudinal character of students leaving." *Journal of Higher Education,* 59 (July/August), 438–55.

———. (1993). *Leaving College.* (2nd Ed.) Chicago: The University of Chicago Press.

Turner, C. S. V. (1988). "Organizational determinants of the transfer of Hispanic students from two- to four-year colleges." Unpublished Ph.D. dissertation. Stanford University.

Van Gennep, A. (1960). *The rites of passage.* (N. Vizedon and G. Caffee, translators). Chicago: University of Chicago Press.

Weis, L. (1985). *Between two worlds: Black students in an urban community college.* Boston: Routledge & Kegan Paul.

Yin, R. K. (1984) *Case study research.* Beverly Hills: Sage.

C H A P T E R   1 0

Toward a New Vision of the Multicultural Community College for the Next Century

LAURA I. RENDÓN

The time has come for a new vision of the democratic, open-access, community college for the next century. This new vision needs to build on the strengths of past research and practice. More importantly, it needs to incorporate the work of new thinkers, new voices, and fresh perspectives that are being offered by scholars and practitioners who are able to think "outside the box," with courage, conviction, inspiration, and creativity. As such, this book represents what could be called the best compendium of qualitative research that provides the framework and the building blocks necessary to create the contemporary community college of the next century.

It is interesting that the model of a multicultural community college emerges from a qualitative paradigm, as opposed to the classic, quantitative mode that celebrates objectivity and distance. In the book *Culture and Truth: The Remaking of Social Analysis*, anthropologist Renato Rosaldo (1993) presents a critical contestation of scientific objectivity and argues that social scientists should study their subjects through numerous positionalities. The authors of this text are social critics who are informed by conceptions of social justice, democracy, fairness, and human dignity. As such, they are not utterly detached from their subject matter. This in itself is not a weakness, for Rosaldo (1993) argues that "social analysts can rarely, if ever, become detached observers" (p. 169). Moreover, a critical analysis of the community college culture calls for a qualitative approach that brings researchers closer to their subjects, allowing them to explore the complexities and nuances of truth, meaning, and understanding.

The framework for the democratic community college is based on the notion of what Robert Rhoads calls "multiculturalism," a widely-used term that here refers to the incorporation of a wide range of perspectives that are representative of culturally diverse peoples. Bensimon & Tierney (1993) note that

> multiculturalism is a complex set of relationships framed around issues of race, gender, class, sexual orientation, and power. Multicultural organizations struggle to understand commonalties and differences among underrepresented groups, and develop an appreciation of how an understanding of these characteristics might create alliances for change . . . Multicultural excellence [is] based on democratic acceptance of both the commonalties and differences of all groups on campus (p. 68).

In essence, multiculturalism is the conceptual framework by which traditional views of learning, organization, identity, and power relationships can be challenged, debated and resolved. Multiculturalism is contrasted with monoculturalism, an adherence to homogeneity accompanied by the view that cultural diversity is a threat to dominant conceptions of education and social life.

What do the next generation of community college leaders need to know about what it takes to construct a multicultural institution? Perhaps the first step is to come to terms with the nature of community college students, their histories, their hopes and dreams. It is with this understanding that the colleges can employ multicultural organizational structures, as well as create inclusive, democratic classrooms.

Community College Students

A multicultural community college begins with the recognition that the colleges need to reflect student lives—their in- and out-of-class experiences, their ways of knowing, their histories. As Kate Shaw notes, there is a need for these colleges to recognize the multiplicity of student identities. Perhaps it is appropriate to review what scholars have learned about these students over the past few years. While community colleges differ in their student body composition, the authors of this text are addressing the issues of the majority of students that these colleges were designed to serve—low-income, working-class, academically underprepared, first-generation students, many who are ethnic or racial minorities.

Many of these students, often labeled "nontraditional," do not consider themselves to be college material, have never made an "A" in their lives, and have been retained in high school. Some were involved in gang life. This cohort also includes single mothers and fathers coming back to college after a long period of time, students who have been told they will never amount to anything, and who view the community college as their only hope to restart their lives. The profile of nontraditional students is in sharp contrast to that of traditional students whose parents and siblings have attended college, who come from middle-class backgrounds, who grow up feeling empowered to reach their goals, and who view college as a continuation of their life trajectory. For traditional students the transition to college is much easier. The passage represents a continuation of family expectations and traditions. Nontraditional students, on the other hand, break and often redefine their family history. In the process they must learn to operate in multiple worlds—the world of family, work, barrio or ghetto, and the new academic world (Rendón, 1996; Terenzini, *et al.*, 1994; Jalomo, 1995; Weis, 1985).

Bourdieu (1977) notes that children from dominant group families possess a specialized kind of "cultural capital"—that is, they possess a working knowledge of the values and traditions of educational institutions acquired through early socialization in middle- and upper-class families. Conversely, children from low-income families lack the benefits of privilege and status. Their cultural capital is incongruent with the symbolic and social expectations of the existing educational system. Educators tend to stereotype students who lack the "right" cultural capital as underachievers who are not interested in social and class mobility. This happens in spite of the fact that many students from modest origins are very bright and have high aspirations.

In a study that examined the aspirations of 6th-, 8th-, 10th-, and 12th-grade urban students, a key finding was that the vast majority of these students wanted to graduate from high school, attend college and graduate from college (Rendón & Nora, 1996). And numerous other scholars have found that African American and Hispanic community college students do have transfer aspirations (Rendón, Justiz, & Resta, 1988; Richardson & Bender 1987). The problem is not so much that low-income students lack ambition, it is that these students have not received the socialization, encouragement, or mentoring to take full advantage of higher education. Further, higher education has yet to validate and incorporate the cultural capital that these students do have—their prior learning experience, their music, art, and literature, their diverse ways of knowing. Scholars who have studied first-generation and working-class students (Zwerling & London, 1991; Jalomo, 1995; Rendón, 1996) would tend to agree with Dennis McGrath and Bill Van Buskirk when they indicate that students want an education, not just training. They want a career, not just a job. They want a future, not just a course or two.

Lamentably, many community colleges have operated employing quite the opposite view, with vocationalism framing almost all educational policy for nontraditional students. The promise of the multicultural community college lies in the extent to which it is able to convince immigrant students—those that cross the academic border—that it is possible to attain an education that goes beyond performing menial tasks, obeying authority, and getting a low-paying job. If all the community college emphasizes is the opportunity to learn vocational skills at the expense of diminishing other possibilities and dimming student futures, it reproduces a class structure. The challenge is to help students envision the broad array of career possibilities, and to arm students with enough information that will allow them to see the pros and cons of each of those possibilities in order to make an informed decision that will ultimately shape the rest of their lives.

Organizational Elements of the Multicultural Community College

Diversity and multiculturalism are not new to the American community college. Built on the egalitarian philosophy of open access, the community college often takes pride in the diversity of its students, faculty and staff, the multiplicity of its programmatic offerings, the diverse definitions of "success." This is an institution in which one would expect to find a wide range of examples that the college truly abides by the philosophy of multiculturalism— inclusiveness in decisionmaking, a sense of community, and a conscious and concerted emphasis on recognizing, respecting and validating diverse identities and diverse ways of thinking and knowing.

Trujillo and Diaz, as well as Laden and McGrath and Van Buskirk, provide examples of the power of a college and of student services that support a multicultural organizational culture. In the examples the authors present, access is more than an open door. Access is creating an organizational culture that is responsive to student lives. It is working with students to build their stock of social and emotional capital, providing validating environments, emphasizing intellectualism, and helping students to see themselves as capable learners while creating a powerful image of their future. Yet, one cannot negate what Amey and Valadez found in their studies—that while many community colleges preach diversity, they fail to provide for it. Behind the gloss of the rhetoric of access and diversity is the reality of monoculturalism that permeates the college culture of some, and perhaps too many, two-year colleges.

If one can consider the community college a "border zone," a place where diverse students, much like immigrants who cross national borders, enter a new world, then one can, as Rosaldo (1993) suggests, view such borderlands "not as empty, transitional zones, but as sites of creative cultural production that require investigation " (p. 208). Using Rosaldo's conceptualization of culture, community colleges are not self-contained, homogenous places. Instead, they are cultural border zones that are dynamic, fluid, and ever-changing. As such, the pretense that the community college culture is internally coherent or monocultural is a distortion of reality. Community college leaders and faculty who adhere to a monocultural orientation are operating in direct opposition to the rich multiculturalism that superimposes them.

Figure 10.1 summarizes what the authors of this text found to be the monocultural organizational elements of community colleges, as contrasted with what could be a community college organized around multiculturalism. What is proposed is a transformation of the community college culture, involving a critical analysis of its values, beliefs, norms, power structures, attitudes and old conceptions of static, monolithic culture. A multicultural community college embraces multiple forms of cultural knowledge, organizational complexity, plural organizational identities and critical thinking. It is guided by a philosophy of full access, it is humanistic, and its faculty and staff are representative of different cultures.

Classroom Elements of a Multicultural Community College

One of the greatest challenges in this new vision of a multicultural community college is building a democratic curriculum based on varying representations of people. The democratic classroom embraces traditional and nontraditional students, as well as gender, race, and sexual orientation. Figure 10.2 summarizes what the authors of this text would differentiate as monocultural and multicultural classroom elements.

The remaking of the classroom is essential in the creation of a multicultural community college. The model the multicultural community college classroom that emerges from this book's studies is very much in line with what Belenkey and others (1986) call "connected teaching" and elements of the model of validation that I have described elsewhere (Rendón, 1994). The reader will note that a democratic classroom is one of inclusion, one that realigns power between the professor and students, one that challenges privilege and authority. Equally important is that students are viewed in broad terms, as knowers and as potential contributors to the well-being of society.

This model of the democratic classroom is in sharp contrast to "Prescott College," described by Valadez, that responds to the needs of employers, as opposed to the needs of the students. It is not necessary to be a critical thinker or even to have a holistic view of the world at Prescott—all students have to do is to learn the skills, obey the rules and respect authority. What is conveyed in this example is a culture clash that puts institutional survival in direct conflict with what is in the hearts and minds of students. Many community college leaders believe that the colleges survive because they provide a service to the community. The more graduates that are placed in community jobs, the better the image of the college and the more resources it is able to leverage.

This is where community colleges miss their mark. The challenge is not simply to offer open access to students in the green card phase (Rosaldo,

Table 10.1   Organizational Elements of a Monocultural and Multicultural Community College

Monocultural Elements *Organizational Elements*	**Multicultural Elements** *Organizational Elements*
• The college operates as if a single culture prevails reflecting mainstream values.	• College reflects multiple identities in society and diverse ways of knowing and operating.
• The administrators and faculty are predominantly white and male.	• Administrators and faculty are representative of different cultures.
• The ethos of the college is on careerism.	• The ethos of the college goes beyond envisioning students as prospective employees. Students are prepared to be responsible and active citizens of society.
• College culture fosters assimilation and sameness.	• College culture affirms cultural identities and embraces a wide range of cultural knowledge.
• Transfer and intellectualism are not given a high priority.	• The college is guided by the philosophy of full access to all of higher education, especially for underrepresented students.
• Students are described in narrow terms.	• The college recognizes multiple representations of identities.
• The organizational structure perpetuates social stratification and precludes upward mobility.	• Students are given positive appraisals and encouraged to have a powerful image of the future.
• Power structures are not humanistic.	• College adopts a humanistic approach to governance. Power structures are reconstructed and a critical review of institutional policies and practices is conducted.
• Professionals work in isolation from each other.	• College works to promote community.
• Faculty harbor patronizing views about students.	• Faculty engaged in a critical discourse about education and its role in developing responsible citizens.
• Students support services are inappropriate to student lives and needs.	• College staff helps students develop their stock of cultural and emotional capital through student-centered services.
• Low expectations are set—narrow career choices are offered.	• Education is more than preparation for a job. Students prepared for multiple roles in their communities and in the larger society.

Note: Figure 10.1 represents a summary of organizational elements as presented in Shaw, Valadez, and Rhoads (1999). *Community College as Cultural Texts: Qualitative Explorations of Organizational and Student Culture.*

Table 10.2 Classroom Elements of a Monocultural and Multicultural Community College

Monocultural Community College *Classroom Elements*	**Multicultural Community College** *Classroom Elements*
• Students are engaged in menial tasks.	• Students are engaged in critical thinking and problem solving.
• Faculty employ authoritarian forms of pedagogy.	• A democratic classroom is created.

—Culturally different views are devalued.
   —System of rewards and punishment prevails.
   —Linear teaching is employed.
   —Faculty are authority figures and keepers of knowledge.
	—Diverse voices are represented.
	   —Faculty and students are open to diverse points of view.
	   —Students are equal partners in teaching and learning.
	   —Faculty share knowledge and learn from students.

• Students are not viewed as knowers.	• Students have the opportunity to discuss their own experiences and write their own histories.
• Student docility and passivity are viewed as positive qualities that help faculty work with students.	• Students are active learners and assisted to negotiate the college environment.
• Students expected to conform to predetermined standards of academic proficiency.	• Standards are set with students.
• The curriculum is Euro-centered.	• Diverse forms of knowledge are recognized and legitimated.

Note: Figure 10.2 represents a summary of classroom elements as presented in Shaw, Valadez, and Rhoads (1999). *Community College as Cultural Texts: Qualitative Explorations of Organizational and Student Culture.*

1993) of college admission. Neither is the challenge as narrow as producing workers to fill low-level, short-term, dead-end jobs. Rather, the challenge is to assist students to set their goals higher than what they think they should be, to broaden the array of career choices, to foster intellectualism and critical thinking, and to institute changes in the curriculum and pedagogical practices that are important for democratizing college classrooms. The moment that a classroom begins to take on a democratic character, a true revolution in teaching and learning begins. And a democratic classroom can be found in either a vocational or academic department. These are "contact zones" (Pratt, 1991) where, as Stanford Goto notes, individuals engage in classroom interaction where conflicting ideas with any individual (including the instructor) potentially influencing any other.

According to Rosaldo (1993): "The moment classrooms become diverse, change begins. There is no standing still. New students do not laugh at old jokes. Even those teachers who do nothing to revise their yellowed sheets of lecture notes know that their words have taken on new meanings. New pedagogies begin" (p. xiii). The impact of a democratic classroom can be phenomenal, for it is here that a change in the students' habitus can occur. As Valadez points out, changing the habitus of working-class students in vocational classrooms would see students questioning why prospective employers offer only minimum-wage jobs and why so many of the jobs are filled by women and minorities. Students would critique their positions in society and broaden their horizons. In short, students would be transformed into powerful thinkers, knowers, and contributors to society.

Toward a New Vision of the Multicultural Community College

Traditional models of leadership, much like stale conceptions of monolithic culture, will not take the community college into the next century. The next generation of two-year college leaders will need to broaden their thinking about access, student aspirations, organizational change, and classroom policy and practice. New community college administrators and faculty will have to engage in a critical analysis of the definition of student success and how the colleges can best serve the full diversity of their student clientele. The future of the community college lies more in having futuristic leaders bound by a sense of social justice and democratic ideals than by the belief that the colleges should continue to do the same things they have done in the past. Helping nontraditional students cross academic borders requires more than opening the admissions door, paying scant attention to the transfer mission, or preparing students for entry-level jobs. The community college of the next century ought to produce students who understand and appreciate the full range of opportunities available to them, who are able to make informed choices about their future, who leave the colleges as critical thinkers who can engage in civic life, and who are able to operate in multicultural environments. To do this, the authors of this important book are calling for the transformation of the community college. New leaders ought to heed this challenge as they engage in creating a new vision of the community college of the next century.

References

Belenkey, M.; Clinchy, B.; Goldberger, N.; & Tarule, J. (1986). *Women's ways of knowing.* New York: Basic Books.

Bensimon, E. M., & Tierney, W. G. (1992–93, Late Winter). "Shaping the multicultural college campus." *The College Board Review* 166, 4–7.

Bourdieu, P. (1977). "Cultural reproduction and social reproduction." In Karabel, J. & Halsey, A. H. (Eds.), *Power and ideology in education,* (pp. 487–511). New York: Oxford University Press.

Jalomo, R. E. (1995). "Latino students in transition: An analysis of the first-year experience in the community college." Unpublished doctoral dissertation. Arizona State University.

Pratt, M. L. (1991). "Arts of the contact zone." *Profession* 91, 33–40.

Rendón, L. I. (1992). "From the barrio to the academy: Revelations of a Mexican American scholarship girl." In S. Zwerling & London, H. (Eds.) *First generation students: Confronting the cultural issues.* New Directions for Community Colleges 80 (4), 55–64.

Rendón, L. I. (1994, Fall). "Validating culturally diverse students: Toward a new model of learning and student development." *Innovative Higher Education* 19 (1), 33–51.

Rendón, L. I. (1996, November/December). "Life on the border." *About Campus* 1 (5), 14–20.

Rendón, L. I.; Justiz, M.; & Resta, P. (1988). *The transfer function in southwest border community colleges.* Columbia, SC: University of South Carolina. ED 296 748.

Rendón, L. I., & Nora, A. (1996). "It takes a partnership: Student victories in the Ford Foundation's Urban Partnership Program." Internal report prepared for the Ford Foundation. Tempe, AZ: Arizona State University.

Richardson, R. C., Jr., & Bender, L. W. (1987). *Fostering minority access and achievement in higher education: The role of urban community colleges and universities.* San Francisco, Jossey-Bass.

Rosaldo, R. (1993). *Culture and truth: The reordering of social analysis.* Boston, MA: Beacon Press.

Terenzini, P.; Rendón, L. I.; Upcraft, L.; Millar, S.; Allison, K.; Gregg, P.; & Jalomo, R. (1994, Winter). "The transition to college: Diverse students, diverse stories." *Research in Higher Education* 35 (1), 57–73.

Weis, L. (1985). *Between two worlds: Black students in an urban community college.* Boston: Routledge & Kegan Paul.

Zwerling, L. S., & London, H. (Eds.) (1992). *First–generation students: Confronting the cultural issues.* New Directions for Community Colleges.

Contributors

Marilyn J. Amey is an Associate Professor in the Higher, Adult, and Life-long Education Program at Michigan State University. Using leadership as a conceptual framework, her scholarship addresses cognitive and functional issues in collegiate organizations, including community colleges.

Eusebio Diaz received a masters degree in Bicultural Studies from the University of Texas, San Antonio. He is currently the director of community outreach for the American Cancer Society in San Antonio.

Stanford T. Goto received his Ph.D. from University of California at Berkeley and is a Postdoctoral Research Fellow at Teachers College, Columbia University. He is currently conducting an historical study of reform movements in remedial education.

Berta Vigil Laden is an Assistant Professor at Vanderbilt University in the department of Educational Leadership. She has both taught and served in various administrative positions in the community college sector.

Dennis McGrath is a Professor of Sociology at the Community College of Philadelphia and Senior Fellow for Assessment at the National Center for Urban Partnerships, a sixteen city educational reform project funded by the Ford Foundation. He is the author of *The Academic Crisis of the Community College* (with Martin Spear).

Laura I. Rendón is Professor of Educational Leadership and Policy Studies at Arizona State University. Since 1992, Dr. Rendon has served as Director of Assessment for the Ford Foundation's Urban Partnership Program. She is the author of numerous publications, including *Educating a New Majority: Transforming American's Educational System for Diversity* (with Richard Hope). She currently serves as President of the Association for the Study of Higher Education.

Robert A. Rhoads is an Associate Professor in the Department of Educational Administration at Michigan State University. He is the author of several books, including *Democracy, Multiculturalism and the Community College:*

A Critical Perspective (with James Valadez); *Coming Out in College*; *Community Service and Higher Learning: Explorations of the Caring Self*; *Freedom's Web: Student Activism in an Age of Cultural Diversity;* and *Academic Service Learning: A Pedagogy of Action and Reflection* (with Jeffrey Howard).

Kathleen M. Shaw is an Assistant Professor in the Educational Leadership and Policy Studies Department at Temple University. She is also the Coordinator of the College of Education's Interdisciplinary Urban Education Program. She is the co-director of a national study of urban community colleges, and is currently completing a book manuscript entitled *Where Dreams Cross: Urban Community Colleges and the Search for Educational Mobility* (with Howard London).

Armando Trujillo is an Assistant Professor of Bicultural and Bilingual Studies at the University of Texas at San Antonio. He is the author of *Chicano Empowerment and Bilingual Education: Movimiento Politics in Crystal City, Texas.*

James R. Valadez is an Associate Professor of Educational Leadership and Policy Studies at the University of Washington. He is co-author, with Robert Rhoads, of the 1996 book *Democracy, Multiculturalism and the Community College: A Critical Perspective*, and *Portrait of the Rural Community College*, with C. J. Killacky.

William Van Buskirk is Professor of Sociology at La Salle University in Philadelphia, Pennsylvania.

Index

207

SUNY series: Frontiers in Education
Philip G. Altbach, Editor

List of Titles

College in Black and White: African American Students in Predominantly White and in Historically Black Public Universities—Walter R. Allen, Edgar G. Epps, and Nesha Z. Haniff (eds.)

Critical Perspectives and Early Childhood Education—Lois Weis, Philip G. Altbach, Gail P. Kelly, and Hugh G. Petrie (eds.)

Textbooks in American Society: Politics, Policy, and Pedagogy—Philip G. Altbach, Gail P. Kelly, Hugh G. Petrie, and Lois Weis (ed.)

Black Resistance in High School: Forging a Separatist Culture—R. Patrick Solomon

Emergent Issues in Education: Comparative Perspectives—Robert F. Arnove, Philip G. Altbach, and Gail P. Kelly (eds.)

Creating Community on College Campuses—Irving J. Spitzberg, Jr. and Virginia V. Thorndike

Teacher Education Policy: Narratives, Stories, and Cases—Hendrik D. Gideonse (ed.)

Beyond Silenced Voices: Class, Race, and Gender in United States Schools—Lois Weis and Michele Fine (eds.)

The Cold War and Academic Governance: The Lattimore Case at Johns Hopkins—Lionel S. Lewis

Troubled Times for American Higher Education: The 1990s and Beyond—Clark Kerr

Higher Education Cannot Escape History: Issues for the Twenty-first Century—Clark Kerr

Multiculturalism and Education: Diversity and its Impact on Schools and Society—Thomas J. La Belle and Christopher R. Ward

The Contradictory College: The Conflicting Origins, Impacts, and Futures of the Community College—Kevin J. Dougherty

Race and Educational Reform in the American Metropolis: A Study of School Decentralization—Dan A. Lewis, Kathryn Nakagawa, and Hugh G. Petrie (eds.)

Professionalization, Partnership, and Power: Building Professional Development Schools—Hugh G. Petrie (ed.)

Ethnic Studies and Multiculturalism—Thomas J. La Belle and Christopher R. Ward

Promotion and Tenure: Community and Socialization in Academe—William G. Tierney and Estela Mara Bensimon

Sailing Against the Wind: African Americans and Women in U. S. Education—Kofi Lomotey

The Challenge of Eastern Asian Education: Implication for America—William K. Cummings and Philip G. Altbach (eds.)

Conversations with Educational Leaders: Contemporary Viewpoint on Education in America—Anne Turnbaugh Lockwood

Managed Professionals: Unionized Faculty and Restructuring Academic Labor—Gary Rhoades

The Curriculum: Problems, Politics, and Possibilities; Second Edition—Landon E. Beyer and Michael W. Apple

Education/Technology/Power: Educational Computing as a Social Practice—Hank Bromley and Michael W. Apple (eds.)

Capitalizing Knowledge: New Intersections of Industry and Academia—Henry Etzkowitz, Andrew Webster and Peter Healey (eds.)

The Academic Kitchen: A Social History of Gender Stratification at the University of California, Berkeley—Maresi Nerad

Grass Roots and Glass Ceilings: African American Administrators in Predominantly White Colleges and Universities—William B. Harvey (ed.)